EDITING YOUR NEWSLETTER

(Fourth Edition)

Mark Beach

**WRITER'S
DIGEST
BOOKS**

Cincinnati, Ohio

99 98 97 96 95   5 4 3 2 1

Library of Congress Cataloging-in-Publication Data

Beach, Mark.
    Editing your newsletter / by Mark Beach. — 4th ed.
               p.   cm.
    Includes index.
    ISBN 0-89879-641-5
    1. Newsletters. I. Title.
PN4784.N5B4   1994
070.1'72—dc20   94-29802
                                                              CIP

Edited by Dawn Korth
Interior and cover design by Leslie Meaux-Druley

The following page constitutes an extension of this copyright page.

PERMISSIONS

Ah Ha! © Caton Graphics & Marketing Communications

Atlanta History Center News © the Atlanta History Center

Behind the Seams. Design by Shelby Putnam Tupper and Rick W. Sams. Illustration by Rick Sams. Production by Emily Cotler

The Business Report © Franson, Hagerty & Associates

Chateau Montelena Winery Newsletter © Yates & Associates

Currents in Emergency Cardiac Care © American Heart Association/Citizen CPR Foundation, Inc.

dBug ReView © Seattle Mac dBug

Dick Davis Digest © Dick Davis Digest

Eastern European Outreach © Eastern European Outreach

Focus © Federal Reserve Bank of Cleveland and Don Borger, Design Associates, Inc.

The Green Business Letter © 1993 Tilden Press Inc. All rights reserved

Heart Health © Ariad Custom Publishing Limited, Toronto, Canada

Mayo Clinic Health Letter. Reprinted from September 1993 *Mayo Clinic Health Letter* with permission of Mayo Foundation for Medical Education and Research, Rochester, MN 55905

Mutual Matters © CUNA Mutual Insurance Group

The Numbers News © American Demographics, Inc.

Piedmonitor © Piedmont Hospital

The Public Pulse © The Roper Organization

Random Lengths © Random Lengths Publications, Inc.

Random Lengths Export © Random Lengths Publications, Inc.

Random Lengths Yardstick © Random Lengths Publications, Inc.

Renaissance © The Bank Marketing Association

Samaritan Today © Samaritan Health System

School Matters © Southern Westchester BOCES

Ships and Shipwrecks © Riderwood Publishing Company

Stagelines © Wells Fargo Bank

Syva Monitor © Syva Company

The Technology Monitor © Cadbury Beverages Inc.

Think & Grow Rich Newsletter © Think & Grow Rich

Watkins Motor Lines *Dispatcher* © Watkins Motor Lines, Inc.

Wildflower © National Wildflower Research Center

WordPerfect Report © WordPerfect Corporation

CONTENTS

INTRODUCTION

This book helps anyone who plans, produces or pays for a newsletter. It makes your publication more effective and your work more efficient and satisfying.

If your newsletter is new, this manual gives you a good start. If your publication is already established, it helps you reach full potential.

The value of your skill to produce a successful newsletter on schedule and within budget grows each day. Organizations produce more newsletters than ever and consider them more important as couriers of specialized information.

Effective newsletters have clear objectives. This guide explains how to establish objectives and use them to select content, graphics and design. It describes how objectives determine methods of printing and distribution.

Whether you edit as an employee or volunteer, you find techniques and examples in this book to help you. They come from publications in business, education, religion, government and health, and from commercial publications.

Throughout this guide, I refer to other publications about special topics, such as writing and design. I list the title and author, but depend on you to consult *Books In Print* for current order information. Prices, publishers and editions change so fast that information goes out-of-date quickly.

The illustration on the opposite page shows standard terms for elements of a newsletter.

Definitions for these and other terms are in the glossary.

This guide includes reproductions from dozens of newsletters—nameplates, front pages and inside spreads. As you examine these examples, you become more aware of the design characteristics of effective newsletters. You discover ways to improve your own publication.

This is the fourth edition of *Editing Your Newsletter*, first published in 1980. During the fifteen years between the first edition and the guide you have now, the number and importance of newsletters have grown along with many other forms of specialized information. In our electronic age, newsletters remain popular because readers find them convenient and portable. And they keep the secure feel of words on paper. Effective newsletters are "user-friendly" in the fullest sense of the term.

The first newsletter in North America began in 1704. The *Boston News Letter* reported commercial information, such as ship arrivals, that people no longer learned efficiently by word of mouth. Editor John Campbell wrote articles, selected illustrations, composed type, supervised printing and kept address files. Versatility paid.

Versatility still pays. This guide describes and demonstrates the many skills that you need to produce a newsletter that accomplishes your objectives.

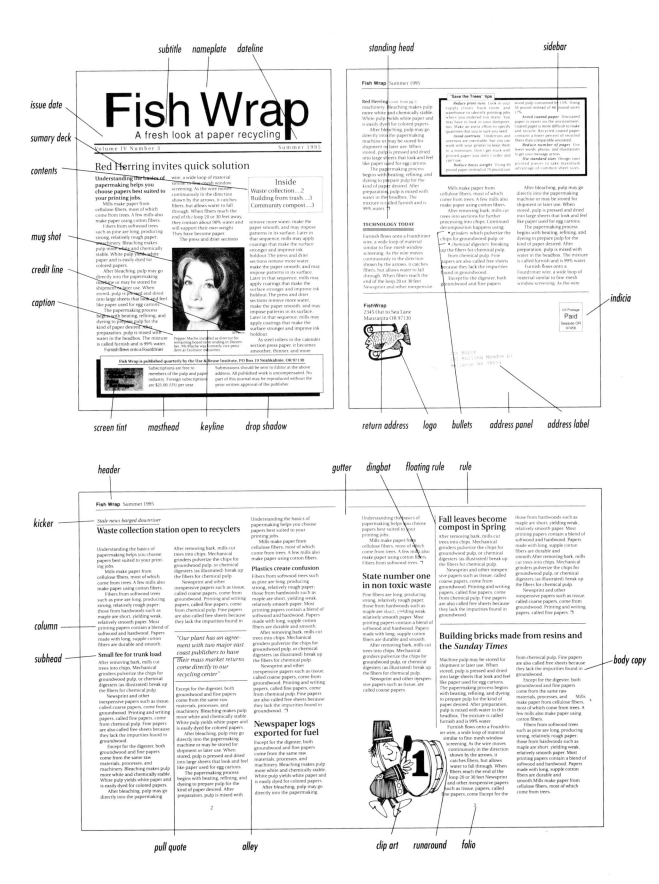

Standard newsletter terms *Professionals use the terms shown above to refer to design elements of newsletters. To ensure clear communication, use these terms consistently when dealing with writers, designers, printers and mailing services.*

1. PLANNING

Newsletters give specialized information to limited audiences on a regular basis. Most have four or eight pages with a page size the same as business stationery. They have short articles written in an informal style.

As a newsletter editor, you need to know what results management and readers want from your publication. Goals, objectives and audience determine results and shape decisions about content, design and printing.

The results expected from your newsletter establish its objectives. Try to define them as specific, measurable benefits to your organization.

In this chapter, you learn under what conditions to use a newsletter to meet communication goals and how to define your publication's major purpose. You learn how to set goals, establish objectives and identify your audience. You discover how to decide about quality, length, frequency, timing, schedule, quantity and budget. The chapter ends with a discussion of newsletter names and subtitles that includes sources for ideas and standards to use when deciding.

Decisions about newsletters involve both business and technical information. This chapter deals with business considerations as a basis for technical judgments about type, graphics and printing discussed in chapters five, six and ten.

CHOOSING A NEWSLETTER

People often decide to publish a newsletter because it seems easy and inexpensive. They believe a newsletter will help solve a problem or achieve results simply by "improving communication." Yet cable television, posters, meetings, computer bulletin boards, electronic mail and many other media can accomplish some of the same results as newsletters.

A newsletter can work well for your organization under certain conditions. Effective newsletters meet the following guidelines.

Print is sufficient

Print works best when information must be portable, available at the convenience of the audience and inexpensive. Media such as slides, video and meetings work better than print in situations needing oral and visual presentation and constant audience interaction.

Homogeneous audience

Newsletters work best when published for people with an obvious common interest. And newsletters are easy to write for a highly targeted audience. Readers themselves tell you what they want to read about.

Homogeneous content

When content stays within a narrow field of interest, a newsletter does its best work. Pony Express News shouldn't deal with both Arabians and Percherons; each breed needs its own special newsletter.

Valuable information

An effective newsletter gives readers information they can use. It doesn't try to compete with books, movies or TV as entertainment.

The most successful newsletters blend the self-interest of reader and sponsor. Both perceive the publication as a service.

Trustworthy

Readers want inside information and trust a newsletter because it resembles a personal letter. Don't let outside pressures influence content.

Paid advertising has no place in a newsletter unless readers (not advertisers) perceive the ads as part of your service. Readers often feel suspicious of editorial content when you also have paid advertisements.

Personal

Readers know the editor's name, think of the editor as an individual writing a letter, and can reach the editor easily by phone or mail.

Short

Your audience can read the news in a few moments. Sentences, paragraphs, articles and the newsletter itself are all brief compared to other publications.

Timely

Content relates to the recent past, present or near future. You publish often enough to keep each issue current.

DECIDING YOUR PURPOSE

Key people in your organization should establish the purpose of your newsletter. You help them select one of the following categories.

Marketing

Newsletters that try to sell ideas, products or services are for marketing. They focus on actions you wish readers to take and include publications to raise money, increase membership, influence votes, or promote greater use of facilities.

To learn more about marketing newsletters, read the book *Marketing With Newsletters*, by Elaine Floyd.

Public relations

Newsletters for public relations focus on attitudes instead of actions. Successful public relations efforts make the newsletter's readers more receptive to marketing or to the mission of an organization.

Public relations newsletters need the highest possible standards of writing and design. Furthermore, the enthusiasm that PR editors feel for their causes must help, not prevent, analysis of objectives and audiences. Don't let your zeal blind you to self-serving or pointless content. Keep your red pencil sharp and use it ruthlessly.

Internal relations

Publications for employees or members are for internal relations. They give information about people, places and ideas that readers already know about and describe coming events. Their goals may include honoring outstanding performance, building morale, and stimulating attention to quality.

Too often internal relations newsletters promote the viewpoints of management in a condescending "top-down" style. Readers feel excluded from complete, honest, useful information. A newsletter full of lectures makes a short trip to the wastebasket.

The best internal newsletters help shape organizational vision and promote the feeling that "we're all in this together." They establish direction, present agenda, build morale, inspire loyalty and stimulate quality.

Many internal newsletters are published by a church or synagogue. To learn more about newsletters for religious organizations, read the book *How to Publish a Church Newsletter*, by Robert W. Fisher.

Profit

A commercial newsletter tries to make money for its publisher and editor. Often the same person does both jobs.

Newsletters for profit reach individuals through mail or fax. Subscribers pay anywhere from $50 to $500 per year, with a median price of about $100. Readers expect valuable information to justify the high cost.

Another kind of newsletter for profit goes to organizations that redistribute them to employees or clients. When buyers redistribute, they imprint their name on the front page, making it appear like their own product. Publications from professional services, such as insurance agents, realtors and medical clinics, often fall into this category.

Publishing a newsletter as a business requires little capital, but lots of time; success requires skills in marketing, management, reporting and production—and lots of self-discipline. A few thousand individual subscribers or a handful of bulk subscribers can yield a comfortable income.

If you are considering a commercial newsletter, read the book *Publishing Newsletters*, by Howard Penn Hudson. Also, seek advice from the publisher of a commercial newsletter that has been published continuously and profitably for more than three years. Consult *Hudson's Directory of Newsletters* or call the Newsletter Clearinghouse in Rhinebeck, New York, to learn about a publisher in your area. If the local publisher charges a consulting fee, pay it. The small investment may save you thousands.

DEFINING GOALS

Although your sponsor or supervisor may specify the purpose of your publication, you may feel uncertain about how to fulfill it. Begin by establishing goals.

Goals are guides to content, design and budget. They suggest what stories to write and photos to use and how well you should design and print your publication.

To define goals, choose three or four words from the list in Visual 1-1. Write them in sentences that relate to your audience. Reviewing the sentences with your supervisor or leadership helps produce a statement of goals.

Here are some examples of goal statements that are useful because they are specific:

- Persuade our members to contribute money and time and to recruit new members
- Impress elected officials at the local and state levels with how serious we are

about delivering or withholding votes.

- Interpret our views about residential property taxes to business leaders statewide.
- Explain to employees our plans, policies and progress.
- Inspire a feeling of fellowship and cooperation among our volunteers.

A complete statement of goals might include four or five phrases such as those above. Wanting to accomplish more than four or five tells you to consider more than one newsletter.

ESTABLISHING OBJECTIVES

The objectives of your newsletter are the results it should produce for your organization. Goals point the direction of travel; objectives describe the destination. Well-stated objectives tell why your newsletter deserves the time and money to produce it.

Useful objectives describe benefits both to those who produce the newsletter and those who read it. They leave no doubt about the value of your publication.

Objectives should include criteria for evaluation that tell how readers would behave if you meet an objective. Here are some examples:

- *Tricky Times* explains to our members our stand on key issues so **we spend less time at meetings interpreting decisions already made.**
- *Tricky Times* describes emergency preparations so well that **employees no longer report feeling unsafe or unaware of what to do.**
- *Tricky Times* stimulates enough interest in our services that **at least five new clients visit our drop-in center each week.**

The ideal objective describes a result that you can measure. For instance, it tells how many dollars you will save or the date on which you will finish a project.

An objective without a measurable result should be specific enough for people to agree about its outcome. Writing such an objective may require several revisions before it

advise	honor	praise
advocate	illustrate	predict
analyze	impress	prepare
announce	improve	prevent
assure	influence	raise funds
clarify	inform	recruit
condense	inspire	report
define	interpret	simplify
describe	justify	solicit
digest	lead	stimulate
evaluate	motivate	suggest
explain	notify	support
guide	persuade	teach
help	portray	train

1-1 Goals *Use any of the verbs above in sentences about goals or objectives. If you have a thesaurus, look up some of the above words to find alternatives to help you write more precise statements.*

becomes a precise guide to action. Here's an example.

Goal. Contribute to success of capital campaign.

Objective. Help people who solicit contributions be more effective.

Better objective. Help volunteers get larger contributions with less time spent soliciting each gift.

Specific objectives help reveal whether or not you can attain a goal. They make you ask if a newsletter is a practical way to accomplish this precise goal with this specific audience.

IDENTIFYING YOUR AUDIENCE

The readership for most newsletters seems obvious: all employees or members; everyone who subscribes; retailers in the region. What seems obvious, however, may not be correct.

Most audiences are more complex than they appear. You may have only one marketing department, but that doesn't mean you have only one market to consider. All employees may have the same company address printed on their paychecks, but management and labor, day shift and night shift, and clerical and maintenance all have very different interests.

Newsletters typically start with one or two audiences in mind; editors add other audiences as production becomes routine. No one asks if the newsletter can accomplish the old objectives with the new audiences.

You may think that success with one audience means equal interest from others. This belief seems strongest with messages that appear most important. A publication for volunteers might not, however, interest paid staff, legislators, potential donors or colleagues at other locations.

To help ensure success, divide your audience into categories having the fewest possible readers. Ask yourself the best way to accomplish your objectives with each category. Perhaps people in some groups would prefer learning news via electronic mail or at a luncheon meeting. Maybe VIPs should get personal letters instead of a printed newsletter.

Strong newsletters specialize. If you have more than one audience, consider more than one newsletter. You can use some of the same articles and photos for the different publications and make their design similar. As an alternative, produce special inserts for specific portions of the audience.

Try to define your readership so clearly that you can describe it in one sentence. That sentence might include some of the words in the list that follows

- current or prospective members, employees, residents, buyers, voters, clients
- managers, directors, stockholders, department heads
- leaders in community, politics, industry, associations, religion, education, government
- reporters for radio, TV, newspapers, magazines, other newsletters

- product dealers, distributors

Newsletters that best accomplish their goals have both audience and content highly targeted. Deal with other audiences and content outside the field with another newsletter or in some other way. Resist the temptation to make one newsletter serve many audiences.

If you have information about your readership on a database, use your computer to help analyze your audience. You might learn that certain categories are larger than you thought—or smaller. You might discover how many readers live nearby, are married, or have incomes over a certain level. Put Your computer to work to keep your audience in short focus.

DETERMINING QUALITY

How your newsletter looks and reads affects how well it accomplishes its objectives.

Readers notice tangible traits, such as paper and printing, and intangible features, such as design and writing. The intangible aspects matter more than the tangible ones. Fancy paper or color printing cannot make up for dull writing, careless editing or poor design.

Money helps buy quality, but isn't the only factor. Time and skill make a big difference. Design of the nameplate alone heavily influences perception of quality.

Quality reflects personality. Your publication may seem neighborly, concerned or authoritative. You may want readers to regard you as an objective observer or as an enthusiastic insider. Your writing can seem intimate or detached.

The way you want readers to perceive your organization should affect quality. Filling each issue with professional photos may suit the marketing department of a bank, but would seem excessive from a neighborhood volunteer agency.

Quality in a newsletter means that you define objectives and audiences so clearly that every issue has a sense of clarity and attention to detail.

Each newsletter has its own appropriate quality level. Try to keep type, photos, paper, printing and other components all consistent with that level. Components below the average quality level drag down the others; components above average don't look as good as they should, and thus waste your time and money.

MAKING FINAL DECISIONS
You have several administrative decisions to make in consultation with your supervisor and perhaps colleagues and readers.

Length
Most newsletters have four pages (one folded sheet 11" x 17" or A3) or eight pages (two folded sheets). These lengths and sizes are most common because printers can produce them quickly at low cost. And they comply easily with postal regulations.

Readers finish with a newsletter in four or five minutes. If your newsletter has more than eight pages, it's probably too long to hold readers' attention. Publish more frequently, cut some content, or use a more efficient format.

Frequency
Publish often enough to report information while it's still news. Four times a year is minimum. Quarterly works for a school district report to taxpayers, but monthly works better for a school report to parents. Weekly is more often than you need unless you report weekly functions, such as church activities.

As a general rule, a shorter newsletter arriving more frequently works better than a longer publication arriving less often. Increasing the number of issues means higher distribution costs and more deadlines, although meeting each deadline requires less time writing and producing.

Timing
When readers receive each issue shapes how well your newsletter meets objectives. Readers should have copies at least a week before the

Plan content	Final approval copy
Get information	Insert or key photos/art
Choose photos/art	
Make dummy	Make mechanicals/proofs
Write headlines	
Write articles/captions	Transmit to printer
	Check proofs
Write sidebars/pull quotes	Printing
	Trimming/folding
Copyedit	Addressing
Proofread	Bundling/sacking
Copy approval	Take to Post Office
Design layout	Readers receive
Final edit copy to fit	

1-2 Production activities Because your have so many ways to handle the various stages of production, a newsletter has no correct or typical schedule. To develop a schedule that works for you, assign an approximate amount of time to each activity. Count the days from when you begin to when readers receive your publication. After making your best final estimate, add at least 25 percent more time.

first date on the calendar of coming events.

Timing determines deadlines. Working backward from when you know copies must reach readers allows you to set a schedule. When setting the schedule, consider distribution speed. The production sequence ends when readers have newsletters in their hands, not when copies leave your hands.

Schedule
How long it takes to produce your newsletter depends on how quickly you write, how much help you get, and dozens of other factors. After the first few issues the production sequence for one issue becomes routine. Something may go wrong at any point, but it shouldn't disrupt the overall schedule.

Visual 1-2 lists typical production tasks. Few newsletters require them all, but every publication requires some. A clear schedule that everyone can depend on eliminates many excuses for missing deadlines.

Quantity

It may seem obvious that you need just enough copies to reach everyone in your audience, but factors other than number of readers determine how many copies to print. For example, if readership grows, new people may want back issues.

Printing 10 percent or 15 percent more copies than you need adds very little to overall production costs, but can lead to wasted money elsewhere. Those extra copies may go to people who should get a separate newsletter, be reached via another medium, or be dropped from your address list. Consult chapter eleven about cutting costs by keeping your mailing list clean.

DEVELOPING A BUDGET

During early planning, you can only estimate how much your newsletter will cost. Base your guess on initial answers to questions in this chapter plus projections of costs for printing and distribution.

Your best guess about cost during the first year is probably between 50 and 100 percent too low. It's easy to underestimate development cost, especially the cost of time spent in meetings needed for a proper launch.

Experienced editors distinguish between fixed and variable costs. Fixed costs stay the same whether you print one copy or one million. They include writing, design and layout. Variable costs depend on quantity. They include what you pay for paper, printing and distribution.

If you are an employee, the value of your time represents the largest fixed cost of your newsletter. Newsletters are labor intensive, but editors often ignore that fact when planning budgets.

Money required for a good start is easiest to deal with if you think in terms of unit cost for two or three years. For instance, paying a graphic designer $1,000 for a nameplate to print on 250 copies of a quarterly newsletter may be extravagant. The same $1,000 spent

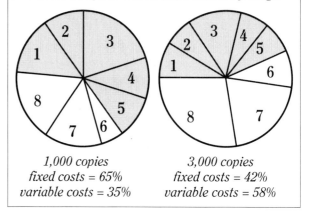

Fixed costs: 1 Gather information, 2 Administration/overhead, 3 Write/edit/proofread, 4 Make/select photos/drawings, 5 Type/layout/camera-ready. Variable costs: 6 Paper, 7 Print/fold, 8 Address/postage.

1,000 copies
fixed costs = 65%
variable costs = 35%

3,000 copies
fixed costs = 42%
variable costs = 58%

1-3 Production costs *The relationship between fixed and variable costs depends on the number of copies you need. The charts above show that variable costs become a larger percentage of your budget as production runs increase. The percentages in these charts apply to newsletters whose production has become routine, not to publications during the start-up phase when fixed costs are relatively high.*

To ensure best cost control, use the following guideline: With relatively few copies, pay most attention to fixed costs. As quantities increase, shift your attention to variable costs.

for a monthly with a print run of 2,000 may be a bargain.

Another way to approach budget planning is to estimate the value of achieving your goals. A publication that builds customer loyalty to $50,000 cars has more value than one that solicits $50 donations to a political campaign.

Translating goals into objectives helps define value. Even if your newsletter does not lead directly to financial profit, its objectives have at least some relationship to money, such as helping workers be more efficient. Precise objectives help make the relationship clear.

SELECTING A NAME

An effective newsletter name describes subject matter and offers readers a benefit. Great names also sound lively to attract attention. Readers remember them.

Good names build on content or publisher. *Metal Collecting*, *Venture Capital* and *Hospital Purchasing* convey content; *Hilltop School*

accents	guide	post
advisory	highlights	profile
advocate	horizons	report
alert	hotline	reporter
almanac	ink	resources
briefs	insider	review
briefing	interchange	scene
bulletin	intercom	scope
channel	journal	spotlight
connection	keynote	survey
context	letter	tab
digest	light	times
dimensions	line	topics
eye	link	trends
examiner	list	update
facts	log	viewpoint
file	monthly	views
focus	news	voice
forecast	notes	weekly
forum	outlook	wire
gram	perspective	world

1-4 Key words in names *Newsletter names often build on communication terms such as those above. Use this list to suggest possible names for your publication.*

Bulletin, Franklin Real Estate Review and *St. Mary's Report* reveal the publishers.

Use an active communication term to describe a benefit. *Loggers Alert* works better than *Loggers News*. Readers yawn at *School of Education Newsletter*, but reach for *Teachers Success Bulletin*.

If you publish for an external audience—marketing, public relations or profit—put your audience into your name. Call it *Working Woman*, not *Knowledge Power*. Think about the attraction of the perfect magazine name, *Reader's Digest*.

Subscription and marketing newsletters often build on the names of their publishers, such as *Ruff Times* (financial analysis from Howard Ruff) and *Publishing Poynters* (news about book publishing from Dan Poynter). Titles can play on jargon, such as *Thruput* for computer programmers. Even initials can sometimes fit into a title, such as *ARTAFacts* from American Retail Travel Agents.

Use Visual 1-4 to help you compose a good name. If you want further ideas, browse one of the following directories: *Newsletters In Print* (Gale Research Company), *Hudson's Newsletter Directory* (Newsletter Clearinghouse), *Oxbridge Directory of Newsletters* (Oxbridge Publishing), and *Working Press of the Nation*, volume 5 (National Research Bureau).

The Clean Yield
Principles and profits working together

Retail Vacancy Reporter
Monthly information about store, strip and surplus property.

Customers
Up-to-the-minute ideas on how managers achieve excellence in customer service/relations.

Ways and Means
Reporting on innovative approaches to state and local government

The DMSO Report
Accurate and timely information about dimethyl sulfoxide for general and professional readers

Whirlpools
Pooled information for professionals on preventing and treating alcoholism and drug abuse

Energy News
A pipeline and gas utilities bi-weekly, edited for management, users and producers, and reporting on supplies, prices, regulations and construction in the natural gas industry

1-5 Newsletter subtitles *Your newsletter needs a subtitle as well as a name, especially if you publish for an external audience. A subtitle, also called a tag line, makes your purposes and readership clear. Pay as much attention to its wording as to the name of the newsletter itself. Keep tightly focused, resisting the impulse to serve too many audiences with the same publication.*

2. EDITORS

Whether you are an employee or a volunteer, and whether you carry out every aspect of production or only parts of it, you must work with other people. Supervisors, leaders, colleagues, vendors and readers all have expectations. And all can help. You can't do your job without them.

Controlling costs, schedules and quality requires good communication among people who work together. Chapter one explained how to develop clear goals and objectives; this chapter describes how to deal with management, colleagues and suppliers.

You have your most important relationship with the person or group who represents your sponsoring organization—your publisher. If you are an employee, your publisher is probably your supervisor. This relationship can be awkward, especially when the supervisor has unrealistic goals or knows little about producing a newsletter.

Much of this chapter deals with how you and your publisher work together and the rewards, training and help you deserve. It outlines the routine tasks most editors carry out and includes a form, the Editor's Job Organizer, to help you decide which tasks to do yourself and which to delegate.

This chapter includes a list of suggestions for supervisors who want to ensure good working relationships with editors. The list, shown as Visual 2-1, gives recommendations in a form that your supervisor can read quickly as a basis for discussion with you.

The following pages raise the question of whether you need desktop publishing skills and software. The answer is "definitely yes" if you regularly produce several newsletters or other publications, such as reports, books and magazines. The answer is "probably no" if most of your keyboard work is word processing and the newsletter is your only publication.

This chapter explains how to work with graphic designers and newsletter services, how to evaluate workshops and training programs, and how to operate if you produce newsletters as a freelancer.

WORKING WITH YOUR PUBLISHER

You produce a newsletter to benefit your publisher, the sponsor that pays for it. Your publisher may be an individual or an organization, such as a business, agency, club, association or school.

Your publisher has a purpose in mind and expects you to accomplish it. To define your job clearly, you must understand that purpose; to do your job well, you must agree with it.

Some person with whom you have frequent contact should represent your publisher to you. That person might be your supervisor or an officer of your organization. As an alternative, your publisher might be represented by a small committee.

The person speaking for your publisher is both supervisor and advocate. As supervisor, the person should interpret goals, help define objectives and audiences, and evaluate your work. As advocate, the person should try to get the time, money, training and help you need to produce an effective newsletter.

Your management needs to understand newsletters. You can help build that insight by asking good questions and presenting thoughtful options. It also helps to show your supervisor successful newsletters from other organizations similar to yours.

If you don't have a person or committee acting as publisher, ask for one. Try to make sure that person carries out the responsibilities described in this chapter.

Even with one person as supervisor, it helps to have a newsletter committee of two or three others. Meeting informally with them every few months can build support for the newsletter job, which other people often understand poorly. Members may suggest ideas and sources of help that might not occur to you on your own. These suggestions are especially important if you are new to your organization.

Publishers sometimes do not carry out their end of the bargain. Some won't take the time, or some think that having you in charge has solved all their problems. Others write articles twice as long as they promised and ignore the deadlines that they helped set.

The most frequent problem involves control over content. The editor feels responsible for content, loyal to readers, and pressured by the deadline. The publisher wants to approve every word.

When meeting with your publisher, try to solve problems within the overall context of your newsletter instead of as isolated headaches. Start with a review of objectives and what achieving them is worth in time and money. Focus the conversation on basic questions to keep responsibility for support and advocacy on the publisher's desk, where it belongs.

No one has discovered one correct way to resolve the issue of editorial freedom, but you can find ways of handling it to reduce tensions and keep responsibilities clear. Here are ideas that work for many editors:

• Agree with your publisher who has the final word, then print that person's name in the masthead as senior editor.

• Make your production schedule begin when approved copy comes off your publisher's desk, not when your draft goes on it.

Ideally, you control content because your management feels confident that you understand objectives and feel responsible for achieving them. If your supervisor insists on being editor too, I recommend taking both steps suggested in the previous paragraphs.

Visual 2-1 provides a list of guidelines that may help your supervisor create conditions for producing an effective newsletter.

TASKS

You may not actually do everything needed to produce and distribute your newsletter, but you should know enough about each task to judge whether it's done well. Defining your job requires knowing what to do yourself and what to delegate. Here are some guidelines.

Planning

Your publisher decides policy, but you can help. The process might be as simple as a few conversations with your boss or as complex as a membership survey; it might take a few moments or a few months.

Administration

After consulting with your publisher, colleagues and perhaps outside specialists, you decide about such topics as frequency, quantity and methods of production and distribution.

Content

With regular help from others and comments from readers, you select and prepare content.

Production

Working with designers, printers and other specialists, you produce each issue.

Distribution

You coordinate addressing and distribution or mailing services.

Evaluation

Working with your supervisor, you determine how well each issue meets objectives. You also judge the process—how efficiently issues are produced and whether they meet the budget.

Visual 2-2 is a form that lists the tasks involved in producing most newsletters and lets you identify who is responsible for each task. You may copy the form for your supervisor, colleagues and vendors.

Although not part of the production sequence for each issue, keeping records is part of your overall job. Complete, accurate records help spot problems and ensure that the next editor doesn't feel as overwhelmed as you did when you started.

2-1 SUCCESSFUL SUPERVISION

Whether one person or a group represents your publisher, following the suggestions below helps makes your newsletter effective and your production process enjoyable.

Goals, objectives and audience Make sure they are carefully defined, clearly understood and expressed in writing.

Responsibility Verify that each production task is clearly assigned and that other people know who is responsible for what.

Authority Confirm that each person with a production task has the authority to carry it out.

Money Make sure that your budget covers the publication you want; clarify how much the editor can spend without your approval. Set aside some money for training.

Example Set an example to others in your organization by meeting deadlines, respecting space allotments and reading the newsletter.

Evaluation Plan with the editor how to evaluate success. Tell the editor how producing the newsletter relates to other job responsibilities.

Your records should include one copy of each issue and the basic documents that tell about your publication. Those documents include those on the following list:

- statement of goals, objectives and audience
- completed Job Organizer (Visual 2-2)
- style sheet
- type specifications (similar to Visual 5-6)
- printing specifications (Visual 10-3)
- contracts for printing and other services
- postal permits, classification forms
- names, addresses and phone numbers for sources of information, services and helpers

Keep copies of your newsletter and the key documents listed above in a file folder or ring binder. You should also have computer files to back up the records on paper.

TIME

You may wonder about how much time you should need to produce your newsletter. The question grows from the tension and frustration that so often go with the job. I wish I could give an answer for every situation, but that's not possible. There are too many variables in production methods, ease of writing, and other demands on time.

Instead of guessing how many hours should go into a newsletter with specific characteristics, consider factors that create delays. When you reduce the influence of those factors, you make production more efficient and pleasant.

Understanding

Supervisors easily forget how much work goes into a good newsletter—if they ever knew in the first place. Perhaps you would be given more time if you and your management went point by point through your list of tasks, discussing how long each might take.

Planning

Efficiency begins with detailed specifications for format and type, and involves having a clear understanding of responsibilities.

Concentration

Too many editors must produce newsletters while also answering the phone and managing other projects. You must have the time and quiet surroundings to work, especially to write, edit and design.

Even with the best of supervisors, plans and working conditions, you may never seem to have enough time. Don't worry about it. Pressure is a normal part of publishing a periodical. Every newspaper, magazine and newsletter editor feels it.

Editors without ulcers know how to ignore the pressure when it doesn't matter, which is most of the time, and respond to it when it does.

TRAINING

The fact that you have this book means you want to improve your newsletter skills. There are other books that can help, many of which are mentioned throughout this guide.

If you're like most editors, you haven't learned more than 50 percent of the writing and design potential of your computer software. Ask for additional training and time to study the manuals.

People in public relations or marketing receive direct mail advertising for workshops on topics such as copywriting, pasteup and computer graphics. Most workshops are produced by companies that specialize in teaching professionals. Some workshops are produced by universities or nonprofit agencies.

Workshops range from invaluable to useless. Here are some guidelines to consider before signing up.

Instructor

Advertising should tell you the name and experience of the teacher, not just assure you that "all our instructors are highly qualified professionals." You should be able to phone the instructor for details about content.

Editor's Job Organizer

Newsletter name _____ Editor _____

Phone _____ / _____ Fax _____ / _____

Organization _____

Address _____

Function	Person responsible	Vendor
Decide purposes/goals		
Establish objectives		
Identify audience		
Set schedule		
Develop budget		
Select name/subtitle		
Choose distribution method		
Design format/nameplate		
Specify typography		
Select production services		
Specify paper/printer		
Verify work completed		
Approve/pay invoices		

2-2 Editor's Job Organizer *Even simple newsletters involve many of the tasks shown above. Complex publications may require them all plus more. Use this list to help plan time and assign tasks. Clearly assigned tasks help ensure efficient production and reduce mistakes due to misunderstandings.*

Function	Person responsible	Vendor
Gather information		
Select content		
Write copy		
Select photographs/drawings		
Select charts/graphs/maps		
Copyedit text/visuals		
Proofread text/visuals		
Approve text/visuals		
Final output		
Make dummy		
Create mechanicals		
Prepress service		
Printing Company		
Maintain address files		
Prepare for mailing		
Evaluate production process		
Evaluate achieving objectives		
Evaluate address lists		
Evaluate newsletter costs		

Recommendations

Workshop producers should offer to tell you names of some people who attended previously. If they don't offer, forget about that workshop. If they do offer, call some of those people to learn whether they felt satisfied.

Price

A good workshop is worth whatever it costs. A poor one isn't worth attending, even for free.

Most editors spend more time on writing than on other tasks. A workshop or course can cut that time by making you more skillful and confident. Look for training in business or technical writing, not general composition.

REWARDS

If you are like most newsletter editors, you have little specific training for the task and plenty of other tasks within your organization. You have to learn fast and work hard.

You deserve several benefits for producing an effective newsletter. Some are inherent in the job itself; others must be given by your publisher.

Sense of worth

The adage that knowledge is power becomes more true each day. Editors of effective newsletters share information that helps both readers and publishers and get personal satisfaction from being an authority.

Creative satisfaction

Most editors control all aspects of their newsletters, from planning through distribution. They create the entire product and are largely responsible for its success.

New skills

Successful production requires so many talents that few editors have them all, especially when new. You should build skills in general editorial areas, such as writing, photography and design, and continue to learn in the field of your publication.

Job opportunities

Newsletter editors publicly demonstrate their commitment and range of skills. Loyalty and ability should bring opportunities for advancement.

Appropriate compensation

You deserve rewards commensurate with the value of the newsletter to your publisher. If you are a volunteer, compensation may take the form of status and frequent expressions of appreciation. If you are an employee, what you are paid should reflect, in part, what your newsletter is worth.

If you are trained in graphics, public relations or marketing, you already have a rough idea of the pay for people with your experience. You can get more data from professional organizations, such as Graphic Artists Guild (New York), International Association of Business Communicators (San Francisco), Public Relations Society of America (New York), Society for Technical Communication (Washington), and the Council for the Advancement and Support of Education (Washington), that survey salaries of their members.

People trained in a field such as secretarial work can look at salary in one of two ways: (1) decide that the boss defines the job, so don't worry about how producing a newsletter affects income; or (2) decide whether being editor should increase salary.

If you want a raise, prepare your case by learning hourly fees in your area for services that you provide. Copywriters and service bureaus often charge by the hour. You might also learn what local freelancers charge to produce newsletters similar to yours. Salaries for people with your experience who hold public relations jobs that focus on printed products could also guide you.

Effective newsletters bring value to their publishers. If yours doesn't, stop producing it. Continuing makes that portion of your time worthless to your organization.

COMPUTERS

Use the most appropriate production system your organization has—not necessarily the best, but the machines most suited to your task. You don't need the computer with a 486 chip and 100MB disk, but neither should you have to fight the old machine that only uses floppies.

When used well, computers help create quality and efficiency; when used poorly, they help make a mess. Let the machines help you keep track of stories and write precisely. Learn how to create consistent formats with macros or style sheets. But avoid the temptation to use the computer's power to create almost infinite variety. Just because you can easily create clever drawings or exotic type doesn't automatically make them useful for your newsletter.

If you are thinking about buying software for newsletter production, especially if it's desktop publishing software, make absolutely, positively, 100 percent sure that it will run on your machine with your current operating system and that it suits your needs—before you pay for it.

Ask for an intensive demonstration. Work with some files of the size that you typically use to verify that the program does everything you want. Test it again. Make some major changes in files, then print them out. Make sure that the machine doesn't give you time to play in a chess tournament while it searches, manipulates, stores or prints.

Test the software until you are so bored you could scream. And remember that it will take twice as long to learn as you think.

You can produce a first rate newsletter with word processing programs, such as *WordPerfect* and *Microsoft Word*. Even if you use *PageMaker*, *Ventura Publisher*, or another desktop publishing program, write and edit using the word processor, then import files into the graphics program. Word processing software keeps your production sequence clear by focusing your attention on writing. Design and graphics come later.

When thinking about help from a computer, keep in mind the needs of distribution and internal communication.

Distribution

Keep addresses of readers in a database that can generate mailing labels in the sequence and format you need. Up-to-date word processing programs include mailing features that handle a few thousand names, plenty for most newsletters. To save time and money, take advantage of the methods to keep mailing lists clean described in chapter eleven.

Communication

If your organization uses electronic mail or a groupware program, such as *Notes*, make sure to tag your files with version numbers and due dates. To reduce confusion, only put duplicates on the system. Locking other users out of latest versions lets you compare their work to yours.

HELPING SERVICES

You don't have to produce the newsletter by yourself. Usually you have the previous editor and one or two other people within your organization to lend a hand. When a newsletter gets a new editor, it's a good time to evaluate the publication. The analysis should include reviewing goals and objectives, format and design, and budget.

Evaluation may benefit from the views of someone not directly associated with your newsletter. Most organizations have leaders skilled at posing the right questions about virtually any activity. Ask one of them to help review goals and objectives. Perhaps the right person is in another department or on the board of directors.

The cost of a graphic designer to develop a nameplate and fine-tune format is usually a good investment. The designer might also consult with you occasionally about layout, production and working with printers.

Graphic designers have their own separate

category in classified directories. You can also get referrals from people in public relations, advertising and marketing who are regular clients of design studios.

When discussing your project with a designer, keep in mind the following guidelines.

Newsletter experience
Ask to see examples of newsletters produced by the designer. Design work for brochures, annual reports and menus may look beautiful, but it's not relevant.

Practical design
Insist on seeing samples of printed newsletters, not dummies or comps. Only the final product tells how ideas translate from design to paper.

Good listener
Look for a designer who asks the kind of questions found in chapter one of this book. Designers should understand your needs before visualizing compositions produced at your expense.

Recommendations
Call some previous clients to check on deadline dependability and overall satisfaction.

Price
Pay by the job, not by the hour. When you find the designer who seems absolutely right, don't quibble. Your design should stay appropriate for at least five years, thus worth every dollar.

If your time is too valuable to spend producing a newsletter, consider hiring an outside service. You might use a public relations or ad agency, or a freelance writer. If you live in a large city, you may also find a newsletter production specialist. If none are listed in the yellow pages, ask for a recommendation from the executive director of any trade association.

Hiring an outside producer requires careful shopping. Apply the guidelines presented pre-

viously with regard to graphic designers, plus the additional standards that follow.

Compatibility
You're going to see the people often, so you should feel comfortable working with them.

Sophistication
Check how up-to-date they are regarding computers. They should have some potential designs and other parts of the production sequence electronically in place and know how to interface with your equipment.

The whole job
Look for people who can handle everything from writing through distribution. If part of the process could stay inside your organization, such as in-plant printing or list maintenance, you can suggest it. Don't just assume, however, that part of the job done in-house will be better, cheaper or faster. Check it out.

If you don't need a newsletter custom-made to your situation, you might consider a franchise publication.

Franchise newsletters, also called syndicated, are produced with generic titles, such as *Executives' Digest* and *Client Advisory*. Most professions have several from which to choose. Subscribers buy them in bulk for redistribution to employees or clients.

Companies that produce franchised newsletters will imprint your copies with your own name and logo and, in some cases, with a front page article that you provide. To locate a publisher, consult with a leader of your trade association or look in one of the newsletter directories referred to in chapter one.

FREELANCING
If you produce newsletters on a freelance basis, consult with potential clients to make a list of every possible production activity. Certify that both you and your client know exactly what your fee includes. Once you define tasks, help clients develop realistic bud-

gets for everything else. That gives you an idea of where to set fees and helps clients understand total costs.

After carefully computing how many hours the job will take, add at least 50 percent more time for delays in approvals, missed appointments and general hassle. And remember that start-up time is high. The first few issues take three or four times longer than the rest.

Watch for the start-and-switch game: You do the development work, then your client's secretary takes over when the going gets easy. Unless you like this kind of work protect yourself with a long contract, high initial fee or termination penalty.

Charge per issue, month or year, not by the hour, and build expenses into fees. If one client insists on knowing the cost of every proof or parking meter, build the extra time for keeping records into your fee.

When setting fees, remember fringe benefits and overhead. You pay for space, heat, insurance, phone, 100 percent of Social Security (FICA) and retirement. Identify a yearly salary that you would receive for compa-rable work from an employer in your locality, then add 100 percent. Use the total as your target gross income for a year.

To keep the jobs separated and on track, create a production cycle for each client. Write and produce at your shop, not the client's, to take full advantage of your computers and other facilities. Make sure you have state-of-the-art software and know how to use it.

Unless you're dealing with print runs over 5,000, don't broker printing; there's too little profit and too much hassle. Instead, make yourself more valuable to your client with advice about how to buy production services.

You may find freelance newsletter production rewarding if you have enough clients and can avoid having two deadlines in one week. It takes skillful marketing, however, because most potential clients feel shocked when they learn the true cost of producing an effective newsletter.

For more information about how to set up and run a newsletter production service, read the book *Making Money Writing Newsletters*, by Elaine Floyd.

2-3 EMPLOYEE VS. FREELANCER

When an organization contracts with a freelance writer or designer, both parties need to ensure that the freelancer is an independent contractor, not an employee. Follow these guidelines to make sure the freelancer preserves independent status.

Define results Freelancers agree to produce specific outcomes, but not what tools or methods to use. They are free to use others (employees or subcontractors) to help produce those results.

Agree on schedule Freelance contracts identify when projects begin and end, but don't set specific working hours.

Pay by the job Payment by the hour, week or month signals employment. Freelancers are paid in lump sums, such as 50 percent to begin and 50 percent on completion.

Multiple contracts Freelancers have contracts with several organizations, not just one. When they work on several projects for one organization, they have a separate contract for each project.

No benefits Freelancers pay their own taxes, insurance and retirement contributions.

1099 form Organizations send a 1099 form to every freelancer with whom they work during the year.

3. CONTENT

The relative ease of producing a newsletter as a physical object may tempt you to consider form more important than substance. Design does add value, but mostly by making content accessible. Without useful content, design means little.

Readers want helpful information. They perceive you as part of leadership or management and assume you have access to facts they can't easily get for themselves. This chapter describes the kinds of topics that interest readers and includes hundreds of ideas for articles.

Your job includes helping readers understand the news. Each time you advise, interpret, show connections and analyze, you make your newsletter more valuable. Commercial newsletters thrive on giving information that other sources lack the energy or nerve to report. Your subject matter may not lend itself to scoops, but you owe your readers insight as well as information.

This chapter explains the advantages of doing your own reporting—not asking others to write articles—and describes techniques for successful interviews. It gives an outline of copyright law as it affects newsletters.

EFFICIENT REPORTING

Presidents, directors and supervisors typically ask people to edit newsletters amid hearty assurances about how much help they can expect. Assurances are especially strong regarding the network of reporters waiting to produce vivid prose on schedule and within space limits.

In most cases, the network is a fantasy. Too often, reality is a file of ideas for you to turn into articles by morning.

Experienced editors find it easier to do the reporting themselves than to rely on others—much easier! Being your own reporter means that you collect information from others, but do all the writing yourself.

Here are some reasons to do your own reporting.

Content
You know whether a story is worth writing and how you want to handle it. Others won't perceive you as a heavy-handed editor for rewriting someone's "finished copy."

Style
When written by you, every article already conforms to your style sheet and to understandings between you and your supervisor.

Copyfitting
You have an idea for layout of each issue, so you know about how many words each story should have.

Production
When you write it yourself, the story is already into production. Your keystrokes begin the process of producing type; as you work, you control layout as well as content.

Deadline
You know the last possible minute for copy and aren't held up when others don't perform.

When you rely mostly on yourself for copy, you gather information with regular phone calls and visits and through systematic review of other sources. You can avoid writer's block by following a few simple tips:

• Keep a list of key names and phone num-

bers. Make the rounds by phone a few days before each deadline to get ideas and information for the next issue.

• Get your name on mailing lists for press releases, government reports and other newsletters.

• Keep an idea file of notes, clippings and references to use at the last minute.

• Make it easy for others to help you. Put your name and phone number in your masthead. Let others know you need information and help.

Visual 3-1 shows how one editor helped his readers provide content. By making it easy, he got a flow of information he could rely on.

EFFECTIVE INTERVIEWS
Readers like interviews because they make information personal and put them in touch with people they might never meet. Editors like interviews because they bring variety to the job and the person being interviewed creates most of the copy.

Interviews get your audience behind the scenes and give meaning to the news. They let you ask the questions that readers have on their minds.

Don't hesitate to ask for an interview. Most people regard them as ways to promote their own interests, so they want to cooperate. If you conduct interviews well, people feel happy to answer your questions.

Effective interviews are carefully planned, carried out and recorded.

Before
When you ask for an interview, tell your subject what topics you want to cover and how much time you want. Ask for materials to read in advance that give basic information and suggest questions. Write in your notebook the two or three questions you most want answered.

Do your homework. Nothing turns an interview cold faster than a question that could have been answered by easy research. Evidence that you arrive prepared also shows

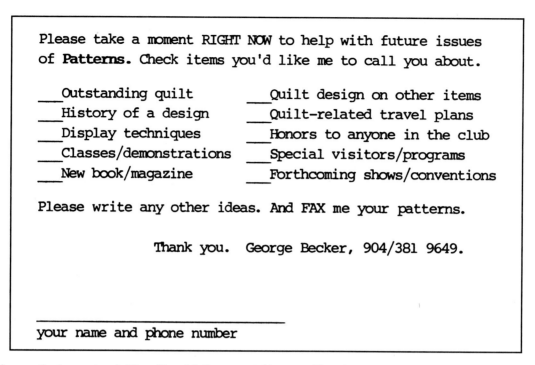

Please take a moment RIGHT NOW to help with future issues of **Patterns.** Check items you'd like me to call you about.

___Outstanding quilt   ___Quilt design on other items
___History of a design   ___Quilt-related travel plans
___Display techniques   ___Honors to anyone in the club
___Classes/demonstrations   ___Special visitors/programs
___New book/magazine   ___Forthcoming shows/conventions

Please write any other ideas. And FAX me your patterns.

Thank you. George Becker, 904/381 9649.

_____
your name and phone number

3-1 News gathering postcard *The editor of* Patterns *sent this postpaid card to association leaders with each newsletter. By making it easy for people to give information, the editor always had plenty of leads for future issues.*

that you take the interview seriously.

Conduct interviews in settings that subjects find comfortable and convenient. It's usually better to visit them, not ask them to visit you.

Ask for a photo to run with the story. If you plan to take photos during the interview, be sure to ask if it's OK. Avoid using flash.

During

Arrive early to become familiar with the setting. Spend a few moments chatting informally before taking out your notebook. Confirm details such as time limits or taboo subjects.

Take charge. Focus the conversation on your priority questions. You don't have to be rigid, but you should keep the discussion on track.

Get specifics. Ask for accurate spellings and correct titles. Check details while your subject is still with you. If your subject talks too fast, ask for a pause to catch up. People appreciate attention to detail during an interview.

Unless the topic is highly technical, write, don't record. Tape recorders make conversa-

tion too formal and distract you and your subject. If your interview is too long for taking notes, it's probably too long to publish in a newsletter.

As you leave, ask for the best way to check last minute details with your subject just before your deadline. Conclude with a thank you for the effort your subject has made on behalf of your readers.

After

Fill in your notes immediately. Don't let quotations and information slip away in the rush of other business. Think of completing your notes as part of the interview itself, not as a task to perform sometime later.

When writing your notes, put the interview in context. Jot down how you felt, how your subject seemed to feel, and observations about the physical setting. Preserve the human feeling that puts personality into quoted words.

Putting the interview in context helps present the subject's viewpoints fairly and accurately.

When writing the interview, get right to the point. Don't hesitate to condense questions and answers to make them more orderly. You may have to cut interesting material, but editing yields a more lively article.

Telephone interviews are often easier to get than personal ones. They are less trouble for both you and the subject. Treat a phone interview as you would a visit in person: Make an appointment, tell your subject what you need to learn, and write down your questions before you call.

COPYRIGHTS

The law of copyright affects your newsletter if you want to reproduce copyrighted material or you want to prevent your own material from being reproduced without your permission.

Creators of literary or artistic products own the exclusive legal right to reproduce, publish and sell their products, such as articles and photographs. Copyright protects the form in which you express an idea—the actual newsletter or illustration—not the idea itself. You cannot copyright the name of your newsletter, but you can copyright the unique graphic rendition of that name in your nameplate or logo. (If you want legal protection for your name, register it as a trademark.)

A person, group, organization or business may own a copyright. Owners of copyrights have rights to:

- reproduce (photocopy, print or copy electronically);
- distribute copies to the public ("to publish");
- prepare derivative works (such as a book based on newsletters);
- perform (a lecture or seminar);
- display (a painting or photograph).

To determine if material has copyright protection, look for the phrase "Copyright (date) (name of owner)." The symbol © may appear instead of the word "copyright." For a newsletter or magazine, the phrase normally appears in the masthead; for a book, on the back of its title page. The phrase protects all material within the publication.

A specific article, photograph or drawing may be copyrighted. In that case, the phrase usually appears as a footnote to the article or as part of the caption for visuals.

Some material is in the public domain because copyrights have expired or were never secured in the first place. Clip art is in the public domain because it is published without copyright. You may, without permission, reproduce articles, drawings and photographs published as clip art.

If you want to use copyrighted material in your newsletter, you must either have the owner's permission or publish under the provisions for fair use.

Permission

A copyright owner may allow you to reproduce material. Owners give permission to reproduce for specific circumstances. Getting the OK to reprint three paragraphs from a magazine article in your newsletter does not mean you may also insert them into a speech.

For permission to reproduce copyrighted material, write to the owner describing what you want to use. Send a sample of your newsletter and a self-addressed, stamped envelope. Tell whether you are profit or non-profit and that you will publish whatever credit line the copyright owner wishes. Attach a photocopy or other precise description of the material you want to use. And state your deadline so your request doesn't go directly to the bottom of the "to do" pile.

Publishers handle routine copyright requests for authors, artists and photographers. You can address a letter seeking permission to the publisher, even though someone else may legally own the copyright.

Owners of copyrights may charge for the reproduction of their material. In practice, you usually get permission at no cost. If your newsletter is for commercial gain, however, you may have to pay.

Fair use

Reproducing small portions of copyrighted material without permission for the purpose of teaching, analysis or review is legal under a provision called "fair use." You may also quote when describing material as news.

Copyright laws do not explicitly define fair use, and there are no clear rules about how much material you may reproduce. Two or three excerpts of fifty words each or one photo or drawing from a book should be no problem. In the case of an article from another newsletter, quoting more than just a few sentences might exceed fair use.

The law tests whether you exceeded fair use by asking whether you deprived the copyright owner of profit. You may not reproduce copyrighted words, photos or drawings simply because you find them interesting or need something to fill space.

Securing a copyright

You should copyright newsletters with writing or visuals that you do not want others to reproduce. For legal protection, put the copyright phrase in the masthead or some other prominent place. The phrase has three elements: (1) the word "copyright" or symbol ©; (2) the date; and (3) the name of the owner. I own the copyright to this book, so my phrase is "Copyright 1995 by Mark Beach."

Because each issue of a newsletter is a publication, each issue needs the copyright phrase. Except under certain circumstances, you cannot copyright back issues.

For official copyright registration, use forms available from the Copyright Office, Library of Congress, Washington DC 20559. Filing adds no rights beyond those you get by simply printing the phrase, but does prove the exact date your copyright took effect. In case of litigation, prior registration is required.

Editors of newsletters that advocate a cause or promote public relations usually want their material reproduced elsewhere. Such newsletters should not have copyrights. In fact, a sentence in the masthead might specifically grant permission to reproduce provided that credit goes to the original publication.

Freelancers

Copyright laws affect freelance writers and artists differently from those on a payroll. Freelancers own copyrights to their products, even if they create them under contract to a client. A freelance artist who made a technical drawing owns its copyright unless a contract includes a clause to the contrary. People on a payroll, on the other hand, create products as part of their job. Work done as an employee is known as "work for hire" and the copyrights are owned by the employer.

Most editors create newsletters as part of their jobs, so they are working for hire. Their employers own the copyright.

Copyright ownership is negotiable. A client and freelancer may agree that the client owns rights; an organization and employee may agree that the employee owns rights. Put agreements in writing. In the absence of a contract to the contrary, work for hire regulations apply to employees.

Most people who contribute to newsletters don't worry about copyrights. For those who do, the standard agreement is for onetime use. The writer, photographer or artist retains rights for repeated use or publication elsewhere.

If you publish material that includes someone else's copyrighted work, you may be liable if the contributor did not obtain permission. If in doubt, ask freelancers and employees to certify the originality of their work.

You may want to print a letter that appeared in another publication or was sent to someone in your organization. The person who wrote the letter owns its copyright. If it was sent as a letter to an editor, there was implied permission to print it only in that editor's publication. If it was sent as private correspondence, there was no permission to reproduce it anywhere. In either case, get permission from the person who wrote the letter before printing it.

To learn more about copyright law and permissions, consult the 1993 edition of *The Chicago Manual of Style.*

4. WRITING

You use writing as the primary method to accomplish the objectives of your newsletter. Content reaches readers mostly by words, not visuals.

Design and graphics help draw attention, but neither holds reader interest in the face of poor writing. Readers feel impatient. You need to get information to them before they get your newsletter to the wastebasket. You compete for attention with jobs, family, housework, computer games and networks, hobbies, television, sleep, shopping, and a dozen pieces of mail.

People often think good writing stems from talent that only few possess. Top professionals may be gifted, but most writers learn their skills. They write, rewrite, then rewrite again. Some write eight or ten drafts before feeling satisfied.

Good writing requires hard work. Neither you nor your management should expect quality articles unless you have the proper time and conditions to craft them. Enough time means at least two or three hours in a row. Proper conditions means working without distractions and interruptions.

Successful writing starts with planning. Knowing why you want an article helps you keep readers in mind. Try to identify which objective each article helps accomplish.

Newsletter writing requires a brisk, informal style. Write headlines and summary decks before writing articles. Keep writing, editing, copyediting and proofreading as discrete activities. Ideally, someone else copyedits and proofreads for you. If you must do every task, carry out each one separately.

Readers skim headlines and summaries first, look at captions and pull quotes next, then—if the topic still interests them—return to the rest of the article. After finishing the article, they may read a sidebar. I have organized this chapter in the order of importance that readers bring to your newsletter: headlines, summary decks, captions and articles.

HEADLINES

For a newspaper or magazine, a specialist writes headlines *after* reading articles. For your newsletter, you should compose headlines *before* writing articles.

Crafting headlines first makes body copy better and production more efficient. It helps you focus on the article. The headline "Fund drive reaches goal" implies a different story from "Pledges ensure new library."

Writing the headline first also suggests how important its article is with regard to other articles in the same issue. The priority of the article tells you the type size of its headline. It helps you visualize the printed newsletter.

Headlines summarize and advertise stories. To make every word count, follow these simple guidelines.

Relate to the story

It seems obvious that a headline should relate to its story, but it's not apparent to every editor. Standing heads for regular features, such as "President's report," invite yawns, not attention.

No   Legislative update
Yes   Senate slates highway hearings

No   Superintendent's corner
Yes   Hometown schools first in SATs

One way to ensure that headlines relate to

stories is to insist they have a verb. The verb can even be implied, as in the second example. A headline without a verb becomes just a dull label.

While standing headlines don't invite attention to articles, they do keep readers alert for collections of short items. Use a standing headline, such as "Washington notes" or "Technology tips," to signal a list of brief (less than one hundred words) items.

Present tense

News is most interesting when fresh. When writing headlines, forget that you know past or future tenses.

No   National officer will attend
        convention
Yes   National rep schedules visit

No   Million dollars sold by Jane Stewart
Yes   Jane Stewart sells million

Writing in the present tense keeps grammar lively and headlines short.

Specific

Tell as much of your story as possible in its headline. Specific heads help readers find exactly the information they seek.

No   Arts and crafts displayed
Yes   Craft fair heralds holidays

No   Production good in eastern mills
Yes   Eastern mills near production record

Writing for specifics is active, not passive. It gets the subject up front and focuses on actions.

SUMMARY DECKS

A summary deck, often just called a "deck," gives a glimpse of the story to follow. Decks create bridges between headlines and articles. They capture the essence of the story, leaving readers free to seek details or move elsewhere in the newsletter. Newspapers, such as *USA Today*, use decks effectively to help readers absorb information quickly.

Most newsletter articles don't need a deck because the article itself is very short—only two or three paragraphs. An article longer than three paragraphs, however, calls for a summary after the headline.

Write decks as one sentence that follows the rules of grammar and punctuation. Make it tell meaning as well as information. Following are some examples.

Headline	New computers raise productivity
Deck	Information Services reports that the seven machines purchased last spring have already increased output 43 percent.
Headline	Smith chosen to lead choir
Deck	Starting January 15th, Sandra Smith steps onto the podium as the first professional director of Hometown Choir.

When you write a deck, keep in mind that many readers will not continue with the story that follows. Make sure the headline and the deck together contain all the essential information.

CAPTIONS

When you print a photograph or infographic (chart, graph, table or map), readers' eyes go from headlines and decks directly to the visual image. Readers examine visuals *before* reading the text of articles.

Every visual needs a caption. This sounds obvious until you examine hundreds of newsletters and realize how often editors print a photo or chart with no caption.

A caption is a major opportunity to connect with your reader. Don't waste the chance to tell your story. Write a caption for every photo and infographic in every issue. Put captions for photos and tables under the image and captions for charts and graphs inside the image right under the headline.

Following are some guidelines for writing captions.

Avoid the obvious

Make the caption add information to the visual, not merely repeat what the reader can already see. Instead of "Officials at awards banquet," write "Jane Smith and Charles Jones celebrate Smith's appointment as corporate counsel."

Convey context and meaning

Tell your readers why the photo or infographic matters to them. Certify that it relates to a communication goal you have for the associated article and the newsletter as a whole.

Print names

Readers want to see names of people in pictures as much as the people themselves do. Unless the photo shows a very large group, such as an orchestra, print the name of everyone in a photograph. If faces look too small to recognize, why print the photo at all?

Relate to the story

Visuals in newsletters rarely stand alone, as they sometimes do in newspapers, but work with an adjacent article. Use captions to reinforce the relationship. Don't hesitate to include words such as "described in the article at the right" or "explained in the sidebar."

ARTICLES

Effective style for newsletter articles is informal and reflects natural speaking.

Newsletters are less formal than magazines, books and reports. The informal style stems from the relatively small amount of space for each article, the value of letting the editor's personality show, and readers' desire for efficiency when seeking practical information.

When you talk, you use plain language and common images. Your words flow easily and sound interesting because they form natural extensions of your personality. You don't worry about rules that seem artificial.

When you organize your thoughts and express them clearly, what you write sounds similar to what you say. The best writing for newsletters has the following characteristics.

Simple

You rarely need complicated language to tell a story—even a complicated story. Everyday words do the job.

INSTEAD OF	WRITE
assist	help
obtain	get
ascertain	learn
attempt	try
facilitate	help, ease
implement	do
indicate	show
insufficient	not enough
numerous	many
terminate	end, stop
as a result of	because
in excess of	more than

Every field has technical terms required for precise writing. But don't confuse technical words with jargon. Trying to seem authoritative may only make you sound pompous.

Write to express, not impress. Jargon drives out simplicity and separates you from readers. Use it only if you want to fill space without saying anything.

Specific

When you talk, you usually refer to things you can sense so you can describe in specific terms. Try to write the same way, using details to tell your story.

General	The annual meeting was well attended.
Specific	Eighty-five people came to the meeting.
General	Members will have an opportunity to give feedback.
Specific	Say what you think by writing

to Ann Hollings before Friday.

General	Financial considerations negatively impacted our sales results.
Specific	Last quarter sales fell by 18 percent because our best customer went bankrupt.

Concrete words create images and examples. When language gets general and abstract, it grows dull and vague.

Compact

Avoid clutter. Get to the point. Purge every useless word. Juggle phrases and sentences until they fit precisely together.

No	All aspects of the situation should be taken into careful consideration prior to the implementation of corrective action.
Yes	Don't change anything until you've checked it thoroughly.
No	Of extreme importance in timely and effective processing of modifications with a minimum of adverse cost impact is the maintenance of upstream visibility to supervisory personnel.
Yes	To keep costs down, tell your supervisor about changes.

Clutter depersonalizes. And it promotes mistakes. When writing isn't clear, don't blame readers if they miss the point. Clutter hides responsibility. Vague messages mean readers can't hold anyone accountable.

Keep sentences, paragraphs and articles in your newsletter as short as in a personal letter. Limit your average sentence to about fifteen words, average paragraph to three or four sentences, and average article to three or four paragraphs. Write some sentences with only three or four words, some paragraphs with only one sentence, and some articles with only one or two paragraphs.

In addition to being easy to read, uncluttered writing keeps production and postage costs to a minimum.

Strong verbs

Verbs form the guts of language, making other words work. Weak verbs kill writing; strong verbs make it sparkle.

Strong verbs link directly to touch, sight, smell, sound, taste and familiar emotions. They are short and personal, such as run, fight, love, say. And strong verbs tend to couple with other short, strong words: drive in, write fast, work hard.

WEAK VERB	STRONG VERB
inform	tell, say
reduce	cut
indicate	show
modify	change
endeavor	try
desire	want

Weak verbs seem abstract and impersonal. They tend to be long words and, moreover, to attract heavy adverbs into phrases such as "frequently employ," "constantly postponing" and "tediously constructing."

Action

Readers want to know who or what the sentence is about, then what happened. Action builds interest. To get action, begin with the subject and follow with a strong verb.

No   A candidate will be Ellen James.
Yes   Ellen James said she would run.

No   The Lincoln auditorium was the site where members congregated.
Yes   Members met in the auditorium of Lincoln School.

Most forms of the verb "to be" produce drab sentences. To perk up your writing, find strong verb replacements for "is," "be," "was" and "were." Replacements almost force you to start sentences with subjects.

Pronouns

Little words such as "he," "she" and "they" help make sentences move briskly.

No   The sales manager informed the audit task force that projections were encouraging a reduction in personnel

Yes   She told them some people would lose their jobs because of falling profits.

Don't hesitate to use "I" and "we." Get rid of those cumbersome phrases, such as "Your editor thinks. . ." and "The committee decided. . ." Tell readers your opinion in clear, simple terms just as if you were speaking directly to them.

Contractions

Yes, I know English teachers say contractions don't belong in good writing. That's not so, at least not for newsletters.

Successful newsletters have personality. Few people talk without using contractions, but most editors turn a spoken "won't" into a written "will not." The two-word version sounds slightly more formal, thus less personal. You do not need to pepper your prose with contractions; neither should you avoid one where it sounds right. It's up to you.

Delete "that"

This common and apparently useful word is a term that clutters language and that encourages writers that are not careful to string out ideas that should be broken into sentences that could be shorter.

Try crossing out every "that" in your last issue. No exceptions. Read the articles aloud and replace "that" only when a sentence makes less sense without it. Perhaps one sentence in ten will get its "that" back.

To improve your newsletter writing skills, study Lionel Fisher's book *The Craft of Corporate Journalism*.

A sidebar is a short news item or feature that supplements a longer article. Sidebars appear in a box or screen tint placed adjacent to articles. You see them frequently in magazines, newspapers, and books.

Newsletter design rarely calls for a sidebar because the articles themselves are short and space is precious. If you print an article longer than 500 words, you might consider a 100- or 150-word sidebar that provides biographical references, gives a detailed example, or summarizes a point of view different from the main article.

AVOIDING BIAS

Good writers want readers focused on the topic, so don't risk offending them with slurs or stereotypes based on gender, race, age, ethnic background, physical ability or sexual preference.

You may find inoffensive prose hard to produce when writing flows from natural speaking. No one, however, can afford the luxury of printing words that slip carelessly from the mouth.

Writing allows for editing. Offensive remarks don't belong in your newsletter. Here are some guidelines to help keep your writing free from bias.

Parallel language

If males are men, call females women, not girls or ladies. Gentlemen may accompany ladies, and boys go with girls, but "man and wife" should be "husband and wife."

Equal respect

Physical traits (beauty, strength) and stereotypes (emotional, logical) are usually irrelevant. So are titles indicating gender.

No Mrs. Rogers, who can still wear her college skirts, takes over as president next month.

Yes Ann Rogers, a graduate of the University of Kansas, takes over as president next month.

No Standing next to her handsome husband John, Carol Simon unveiled drawings of Simon Industry's headquarters building.

Yes Accompanied by her husband John, ...

No John Rogers and Mrs. Thompson planned last year's annual picnic.

Yes John Rogers and Sally Thompson....

or Rogers and Thompson....

or John and Sally....

A married, divorced or widowed woman may use her husband's name, her given name or both. Ask which she prefers. Company policy or your style sheet may require titles for first and subsequent references. Stay consistent.

No Sam Purdy and Julia Brown were promoted. Purdy joined the firm in 1965 and Julia in 1972.

Yes Sam Purdy and Julia Brown were promoted. Purdy joined the firm in 1965 and Brown in 1972.

or Sam joined.... and Julia....

or Mr. Purdy.... and Ms. Brown....

Generic titles and descriptions

Usually it's not necessary to identify a person by gender. Moreover, you seldom need to replace "man" with the cumbersome "person."

NO	YES
businessman	executive, merchant
chairman	leader, moderator, director, head

manned	staffed
middle man	liaison, intermediary, go-between, agent
salesman	agent, clerk, representative
spokesman	representative, advocate

Care with pronouns

Half the population is women, but you don't have to use half your space writing "he/she." Tight writing is harder, but more interesting.

No   A careful housewife keeps XYZ soap near her laundry.

Yes   A careful housekeeper uses XYZ laundry soap.

No   When a salesman is properly trained, he keeps management informed of his prospects.

Yes   Properly trained sales reps keep management informed about prospects.

No   Each employee completes time sheets at the end of his shift.

Yes   Each employee completes a time sheet at the end of a shift.

Or   All employees complete time sheets at the end of a shift.

No   The average parent wants more park facilities for his children and more after school activities for her teenagers.

Yes   The average parent wants more park facilities for children and more after school activities for teenagers.

Avoid irrelevant categories

Do readers really need to know gender, race, age or ethnic group? Only if the information relates to the story.

Would you write: *Allen Bemis, noted white governor....?*

Then why write: *Patrick Buchman, noted Black legislator....?*

Would you write: *Sally, an outgoing English American....?*

Then why write: *Mary, an outgoing Japanese American....?*

Language shapes thought as well as conveys it. Word patterns and meanings define how people view their world.

Racism, sexism and other "isms" are modes of thinking created in part by language. Writing that is free from slurs and stereotypes will not alone end discrimination. Inoffensive prose can, however, help readers build thought patterns suited to a society free from bias.

COPYEDITING

Copyeditors check and correct writing for spelling, grammar, punctuation, inconsistencies, inaccuracies, and conformity to style requirements.

If you write using a computer, you may use a spell checker. The software helps make spelling accurate, but cannot replace the human eye. The spell checker doesn't stop at "fare" to query whether you mean "fair."

Most spell-checking programs let you add a few thousand words to prevent embarrassing errors with personal names and technical terms. Add them.

Computers give easy access to a thesaurus. The instant choice of words improves both style and precision. If you don't use a computer to write, a thesaurus in the traditional form of a book is a must.

To make copyediting easy and accurate, use a style sheet giving rules for use of capitals, numerals, abbreviations and similar topics. When you follow the rules, readers don't feel confused or distracted by variations of style.

Large publishers use a style book giving a rule for every conceivable writing situation. Some use a standard reference such as *Words Into Type* or *The Chicago Manual of Style*; others, such as United Press International and the *New York Times*, develop their own handbooks. In addition, some professional organizations issue guides to style. Two of the best known are published by the Council of Biology Editors and the American Psychological Association.

Base your style sheet on accepted rules, but also include usage specific to your field. If you are part of a large company or organization, there probably is a corporate identity book that includes rules of style. For example, your organization might require that you spell out its own name each time it's used, not abbreviate it or use an acronym.

Style must accommodate feelings about titles and status. For example, some people want all the letters after their names (CEO, Ph.D., ABC). Others want their titles fully announced (Deputy Executive Associate to the Interim Administrative Assistant) when they are first mentioned in an article.

Copyediting is different from proofreading. Don't try to do both jobs at once. Read for style, revise your writing, then proofread.

PROOFREADING

Proofreaders examine final copy for errors in keyboarding. They verify accuracy, not style.

Copyedit as you write. Proofread when you output articles in final form. Proofing is the final stage of producing content.

Ideally, you do not copyedit or proofread your own writing. Newsletter editors rarely enjoy the luxury of that ideal.

Good writers or copyeditors don't necessarily make good proofreaders. Writers and editors strive for style; proofreaders safeguard detail. They compare arithmetic in tables with numbers in text, names in captions with faces in photos, and spellings in the beginning of stories with those at the end. They notice when the calendar says the convention starts on April 31st.

Proofreading involves examining type as well as content. Your proofreader should spot subheads that should be bold or captions that should be italic.

Meditation Preserves Peace

Overgrown hedges, hanging branches, lack of animal control, and loud music are getting on people's nerves these days.

Neighborhood Mediation is keeping a watchful eye on the mood of our neighborhoods during the hot summer months. People are expressing concern and seeking remedies to the issues of importance to them.

With Mediation, a neighbor knows that he doesn't have to take matters into his own hands. Contacting our office is the first step, and a bold step, toward establishing the critical points of communication and understanding that will help resolve conflict. "People help solve their own problems in Mediation," says Eddie Collins, Mediation Specialist.

neighborhood dis[
can escalate into s(
ing injury or crim
focus of our progi
flict and preserve t
borhood.

The staff of N
volunteers have
promptly and eff(
referrals. There is

The following :
the potential sour
can frequently be
diation: Harassme
problems; noise al
nuisance issues, p
and much more.

Call the Mediat
state your proble

4-2 Proofread everyting (sic) If meditation fails, try mediation. And watch those personal pronouns. Only half the neighbors are male. The sentence could say, "...neighbors know they don't have to take matters into their own hands."

5. TYPE

Type forms the most important element of design. Poorly selected type makes content hard to grasp; appropriate type makes your newsletter inviting and easy to understand.

Type is letters, numerals, punctuation marks and other symbols that printing reproduces. You choose what type to use for body copy, headlines and other elements, such as captions. Specifying type involves deciding such additional matters as size, weight, column width, line spacing and alignment.

Although complicated, you need to make decisions about type for a newsletter only once every two or three years. After evaluating some trial layouts and making up your mind, your choice should work for many issues. Efficient production, quality appearance and readable copy depend on consistent typography within each issue and from one issue to the next.

For over five hundred years, printers, publishers and designers have experimented with type. Fads come and go, but standards have emerged that fashion cannot erase. In this chapter you learn how to apply those standards to your publication. In addition to following the standards, type in a publication that appears professional adheres to consistent style requirements. Those requirements are fully presented in books such as *Words Into Type* and *The Chicago Manual of Style*.

SOURCES OF TYPE

Your newsletter may use typewriter type, dot matrix type or laser type.

Typewriter

If you use a typewriter, make sure the machine has a carbon or film ribbon. Cloth ribbons yield fuzzy type because the weave of the cloth is uneven.

Most typewriters produce equally spaced type, not proportionally spaced as in type from a computer. In equally spaced type, each letter occupies the same amount of space regardless of the letter's width. Proportional type has space allocated to letters according to their width, so it uses paper more efficiently.

Equal-spaced type works for a one-column newsletter. You can produce an ideal column of equal-spaced type for a two-column newsletter by using the reduction capability of most photocopy machines.

Dot matrix

Computer printers using the points of pins hitting a ribbon or small drops of ink to form characters make dot matrix type. You can adjust most printers to two or three densities, one of which is near letter quality (NLQ).

Type from dot matrix printers operating in either draft or graphics mode is fuzzy and hard to read for more than a few words at a time. The NLQ setting, even though it reduces printout speed, is the only acceptable density for newsletters.

Dot matrix printers vary widely in their typefaces and their ability to reproduce what appears on the screen. Most machines and software have a greater capability than their operators have explored. If you print out word processing on a dot matrix printer, take the time or ask for the training to learn the full capabilities of the machine.

Laser

Laser printers form characters when a pulsating laser beam places an electric charge on paper. There are two kinds of laser printers: the printer that's part of a desktop system and a device called an imagesetter located at a service bureau or printing company.

Desktop laser printers use toner, a powder, and have output resolutions of 300 dots per inch (dpi) or 600 dpi. Type from a 300 dpi printer meets quality standards for most newsletters, but the machine won't output screen tints or halftones good enough to reproduce. A 600 dpi machine can output tints and halftones suited to any newsletter except one produced in color for an upscale market.

The highest quality type comes from imagesetters using laser beams to form characters on photosensitive paper. For that reason, their output is often called phototype to distinguish it from laser type on plain bond paper. The photo paper is smoother and whiter than paper used in office laser printers, and the dots are much smaller than toner can produce.

An imagesetter outputs at 1,200 dpi, 2,400 dpi or even higher. Any of these resolutions are suited to newsletter production.

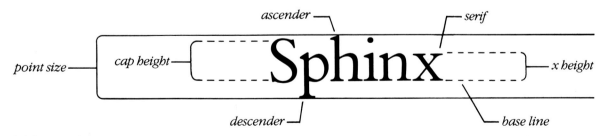

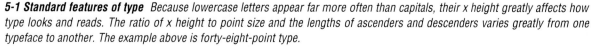

5-1 Standard features of type *Because lowercase letters appear far more often than capitals, their x height greatly affects how type looks and reads. The ratio of x height to point size and the lengths of ascenders and descenders varies greatly from one typeface to another. The example above is forty-eight-point type.*

THE

REFORMER

A PUBLICATION OF THE AMERICAN TORT REFORM ASSOCIATION   VOL. 1 NO. 3 MAY 1987

5-2 Type as graphic *As part of a nameplate, type conveys image. Choose carefully and, ideally, with the help of a graphic designer experienced with publications. For more examples of type as graphics, see Visual 8-18. (Designs by Polly Pattison.)*

SELECTING TYPE

Art applied to letterforms is as ancient as writing itself. Today there are almost five thousand available typefaces. You can, however, produce a successful newsletter by working with only one or two.

Typefaces are grouped into families with similar letterforms and a unique name such as Prestige or Garamond. The "parent" of the family is the letterform in book, light or regular; the "relatives" are all derivations such as bold, italic or condensed. Neither the names of type families nor even designs that seem identical are standard. Helvetica looks similar to Helios, Claro, Newton and Megaron. Courier, a popular typeface for typewriters, looks similar to American Typewriter, available as laser type.

Useful type families include typefaces with a variety of weights, such as light and bold, and come in both italic and roman (upright). In addition, you may find bold weights available

in condensed, extended and other versions for headlines.

A type font is a complete assortment of characters of one typeface, such as Times Roman, in one style, such as bold. Fonts of type may be contained on print wheels, on sheets of dry transfer lettering, in computer memories, and in many other physical forms.

Following are a few simple guidelines that make choosing type for your newsletter easy. After deciding, stick with your choice. Don't change on impulse, especially not while producing a specific issue. If you have too much copy, edit some out or increase the number of pages instead of reducing size of type or space between lines.

Familiarity

People read by the shape of whole words, not the form of individual letters. The shape of words, however, depends on letterforms. Familiar letterforms create words whose meanings readers perceive instantly.

Familiar typefaces for body copy promote efficient reading. New or unusual designs detract from content. Unless you are a skilled graphic designer experienced with newsletter typography, choose type, such as Times or Palatino, with a proven record. Familiar type is also standard, meaning you can change methods of production without changing typefaces.

Family loyalty

Select one family of type and use it for all body copy and other elements, with the possible exception of headlines. Sticking to one family makes your newsletter cohesive. Build interest by changing size and weight or using italic, not by switching from one type family to another.

Choose a type family with a variety of weights (light, medium, bold) that come in upright and italic. You may need the variety to make captions, pull quotes, subheads and other elements.

If you need special punctuation marks,

mathematical signs or symbols, verify that the type you prefer includes all the characters you need or that they are readily available on another font that looks acceptable. Most computers include fonts such as Symbol and Zapf Dingbats that offer plenty of variety.

x height

The size of lowercase letters in proportion to the size of capitals is referred to as x height. Type with a generous x height appears contemporary and looks bigger than type of the same point size with a smaller x height. Legible type is easy to read. In addition to x height, legibility is affected by serifs, weight, size, leading, white space, and the paper on which type appears.

Serifs

Tiny lines that cross the ending strokes of most characters are called serifs. They make reading efficient by helping the eye move easily along the line.

Use serif type, such as Garamond, for body copy. If you think traditional serif type looks too formal, use a modified serif typeface, such as Souvenir or Optima. Type for headlines may be a larger, bolder version of body type or a bold type without serifs. See Visual 5-5 for guidelines.

Type without serifs, known as sans serif, is appropriate for headlines and when characters must be smaller than ten points and include many numerals. Use type such as Helvetica or Avant Garde for charts, tables, lists and formulas, but not for body copy itself.

Weight

Type comes in a variety of weights ranging from light and book through medium and semibold to bold and extra bold. Some weights have different names in different families. For instance, book may be called regular, or extra bold may be known as black.

Body copy should appear in light or book, headlines in a heavier weight. Captions are

Times Roman

1234567890$

8 POINT
abcdefghijklmnopqrstuvwxyz
ABCDEFGHIJKLMNOPQRSTUVWXYZ

9 POINT
abcdefghijklmnopqrstuvwxyz
ABCDEFGHIJKLMNOPQRSTUVWXYZ

10 POINT
abcdefghijklmnopqrstuvwxyz
ABCDEFGHIJKLMNOPQRSTUVWXYZ

11 POINT
abcdefghijklmnopqrstuvwxyz
ABCDEFGHIJKLMNOPQRSTUVWXYZ

12 POINT
abcdefghijklmnopqrstuvwxyz
ABCDEFGHIJKLMNOPQRSTUVWXYZ

14 POINT
abcdefghijklmnopqrstuvwxyz
ABCDEFGHIJKLMNOPQRSTUV

16 POINT
abcdefghijklmnopqrstuvwxyz
ABCDEFGHIJKLMNOPQRST

18 POINT
abcdefghijklmnopqrstuvwxy
ABCDEFGHIJKLMNOPQR

20 POINT
abcdefghijklmnopqrstuvw
ABCDEFGHIJKLMNOP

24 POINT
abcdefghijklmnopqrst
ABCDEFGHIJKLM

5-3 Type size Design, boldness and spacing as well as point size influence how large type seems. When you view type on your computer screen, you get only an approximate sense of how it will look on paper. To ensure more accurate judgments, print out a chart such as this showing the typeface for your newsletter.

Head: Syntax bold, 24pt.   *Kicker: Syntax italic, 12pt.*

Opus sci ent factortum poen legnum quas nulla praid

Tuntung evlent sib conliant

*Text:
Garamond3
11/13
ragged
right*

Lorem ipsum dolor sit amet, con sectetuer adipiscing elit, sed diam nonnumy nibh euismod tempor inci dunt ut labore et dolore magna ali quam erat volupat. Ut wisi enim ad minim veniam, quis nostrud exerci tation ullamcorper suscipit laboris nisl ut aliquip ex ea commodo con sequat. Duis autem vel eum irure dolor in henderit in vulputate velit esse consequat.

Vel illum dolore eu feugiat nulla facilisi at vero eos et accusam et ius to odio dignissim qui blandit prae sent luptatum zzril delenit aigue duos dolore et molestias exceptur sint occaecat cupiditat non simil pro vedit tempor sunt in culpa qui officia deserunt mollit anium ib est abor um et dolor fuga. Et harumd dereud facilis est er expedit distinct. Nam liber tempor cum soluta nobis eligend option congue nihil impediet doming id quod maxim placeat facer possim omnis voluptas assumenda est, omnis repellend.

Temporibud auteui quinusd et aur office debit aut tum rerum necessit atib saepe eveniet ut er molestia non recusand. Itaque earud rerum hic ten tury sapiente delectus au aut prefer zim endis dolorib asperiore repellat. Hanc ego cum tene senteniam, quid est cur verear ne ad eam non possing

accomodare nost ros quos tu paulo ante cum memorite tum etia ergat. Nos amice et nbevol, olestias access potest fier ad augend ascum consci ent to factor tum poen legum odio que civiuda. Et tamen in busdam neque nonor imper ned libiding gen epular reli guard cupiditati quas nul la praid om undat.

Improb pary minuit, potios im flammad ut coercend magist and et dodencendesse videantur. Inviat igi tur vera ratio bene sanos adzum justiatiam, aequitated fidem. Neque hominy infant aut inuiste fact est cond qui neg facile efficerd possit duo conetud notiner si effercerit, et opes vel fortunag vel ingen liberalitat magis conveniunt, da but tuntung ben evolent sib conciliant, et aptis.

*Text:
Garamond3
11/12
ragged
right*

Mosetias simil tempor

*Subhead:
Syntax
bold
12pt.*

Sim est ad quiet. Endium caritat prae sert cum omning nul sit causpeccand quaert en imigent cupidtat a natura proficis vacile explent sine julla inura autend inanc sunt is par end non est nihil enim desidera endis ut lobore et dolore magna ali quam erat volupat. Ut wisi enim ad minim veniam, quis nostrud exerci tation ullamcorper suscipit laboris nisl ut aliquip ex ea commodo con sequat. Duis autem vel eum irure dolor in henderit in vulputate velit esse consequat.

Vel illum dolore eu feugiat nulla

5-4 Patterns of type *Column width of the ragged-right type above is 2¼ inches, the line measure of most three-column newsletters. To ensure legibility, long lines of type need more line spacing than short lines. In the example above, 11/12 seems about right, but would seem too tight for type set 3¼ inches wide for a two-column format. Adding another point of leading often makes text easier to read.*

Opus sci ent factortum poen legnum quas nulla praid

Tuntung evlent sib conliant

Lorem ipsum dolor sit amet, con sectetuer adipiscing elit, sed diam nonnumy nibh euismod tempor inci dunt ut labore et dolore magna ali quam erat volupat. Ut wisi enim ad minim veniam, quis nostrud exerci tation ullamcorper suscipit laboris nisl ut aliquip ex ea commodo con sequat. Duis autem vel eum irure dolor in henderit in vulputate velit esse consequat.

Vel illum dolore eu feugiat nulla facilisi at vero eos et accusam et ius to odio dignissim qui blandit prae sent luptatum zzril delenit aigue duos dolore et molestias exceptur sint occaecat cupiditat non simil pro vedit tempor sunt in culpa qui officia deserunt mollit anium ib est abor um et dolor fuga. Et harumd dereud facilis est er expedit distinct. Nam liber tempor cum soluta nobis eligend option congue nihil impediet doming id quod maxim placeat facer possim omnis voluptas assumenda est, omnis repellend.

Temporibud auteui quinusd et aur office debit aut tum rerum necessit atib saepe eveniet ut er molestia non recusand. Itaque earud rerum hic ten tury sapiente delectus au aut prefer zim endis dolorib

asperiore repellat. Hanc ego cum tene senteniam, quid est cur verear ne ad eam non possing accomodare nost ros quos tu paulo ante cum memorite tum etia ergat. Nos amice et nbevol, olestias access potest fier ad augend ascum consci ent to factor tum poen legum odio que civiuda. Et tamen in busdam neque nonor imper ned libiding gen epular reli guard cupiditati quas nul la praid om undat.

Improb pary minuit, potios im flammad ut coercend magist and et dodencendesse videantur. Inviat igi tur vera ratio bene sanos adzum justiatiam, aequitated.

Mosetias simil tempor

Fidem neque hominy infant aut inuiste fact est cond qui neg facile efficerd possit duo conetud notiner si effercerit, et opes vel fortunag vel ingen liberalitat magis conveniunt, da but tuntung ben evolent sib conciliant, et aptis sim est ad quiet. Endium caritat prae sert cum omning nul sit causpeccand quaert en imigent cupidtat a natura proficis vacile explent sine julla inura autend inanc sunt is par end non est nihil enim desidera endis ut lobore et dolore

5-5 More patterns of type *Columns above have the same line measure as those on the opposite page, but are justified instead of ragged. Note that the text type on these two pages is all eleven-point. The Century type on this page seems bigger because of its generous x height, compared with the relatively small x height of the Garamond text type opposite. Experiment with combinations of type before making final decisions.*

often set in a heavier weight but smaller size than body copy.

When considering the weight of type, take into account how your newsletter will be printed. Photocopy machines tend to fatten type, so a typeface with relatively thin lines, such as Times, might work best. Offset printing should reproduce type accurately, so a typeface with thicker strokes, such as Bookman, might work well.

Size

The height of type determines its size, expressed in units called points. One point equals $1/72$ inch. Visual 5-3 shows examples of type at various point sizes.

Body copy in one-column newsletters

5-6 TYPE SPECIFICATIONS

Body copy 11/13 Times Roman, 2½-inch line measure, ragged-right, ⁴⁄₁₀-inch paragraph indent, ¼-inch alley

Major headlines 36-point Helvetica bold, flush left

Minor headlines 24-point Helvetica bold, flush left

Subtitles 14-point Helvetica bold, flush left

Captions 10/12 Times italic, ragged right

Pull quotes 18-point Times Roman

Footers 12-point Helvetica bold, flush to outside margins

5-6 Type specifications *Clear specifications for type bring two major benefits. They free you to concentrate on content issue after issue, knowing that you have already made major design choices. And they lead to a consistent look that helps readers understand your newsletter quickly.*

Make specifications for type so clear that another person could produce your newsletter without consulting with you. The list above shows how yours might look.

should be twelve-point, the size of pica type from a typewriter. Type smaller than twelve-point, such as elite, for a one-column format produces too many characters per line.

Newsletters in either a two- or three-column format should be in ten- or eleven-point type. Twelve-point is OK if your readers don't see well or if you don't have much to say; nine-point is OK if your readers are under age thirty-five or feel desperate for your information.

If ten-point type seems too large, use a lighter weight typeface; if it doesn't allow enough copy, edit more tightly. Don't switch to a smaller size. If eleven-point seems too small, try a heavier weight and/or slightly more space between lines.

Line measure—the width of one column—should influence type size. The average reader takes in three or four words per eye movement and comprehends best when making two eye movements per line. The ideal line has seven or eight words and contains between 40 and 50 characters.

Newsletters in a one-column format look empty if restricted to 45 or even 50 characters per line. They should not, however, have more than 60 characters. Most publications with a three-column format need ten-point type to assure lines with at least 35 characters.

Leading

Often called line spacing, leading refers to the distance between lines of type. It is expressed in points and measured from one baseline to the next. Type with a point size of ten and with two points of leading is "ten on twelve," written 10/12.

Short lines need less space between them than long lines. Type for two-column newsletters needs at least two more points of leading than the size of type used. Eleven-point type in a two-column format should be set 11/13. Three-column formats may have one or two points of leading; one-column formats should have two or three points. Software for word

Text type	Headline type					
	same family	Orator	Helvetica bold	Univers medium	Avant Guard med	Optima bold
Courier pica	bold					
Prestige pica	bold					
Times Roman	bold					
Garamond light	book					
Bookman light	medium					
Souvenir light	medium					
Optima	medium					

Courier pica

Prestige pica

Times Roman

Garamond light

Bookman light

Souvenir light

Optima

ORATOR ORATOR

Helvetica bold

Univers medium

Avant Garde medium

Optima bold

5-7 Type combinations *The chart shows dependable combinations of text and headline type. The first column after text type gives a headline type in the same family. Cells with screen tints show a sans serif type for headlines to complement the serif text type. Each combination of type gives a different look. Experiment before deciding.*

The typefaces for body copy are commonly found on computers and printers. Courier and Prestige are also the most common typefaces for typewriters. Typefaces for headlines are also available as dry transfer lettering.

processing and desktop publishing defaults to two-point leading, OK for most publications. Visuals 5-6 and 5-7 show variations in leading.

Alignment

Type for body copy may be flush right so the ends of lines are even with each other or ragged right so they are uneven. Visuals 5-6 and 5-7 show examples.

For most readers, flush right type seems more formal, official or technical than ragged right.

Alignment does not influence legibility—unless it affects space between words. When words have too little space between them, readers cannot distinguish them from each other. When words have too much space, they break into distant elements that cause inefficient reading.

Flush right type often comes at the expense of proper word spacing. This situation occurs most frequently with short lines that contain only three or four words.

Paper

Because legibility stems from contrast, it is affected by the surface on which type appears. Use smooth, white paper to get characters in high contrast. White, smooth 80# uncoated book or 28# bond is ideal for output ready to print or photocopy. These are slightly heavier stocks than most offices keep among their paper supplies.

HEADLINES

Headline type is any type fourteen points or larger, whether used for headlines, subheads, logos or other elements. Few newsletters use headline type smaller than eighteen-point or larger than thirty-six-point.

Headlines affect how your publication looks as well as how it reads. Following some simple typographic guidelines makes them work best.

Standard capitalization

Set headlines using upper- and lowercase letters, not all caps. Follow the same rules for capitalizing that you do when writing any sentence.

Headlines are easiest to read when they look like bold sentences because the eye identifies words by their upper outlines. Words in all caps have a uniform outline; readers must comprehend them letter by letter instead of at a glance. Headlines with a beginning capital for each word signal people to read each word separately, not the whole line as one message.

Consistent

Use type from only one family for all headlines. Often the best choice is simply a larger and bolder version of body type. Headline type without serifs also works well. Visual 5-7 presents combinations you can depend on. The newsletters in Visual 8-10 show consistent typography in practice.

When specifying headlines, create emphasis by changing size. Use 36- or 30-point type for your most important headlines, 30- or 24-point for less important ones, and 18- or 14-point for subheads. Don't jump from bold to black or from upright to italic.

Flush left

Align the first letter of the headline with the left side of the article. Flush left headlines are easiest to read. Centered headlines look formal and conservative, but are harder to read.

Row 1

Your Nameplate
Issue Number — Your Subtitle — Date

Headlines run best above text

Lorem ipsum placeholder text.

Start text below the left side of the headline. Keep all text below its headline.

Your Nameplate
Issue Number — Your Subtitle — Date

Headlines read best flush left

Flush left looks familiar

This one, too

Align headlines flush left for easiest reading and informal look.

Your Nameplate
Issue Number — Your Subtitle — Date

Centered heads look formal

They can also look elegant

Use centered headlines to create a formal, conservative, or elegant image.

Row 2

Your Nameplate
Issue Number — Your Subtitle — Date

Make the headline introduce the story

Contents

Make the headline introduce the story

Relate headlines to stories. Avoid standing headlines for articles and regular columns.

Your Nameplate
Issue Number — Your Subtitle — Date

Readers appreciate appealing headlines

Stick with present tense

Write headlines in the present tense.

Your Nameplate
Issue Number — Your Subtitle — Date

Headlines work best in newsletters as complete sentences

Headlines work best as complete sentences

Give headlines a subject and a verb so they read as normal sentences.

Row 3

Your Nameplate
Issue Number — Your Subtitle — Date

Readers understand downstyle best

Don't capitalize every word

Capitalize as a normal sentence. Avoid using all caps or caps for every word.

Your Nameplate
Issue Number — Your Subtitle — Date

Major headlines need bold type

Minor heads need smaller size of the same typeface

Stick with one typeface. Add variety by changing size, not weight or style.

Your Nameplate
Issue Number — Your Subtitle — Date

Use standing headlines to start lists or columns of short items

Use specific headlines to start the story below

Standing head

Use standing headlines to announce groups or lists of short items.

6. GRAPHICS

Graphics is art used to express thought. Both parts of the definition are essential: art and thought. A clear message pleasing to the eye forms the essence of graphics—ideas and information through art.

Graphic art includes typography, photography, design graphics and infographics. Chapter five dealt with typography and chapter seven deals with photography. This chapter deals with design graphics and infographics.

Design graphics for newsletters include rules (lines), screen tints, reverses, symbols and drawings. Infographics include charts, graphs, tables and maps.

Graphics help organize and compress information, so they are especially important for newsletters. Each graphic element should help your newsletter reach its goals. For example, design graphics make reading more efficient by separating and highlighting. They call or direct attention, signal the importance of an article, and break the monotony of solid text. Graphics reinforce text by repeating or elaborating on information.

RULES

When used as graphics, lines for borders, dividers and boxes are called rules. They are the most simple graphics to use.

You can produce rules using a special pen, typewriter, computer, border tape or dry transfer material. Whatever the source, they must meet specific quality standards. Straight lines should look straight, not like sagging telephone wires. Curved lines need uniform arcs.

Like type, rules need clean edges. Border tape that has gathered dust in a desk drawer and pens with felt tips or ball points give poor results. Rules made by laser printers are acceptable and imagesetters are preferable.

In addition to solid, rules come in a variety of patterns consisting of dots, dashes and symbols. Indeed, there are so many ways to make rules that you risk having too much variety. Limit yourself to three kinds. Learn how to get the most out of those three patterns and sizes.

Reducing rules in a photocopy machine or process camera makes them thinner as well as shorter. Be careful not to make them so thin

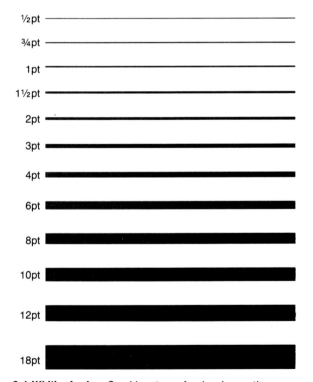

6-1 Width of rules *Graphic arts professionals use the same system of points for expressing the size of type to describe the size of rules. Rules and borders you make using a laser printer also use the point system.*

You can combine rules of various widths and patterns into distinctive graphic effects. Use the rules above as a quick reference when deciding what size to use.

they will not reproduce when printed.

SCREEN TINTS

Screen tints are known also as shadings, fill patterns and tones. They look like light versions of the ink or toner used to produce type. Tints made with black ink appear gray.

Tints are useful ways to highlight blocks, such as mastheads, tables of contents and pull quotes. You can also use tints to give texture to drawings and help organize data within calendars. For examples of these techniques in newsletters, examine Visuals 8-2 and 8-4.

Screen tints create the illusion of lighter printing because they consist of dots that allow the color of paper to show among them. Each dot consists of 100 percent toner or ink.

Dot size and the distance between them determine how dark or light a screen tint appears. Lots of paper showing around the dots makes the tint seem light; not much paper makes it seem dark. Printers use percentages to describe the density of a screen tint. A 90 percent screen looks close to solid; a 10 percent screen seems very light.

In addition to percentage of ink or toner within a screen tint, the tint is affected by the number of lines of dots per inch. As you can see in Visual 6-2, screens with relatively few lines of dots per inch are coarse; fine screens have many lines per inch. The number of lines per inch is called a screen's ruling.

If you want to supply screen tints yourself, you can add them to camera-ready copy or supply them as part of computer files. If you want your printer to add them, you can simply designate the areas for tints. Print shops have different preferences about how customers should identify tints, so ask your printer for instructions.

Catalogs from companies such as Letraset show screen tints and offer tips on using the material. Most art supply stores carry a wide selection.

If you add tints in your computer files, avoid using a 300 dpi laser printer for final out-

	85 line screen	100 line screen	133 line screen
20%	REVERSE / OVERPRINT	REVERSE / OVERPRINT	REVERSE / OVERPRINT
30%	REVERSE / OVERPRINT	REVERSE / OVERPRINT	REVERSE / OVERPRINT
40%	REVERSE / OVERPRINT	REVERSE / OVERPRINT	REVERSE / OVERPRINT
50%	REVERSE / OVERPRINT	REVERSE / OVERPRINT	REVERSE / OVERPRINT
60%	REVERSE / OVERPRINT	REVERSE / OVERPRINT	REVERSE / OVERPRINT

6-2 Screen tints *You can use screen tints to highlight type, accent letters, and give added dimension to illustrations. Overprints and reverses must be carefully planned to assure that words stay legible and fine lines do not disappear. Tints of less than 20 percent tend to look too light; greater than 60 percent, too dark. Percentages above are appropriate for newsletters. Tints in the cattails are 30 percent. The leaves are 20 percent.*

put. A 300 dpi printer works fine for dummies and proofs, but produces tints that look uneven when reproduced by a press. Use at least a 600 dpi printer, or, preferably, have your copy output by an imagesetter.

Reducing or enlarging a screen tint alters both dot size and ruling. For example, a 100-line screen reduced to 75 percent on a photocopy machine becomes 133-line—too fine to reproduce well by quick printing.

You can overlap two screen tints to create the illusion of a third color. Overlapping tints are usually based on black plus one other ink color. Visual 8-23 shows the technique. Books available at agencies, studios and printers show hundreds of combinations of tints.

Note that creating a third color by overlapping two screen tints is different from creating a color build. A color build requires four-color process printing. Equally important, a computer creates colors using methods similar to four-color printing. Colors you see on your monitor do not accurately convey colors you can create by overlapping two screens.

REVERSES

Type, logos and other line images, such as clip art, can be reproduced by printing the background rather than the image itself. When reversed, the underlying color of paper forms the shape of the image. A reverse may also be known as a knockout or liftout.

Like screen tints, you may create reverses as part of camera-ready copy or have a printer create them for you.

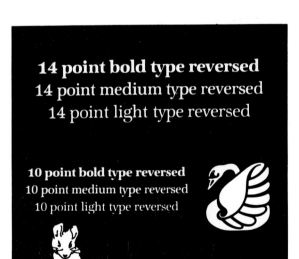

6-4 Reverses *Because the eye is accustomed to dark images against a light background, readers may find reversed images hard to read when made too small or used too often. Furthermore, fine lines, even on bold type, may disappear because they fill with ink during printing. Use reverses only within nameplates and other large elements. Avoid reverses for headlines or text.*

Reverses require heavy ink coverage. A quick printer can give good results with a reverse the size of the one above or smaller. Larger reverses require commercial printing for best results.

6-3 TIPS FOR USING SCREEN TINTS

Rulings Make tints for photocopying 85- or 100-line, for quick printing no finer than 100- or 120-line, for commercial printing 133- or 150-line. Newsletters don't need tints finer than 150-line.

Densities Don't use more than two tints of one color in one publication. If you use a 10 percent and 30 percent black tint, don't also use a 60 percent tint.

Differences Ensure that you have at least a 20 percent spread between tints. Don't print a 20 percent and a 30 percent tint. Raise the 30 percent to 40 percent or 50 percent.

Graduations Make graduated tints end between 10 percent and 5 percent. Most printing processes cannot reproduce tints less than 5 percent.

Upper and lower limits With dark colors, tints greater than 70 percent look solid. With light colors, tints less than 20 percent disappear.

Evaluate ink on paper Tints on your computer screen, especially of light colors, look different from tints on paper. Consult a tint chart available at most printers, art supply stores and graphic design studios.

Desktop publishing software and some word processing software will create reverses of type and line art. You may also make a camera-ready reverse using any method that will put a light image on a dark background. To reverse type, apply white transfer lettering to black paper. Stores selling artists supplies stock white transfer lettering in a limited selection of typefaces and sizes.

Use reversed type only in display sizes for features, such as nameplates and calendars. Avoid reversed body copy.

Visual 6-2 shows that you can reverse type out of screen tints as well as solid ink coverage. If you reverse out of a tint, especially if your screen tint is of a light second ink color, make sure to inspect some samples with the specifications you have in mind.

OVERPRINTS

You create an overprint when you print one image over—on top of—a previously printed image. Overprints are usually type over screen tints, as shown in Visual 6-2.

Overprints require careful planning to ensure sufficient contrast between type and background. You can see in Visual 6-2 that type becomes less legible as the screen tint becomes darker. If you use an overprint, especially if your screen tint is of a dark second ink color, make sure to inspect some samples with the specifications that you have in mind.

To help ensure legible overprints, follow the guidelines for reverses. Use a typeface without fine lines and set type larger than you normally would for placement on a white background.

You can see examples of overprints in the newsletters in Visuals 8-14 and 8-15.

BLEEDS

A bleed is printing that goes all the way to the edge of the paper, seeming to run off (bleed) from the sheet. Printers create bleeds by printing on sheets larger than the trim size, then cutting away the edges. Trims cut into the inked area create the illusion that the press printed to the very edge of the sheet.

6-5 Graphics in page design Each of the six front pages shown above and opposite uses a simple rule, screen or reverse to enhance readability and appearance. Rules keep copy from seeming to float on the page. All of the above graphics could be created using pasteup techniques, computer software, or a blend of the two. For another example of good use of graphics, examine Numbers News in Visual 8-1.

Reverses, screen tints, and combinations of the two create impact, but can also lead to printing problems. Heavy ink coverage, especially when quick printed, increases the probabilities of hickies and mottling and makes variations in density more noticeable.

Newsletters with bleeds require either increasing the size of paper or reducing the final trim size of the publication. Using larger paper may also require using a larger press in addition to consuming more paper, both of which increase production costs.

You can use a bleed to magnify the advantages of color and provide a canvas for other graphic elements. In addition to bleeding elements such as tints and rules, you can bleed photos and illustrations.

You can see examples of bleeds in the newsletters in Visuals 8-13, 8-14 and 8-16.

SYMBOLS

Effective writers use many symbols in addition to letterforms to convey information. There are two categories of symbols.

Symbols that already have meaning include notations such as © for copyright and ∞ for infinity. When using symbols such as these, verify that your readers understand them. Don't assume.

The second kind of symbol is used in newsletters to organize information, usually lists. Also known as dingbats or pi characters, these symbols include bullets, check marks and arrows.

When using bullets or other marks for lists, follow these simple guidelines:

• Introduce the list with a sentence, such as "The committee adopted the new policy for three reasons."

• Rank the items so the most important ones come first.

• Limit the list to four or five items. If you have more items, make another list with another introductory sentence.

• Use the same grammar for all items. If you start the first item with a verb, don't start others with a noun.

Keep dingbats consistent. Don't use bullets to identify items in one list and hearts or apples for other lists. Make dingbats follow the rules of good typography: choose your style, then stick with your choice.

You can find dozens of symbols in your typewriter and hundreds in your computer. Most font menus include Symbol, Zapf Dingbats or both. In addition, most character fonts will produce symbols when you use a combination of keys, such as option-shift.

Because dingbats look bold, they may compete with other elements of text. When using bullets or other symbols, make them one point smaller than the size of text type.

ILLUSTRATIONS

Drawings and technical illustrations for newsletters typically come from clip art or can

6-6 Using clip art *The top two nameplates show creative use of clip art combined with rules, screen tints, reverses and type. Notice how art and type cooperate to project different images of the same newsletter. (Design by Polly Pattison.)*

be obtained from other publications.

Generic drawings ready to add to mechanicals or computer files are called clip art. The drawings are made specifically to sell to designers, printers, and others needing instant graphics.

Clip art comes in a variety of media. Images on film backings are used like transfer lettering. Those on glossy paper are cut out and adhered to mechanicals. Drawings on floppy disks and compact discs are added to printouts through word processing and desktop publishing software.

Many design studios, print shops and ad agencies have books, files or software of clip art. The materials are bought on subscription, from catalogs, or at book and art supply stores.

Drawings for clip art are typically arranged by topic, such as holiday themes, health care or family life. No matter how specialized your newsletter, you can probably find appropriate images. There are entire books with themes, such as early American design, op-art mazes

and flora design. A store or catalog with a good selection could have as many as three hundred titles.

People shown in clip art may look out-of-date because of clothing, hair style, or how they relate to each other. Readers may frown at art that is ten or fifteen years old. Art that is fifty years old, on the other hand, can look nostalgic when used well.

Any dark drawing on light paper is camera-ready. You can add images on white paper directly to mechanicals; images on off-white or colored paper may lack sufficient contrast, but might be enhanced by making a photocopy first.

Clip art was developed for display ads, not editorial matter. When using clip art in a newsletter, keep your objectives clear. Novice editors tend to use too many illustrations and to place them poorly. Even some experienced designers think readers like lots of drawings scattered at random.

Use clip art sparingly. As with writing, take into account gender, age, race, and other possible sources of discrimination when selecting illustrations.

INFOGRAPHICS

The elements of graphics combine in thousands of ways to make the patterns of infographics: charts, graphs, tables and maps. Infographics form powerful tools for newsletters because they pack so much information into so little space.

Software for computing data and graphically presenting results makes creating infographics easy—too easy! Many infographics, even those in leading newspapers and magazines, distort data by showing incorrect relationships between numbers and art.

Useful presentation of numerical data in graphical form requires a head for statistics, an eye for art, and a soul for common sense. To ensure that readers get accurate information from your charts, graphs and tables, follow these simple guidelines.

Appropriate

Create a graphic format to match the data and concepts you want to present. The following four pages explain appropriate uses for the most popular forms of infographics.

Simple

An effective infographic reveals the essence of the information precisely and without visual clutter. Make each element have a function.

Consistent

When using multiple or repeated visuals, don't switch to a different infographic. If you start with a bar chart, stick with it in similar situations. If you run a caption under a headline, keep it there for future infographics.

One color

You rarely need a second color to convey information. Unless you are a highly skilled designer experienced in using color, another color may draw attention away from important concepts in a chart or graph.

If you do want color, use only one. Blue works best because it gives good contrast and a maximum number of people can distinguish it from black. Red and green are worst because some readers may not distinguish them from black.

Words, numbers and visuals together

Don't make readers study a legend outside the graphic to discover the meaning of information inside. Print headlines, captions, labels and sources inside the image.

Integrated into text

Treat a chart or table as part of the story, not a separate design element. Place the infographic in the reader's eye flow. Try to think of it as a paragraph that adds pictures to words and numbers.

Presenting a chart or table as part of text also requires making its design more horizontal than vertical. Design the graphic to maintain eye movement from left to right. Pay particular attention to placing labels so readers see them in left-to-right sequence. Don't stack words on top of each other.

Interpret information

Use captions and some labels to explain what the figures mean, not just identify the data. Make words, numbers and art work together.

Headline and caption

The caption can follow the headline and help explain the information. To help readers understand at a glance, avoid abbreviations and unfamiliar acronyms.

Upper- and lowercase

Help readers focus on the visual images by putting words into familiar patterns. Avoid using all caps and don't capitalize words that you wouldn't in normal text.

Report your source

Tell readers where you got your numbers. And don't forget the person who made the infographic; include a credit line.

Type for infographics may stay consistent with type in the rest of your newsletter or may have its own specifications. Consistency means using the same headline type for text and charts. For numerals and labels, however, use a sans-serif typeface such as Helvetica.

Test every chart, graph or map by showing it to someone unfamiliar with its information. If you have to explain what the infographic is supposed to show, it isn't working. Often the person giving the "cold read" can suggest a new approach that solves the problem.

To see many of the above principles applied in a newsletter, examine *Numbers News* in Visual 8-1. For further information about infographics, study the books *Designers Guide to Creating Charts and Graphs*, by Nigel Holmes, and *Using Charts and Graphs*, by Jan White.

6-7 PIE CHARTS

Pie charts show the proportion of parts to the whole. They are the most simple infographic to create and understand.

Use a pie chart to show market shares; income and expense reports; and data about relative ages, costs or levels of education. Display relative sizes of sections of a population, such as by employment, health or home ownership. Show readers the distribution of their benefits, market or membership. Describe the relative number of patients, clients or customers in categories that help readers understand services or cash flow.

A pie chart shows approximate relationships among pieces of information and encourages readers to absorb its message at a glance. If you need readers to understand precise differences or if you want readers to study data carefully, use a bar or line chart instead. (Charts by Steve Cowden.)

Car dealers' profits
Main profit source for car dealers in 1993:

15% New car sales

30% Used car sales

55% Service and parts

Source: National Automobile Dealers Association

Cautions *Don't divide the pie into more than eight pieces. Make sure that no piece is too small to recognize or label. Don't give mixed signals, such as some pieces with tints and others with crosshatching.*

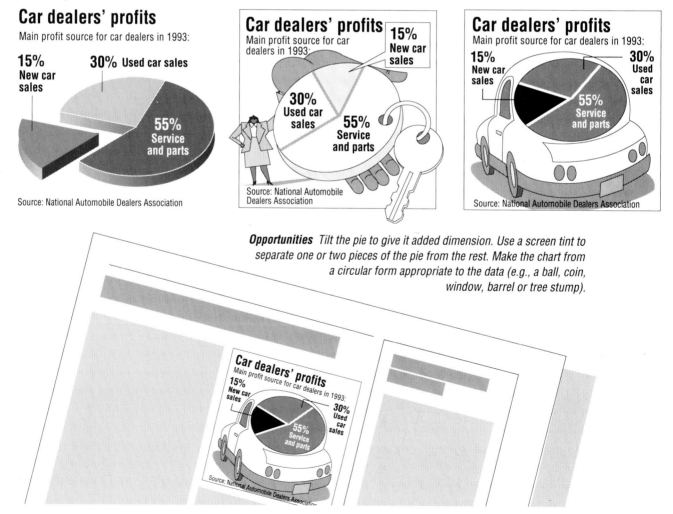

Opportunities *Tilt the pie to give it added dimension. Use a screen tint to separate one or two pieces of the pie from the rest. Make the chart from a circular form appropriate to the data (e.g., a ball, coin, window, barrel or tree stump).*

6-8 BAR CHARTS

Bar charts compare amounts. In a bar chart, vertical or horizontal bars represent amounts and sections or lines designate quantity units.

Use a bar chart to compare income and expense, prices and taxes, supplies or inventory at different times, amounts of goods produced or services rendered. Show percent of populations or rates of change in different countries or industries. Give data about average amounts used or wasted.

Try to put labels that identify each bar inside the bar, not over it (making it too fat) or at the right end (making it too long). Avoid letting words in the label affect perception of the bar itself. Don't hesitate to put lots of information inside only two or three fat bars. (Charts by Steve Cowden.)

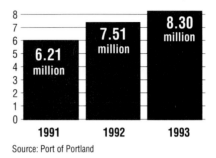

Airport passengers

The number of airline passengers who have flown to or from Portland International Airport:

Source: Port of Portland

Cautions *Avoid having so many bars that all bars look too thin. Make bars and labels all look the same unless you want one to stand out from the others.*

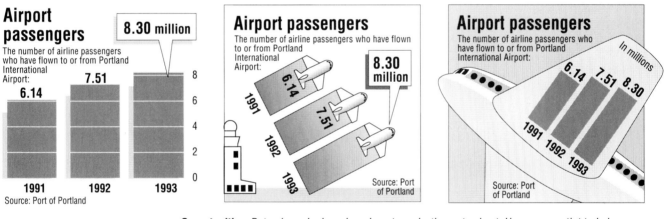

Opportunities *Put a drop shadow along bars to make them stand out. Use a screen tint to help keep bars visually separate. Replace the bars with illustrations (e.g., people of different heights, stacks of coins, chimneys) or with lines of dingbats or graphic symbols.*

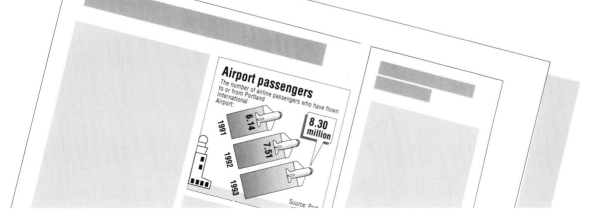

6-9 LINE CHARTS

Line charts, also known as fever charts, show changes of amounts over time. In a line chart, the vertical scale represents quantities and the horizontal scale represents time.

Use a line chart to show changes in income, expenses, prices or weather patterns. Show increases or decreases during months or years. Let two lines compare changing patterns of employment or purchasing. Convey the relationship between profits and quality standards or between educational levels and political beliefs.

When using a line chart, select the time period carefully. Too much or too little time dramatically affects the slope of the line, thus allowing for incorrect interpretation of data. Select units of time that produce obvious changes in the slopes of lines without hiding longer-term patterns. (Charts by Steve Cowden.)

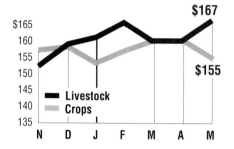

Agriculture prices

Indexes of products for which an Oregon farmer would have recieved $100 in 1977:

Cautions Don't use more than three lines in one chart. Make sure that time and quantity divisions are uniform throughout the chart.

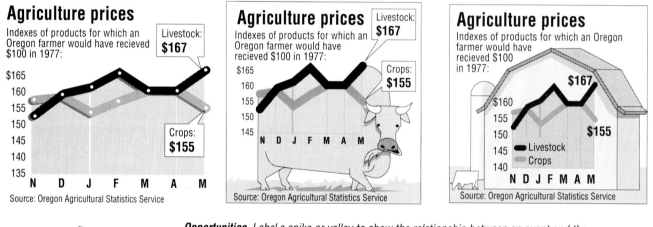

Opportunities Label a spike or valley to show the relationship between an event and the direction of the line. Use a screen tint under the line to separate data from background. Build the line into an illustration or photo.

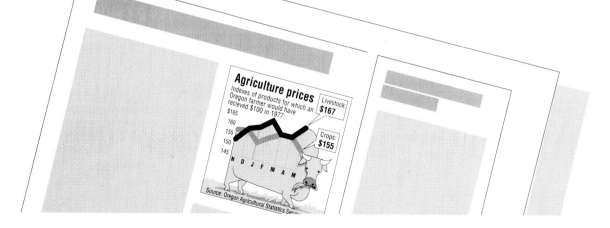

6-10 TABLES

Tables display words and numbers in rows and columns. Use a table

- when readers need exact numbers, not merely lines, bars or pieces of pie;
- when you have too much information to condense into a chart;
- when readers already feel familiar with similar information in tabular form (e.g., calendars and schedules).

A table gives more precise information and a larger amount of information than a chart or graph. Readers need to study a table, not merely look it over. For that reason, a table often calls for a more detailed caption than a chart or graph. You can exploit time that your readers spend with a table by including a three- or four-sentence caption similar to one that you might print under a photograph. (Tables by Steve Cowden.)

Top 5 selling personal computers

1993 U.S. PC shipments

Company	Shipments
1. IBM	2,075,000
2. Apple	2,050,000
3. Compaq	1,418,000
4. Packard Bell	997,000
5. Dell	795,000

Source: International Data Corp.

Cautions *Make sure to label every column and row. If you shorten numbers, make sure to include a phrase such as "population in millions."*

Top 5 selling personal computers

1993 U.S. PC shipments

Company	Shipments
1. IBM	2,075,000
2. Apple	2,050,000
3. Compaq	1,418,000
4. Packard Bell	997,000
5. Dell	795,000

Source: International Data Corp.

Top 5 selling personal computers

1993 U.S. PC shipments

1. IBM	2,075,000
2. Apple	2,050,000
3. Compaq	1,418,000
4. Packard Bell	997,000
5. Dell	795,000

Source: International Data Corp.

Top 5 selling personal computers

1993 U.S. PC shipments

1. IBM	2,075,000
2. Apple	2,050,000
3. Compaq	1,418,000
4. Packard Bell	997,000
5. Dell	795,000

Source: International Data Corp.

Opportunities *Use a screen tint or double rule to highlight rows or columns, thus helping readers keep their place. Build the table into a familiar shape appropriate to the data (e.g., book page, billboard, menu, computer screen).*

Top 5 selling personal computers

1993 U.S. PC shipments

1. IBM	2,075,000
2. Apple	2,050,000
3. Compaq	1,418,000
4. Packard Bell	997,000
5. Dell	795,000

Source: International Data Corp.

7. PHOTOGRAPHS

Photographs are graphics that help you achieve your objectives. Your reasons for using photos should sound similar to the reasons for using other graphics described in chapter six.

Whether or not to use photographs is a decision to discuss with management. Using them adds a little to printing costs, adds a lot to staff time, and changes the image of your newsletter.

Effective photos are made, not taken. You must control them editorially and technically at every stage of creation from concept to camera to printing press.

This chapter deals with black-and-white photos made with the common 35mm camera. Only the rare newsletter needs color photos or studio shots made with a large camera.

In this chapter I explain what kind of camera and film to use, how to compose and edit pictures for maximum impact, and how to evaluate photos technically. I describe how to use photo layouts. Chapter nine tells how to prepare photos for print reproduction.

Many newsletter editors take their own photos. Some have staff photographers or skilled volunteers. Whether you take photos yourself or ask someone else to take them, you should have ideas about the images you want. Your ability to imagine the photos you want largely determines their success in print.

EQUIPMENT AND SUPPLIES

You've seen photographers who need a mule to carry their hardware. Professionals and serious amateurs probably need all that equipment, but you don't for your newsletter. You need only one camera and plenty of film.

Camera

Use a 35mm autofocus camera with a zoom lens. A zoom range of 35mm to 70mm is most common and will handle most of your photo needs.

When you buy a camera for newsletter photos, spend the extra money for a glass lens—approximately one hundred dollars more than cameras made for personal snapshots. Glass lenses yield sharper images, especially in portions of the photo near the edge of the lens.

Read the instructions for your camera and practice using its controls. Shoot one or two rolls of film and inspect the results. When the first pictures aren't as good as you'd hoped, remember that you ignored this advice.

If your newsletter has special photo requirements, consult with a professional photographer or a sales rep at a specialty camera store before buying equipment. Special requirements include photos of

- objects closer than three feet to the camera,
- buildings or rooms free from distorted lines,
- products that require precise focus and lighting.

Film

Select one brand and speed of film and use it exclusively. The brand may be anything you find convenient in places you shop. The speed should be ISO 400 for best flexibility and picture quality. I recommend Kodak T-Max 400 or Tri X.

Use lots of film. Buy it in rolls with thirty-six exposures. If you have a very tight budget and need many pictures, buy film in 100-foot rolls and load your own canisters. It's as easy as loading film into a camera.

Film is the least expensive part of photography—less costly than equipment, much less costly than offset printing, and still less costly than the value of the time required to take, develop, edit and lay out pictures, and get them ready for the printer.

MAKING THE PICTURE

Successful photos begin with the photographer's selective vision, not with the camera. As you gather information for a story, visualize photos you want. Imagine them printed in your newsletter. Then when you look at the original scene, compose it in your camera as closely as possible to what you see in your imagination.

Visualizing helps you control the photographic situation. If you need people grouped more tightly or looking at each other, tell them what you want. If the scene has distractions that you can remove, take them away or shift your position.

Your brain selects parts of a scene to notice, but your camera records everything equally. To help avoid cluttered images, look at the scene with one eye closed to see it in two dimensions instead of three. Imagine it in black and white with the colors gone. Trying to see the finished photo before taking it helps produce an image that contributes to objectives.

Make the effort to get shots that count. Photos that work are created on purpose. They enhance a story because they were planned for it from the beginning.

Photography is a single sequence from visualization to reproduction. Paying close attention to seeing a picture in the camera and controlling light to record it pays huge dividends during the rest of the process.

Keeping objectives in mind is especially important with photos of people. If you need extra credibility, you probably want a picture of the boss or visiting expert. The story might, however, call for a mood shot, in which case you could pay less attention to leaders while

7-1 Good composition *Dynamic photos lead the eye in an S curve through the image and have points of interest placed off-center. An image with only one point of interest in the center looks lifeless. Compose in thirds, not halves. It is especially important to keep the horizon and other strong lines off-center.*

you concentrate on followers or audience.

When you photograph groups, ask people to react to each other or to something of common interest. Obedient stares into the camera are for driver's licenses. To avoid grip-and-grin shots, look for the emotions of the moment, not the convenience of the photographer.

The photo of an audience with the speaker either far away or behind the photographer hardly ever works. To make interesting photos of people in meetings, get the speaker to pose for some close-ups with members of the audience. Or take a number of pictures of just one person in the audience whose expressions and actions represent the group.

If you must do a mug shot, crop tightly. Ask your subject to stand or sit about a quarter turn away from you, not facing you straight on, then to turn the head only to look at the camera. Put a little more space in front of the subject than behind so your subject appears to be looking into the frame of the picture. If your image includes the person's torso, include the hands to ensure that the image appears complete.

Photos often capture emotion more effectively than words. To make them work, however, you have to look for the unusual image, not the safe shot.

To give photos depth and scale, use background and foreground to your advantage. Deliberately place buildings, foliage or props in the picture to reinforce the main subject.

When photographing outside, try to keep the sky out of pictures unless there is a specific reason to include it. Sky almost always dis-

7-2 Editorial angle *Effective photos tell stories from fresh perspectives. In the image above, the photographer got below the scene to give it an added sense of height.*

tracts from the subject matter.

Successful photography may require standing on a chair, moving furniture, wearing a hard hat, or lying on the floor. You can't get good photos when you worry about your clothes. Dress comfortably to work eagerly.

Keep in mind layout as well as content. Your natural tendency is to view scenes horizontally. Cameras reinforce that instinct. Layouts in newsletters, however, benefit from vertical pictures, too. Take both horizontal and vertical shots of the same subject to have lots of options.

LIGHTING

Ideally, you would take all photos using available light. Photos using only the light already falling on the scene, whether from natural or artificial sources, most closely resemble the scene itself.

Most newsletter photography takes place indoors where available light isn't enough for a

7-3 Photos that work *Use photos to capture the essence of a moment, not merely to record who was there. Photos convey feelings more efficiently and often more effectively than words.*

Kathleen Ryan

7-4 Background *Don't overlook potential distractions, which usually appear as white objects, such as coffee cups or lamps. In this case, simply stepping aside removed the clutter from over the subject's head.*

Kathleen Ryan

7-5 Know your format *Keep in mind the size at which photos are likely to be reproduced. Mug shots may be small, but images with more detail must be larger to preserve their impact.*

Mark Beach

7-6 Keep it simple *A good photo delivers an uncluttered image and, therefore, a clear message. Too much information can ruin a photo more easily than too little.*

proper exposure. There are several ways to handle the problem.

Increase available light

Turn on more lights, take shades off lamps, open curtains, move people closer to a window, carry objects outside, wait for the clouds to pass—do anything reasonable to put more available light on the subject.

Pay special attention to light on faces. Often the scene as a whole has enough light, but not enough falls on the faces, which are the real subject of the photo.

Sometimes there is plenty of light, but it makes harsh shadows. The eyes of people standing in bright sun show this effect. Solve the problem by seeking softer light, such as moving to open shade, rather than using flash. If you are indoors, try bouncing available light off a white tablecloth or curtain.

Use flash

Strobe lighting is easy to use, but hard to predict. It can make a scene look stark or washed out and causes unnatural shadows.

If you use flash regularly, learn techniques to reduce its harsh effects. Use your camera's option for fill flash. Learn to combine flash shots with overexposures or underexposures to control the amount of light reflected back to the film.

PHOTOFINISHING

Take developing and printing for your newsletter to companies that do photofinishing for publications. Avoid the one-hour automated services.

To locate a professional service, ask the production manager at an advertising or public relations agency. If you use a classified directory, look under "Photofinishing—Custom" for services that advertise image processing and halftones.

After having film developed, you need to review all images from every roll to select the

7-7 Film is cheap *Take plenty of photos from various angles at various settings to ensure the best possible choices for editorial purposes. When considering the time and effort involved, film is the least costly part of photography.*

ones that work best. You can inspect images either from digital files or as contact sheets. Both have pros and cons.

Digital files

You can ask the photo service to provide images on floppy disks or compact discs. With either medium, you can view results on a computer monitor.

Electronic black-and-white images require relatively little storage memory. If you use electronic images, verify that you have enough RAM and speed to retrieve and display them quickly. If you accumulate a large database of images, use software such as *Aldus Fetch* to keep track of them.

Digital photos have the advantage of moving easily into layouts that you create on a computer. How easily depends on your equipment and your skills with several kinds of software, including a page layout program. And when viewing an image on a monitor, keep in mind that it appears much brighter than it will when reproduced on paper.

Photo services use scanners to convert images on film into computer files. Operators adjust the resolution of scans to suit your needs. You can get low resolution scans to inspect images, then ask for high res scans only for those pictures that you want to reproduce.

The scan resolution of images that you plan to reproduce must take into account the screen ruling of your halftones. Ask your photo service or printer for guidance. Knowledge of resolutions and screen rulings is one reason why you deal with professionals experienced with publications.

Contact sheets

If you produce only a newsletter and not a variety of other publications, you probably will find it easier to deal with photos as prints, not electronic files. And whether or not you get digital images, ask for contact sheets as well. Images on paper give you the best basis for selecting photos because they look most similar to the printed result in your newsletter.

When you get contact sheets, write dates and subject matter on the back. Put negatives in scratchproof sleeves and the sleeves inside business envelopes. Tape the envelopes to the backs of appropriate contact sheets.

Images on contact sheets are too small to inspect without magnification. View them through a loupe, sometimes called a linen tester. A loupe costs only a few dollars at an art

cropping L's Kathleen Ryan

7-8 Cropping *You don't have to use all of an image simply because it's on the negative. Crop to eliminate unwanted portions. Crop when prints are made in the darkroom or when they are prepared for reproduction. Use cropping Ls as shown above to visualize the outcome. Don't hesitate to crop deeply; it often improves the image dramatically. Crop to make the photo more effective or to make the image fit your layout.*

supply store. Place the loupe directly on the photo paper and put your eye to its lens to examine individual images.

Keep in mind that all images on a contact sheet were made with one exposure. Most will not look as good as they would if exposed as individual prints.

When you ask for prints, specify them on paper at least 5" x 7" and with a semigloss or matte surface. The slightly dull surface makes the print look more like a newsletter reproduction than a glossy paper.

While doing layout, it's handy to have duplicates of photos you might use. Ask your finishing service for work prints. Duplicates can even be photocopies.

IMPROVING PHOTOS

Photo services can improve images before you put them in your newsletter. When you ask for improvements, you work with one image at a time. Show the photo service a copy of the image that includes your written instructions. Don't rely only on verbal instructions.

Following are some common improvements relevant to black-and-white photos. All can be done on either electronic files or prints.

Cropping

As shown in Visual 7-8, cropping eliminates unwanted portions of an image around the edges of the photo. Put cropping instructions on contact sheets, prints or laser printouts. Your photo service will produce finished images to your specifications.

When you crop a photo, ideally you also specify the size of the finished image so it fits your layout. Specifying the new size is called scaling and is explained in chapter nine.

Contrast

A photo service can reduce or increase contrast using chemicals, filters or software. Changes usually occur by making blacks either darker or lighter, thus changing your impression of the overall image.

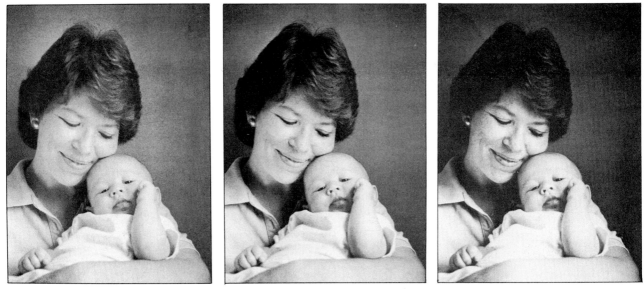

flat contrast   *good contrast and detail*   *detail lost in shadows*

Kathleen Ryan

7-9 Contrast *Lively photos have a full range of tones from white to black. Muddy, washed out or flat images have low contrast; photos that lack detail in shadows or highlights have high contrast. Photos always lose detail in both shadows and highlights when photocopied or offset printed. Quality depends on starting with good images.*

straight print   *sky burned in, truck dodged*

Mark Beach

7-10 Dodging and burning *Prints may be enhanced in the darkroom or using a computer to make them more effective. Dodging, also called lightening, withholds light to bring out shadow detail or create a light area on which to print black type. Burning, also called darkening, adds light to bring out highlights or create a dark area for reverse type. In the image above right, the sky and sign were burned in while the truck was dodged. Decisions about dodging and burning are best made while viewing an enlargement, not a contact sheet.*

24 mm

55 mm

86 mm

7-11 Lens length The three images above and at left were all taken at the same distance from the subject. A wide lens setting of 24mm captures much of the scene from a short distance. A setting of 55mm, considered normal, records what the eye sees at an average glance. Long lenses, such as the 86mm, work well for portraits.

55 mm at f3.5

55 mm at f16

Kathleen Ryan

7-12 Depth of field The ability of a lens to hold both near and far parts of a scene in focus is called its depth of field. Depth of field is affected by the focal length of the lens and the aperture at which it is set. It improves as apertures become smaller and gets worse as they become larger. Most cameras provide a depth of field gauge on the lens that tells the distances within which objects will be in focus for a specific f-stop.

Details

Many photos have details in either shadows or highlights that a photo service can make more clear. The technique of dodging, sometimes called lightening, enhances shadows. Burning, also called darkening, enhances highlights. Visual 7-10 shows the effects of dodging and burning.

Vignettes

Many photos have relatively light areas near outsides of the image. By burning light areas slightly, a photo service increases contrast between the photo and the paper on which it appears. Careful vignetting, especially at corners of the image, draws readers' eyes toward the center of the image.

Silhouettes

To isolate an image from its background, you can specify a silhouette, also called an outline. Your photo service creates this effect by masking on a print or electronic file.

Silhouettes command attention, but are more difficult to work with in layout than photos with corners. You may need to run text around a silhouette or position it so it bleeds off the page.

Retouching

A photo service has many ways to eliminate scratches, glare and miscellaneous flaws. These services fall under the broad category of "retouching" and, with black-and-white images, are relatively inexpensive.

Darkrooms and scanners seem like magnets for small particles of dirt, dust or lint that produce flaws on images. Retouching usually involves some spotting to eliminate those flaws. Using a soft pencil, you can do some spotting yourself on prints made on matte paper.

BLACK AND WHITE FROM COLOR

You get best results when you start with black-and-white originals, but often you have to start

7-13 EVALUATING PHOTOGRAPHS

Focus Check that important parts of the image are sharp. If something is fuzzy that you want sharp, examine the contact sheet to determine if the problem is in the negative or the enlargement.

Grain Certify that further enlargement will not make the image look fuzzy.

Contrast Examine for strong blacks, clean whites, and a full range of grays. If you are not satisfied, ask about improvements using a filter or different paper.

Content Confirm that negatives were enlarged full frame unless cropped accurately according to your instructions.

Detail Inspect shadow areas and highlights for adequate clarity of features. Examine the negative to determine if dodging or burning could produce greater detail.

Critical features Examine the objects, colors or people that you feel are most important to ensure that the image conveys them the way you want.

Flaws Verify that the print is flat and has no scratches, stains, dirt or blemishes. If it has flaws, check the negative and ask about eliminating them.

Paper Ensure that enlargements are on smooth, semigloss paper.

7-13 Evaluating photographs *To ensure quality photos in your newsletter, start with good originals. Verify that enlarged prints meet the technical requirements above.*

with color. But merely getting a black-and-white print of a slide or negative, or a black-and-white laser printout of a color scan, doesn't yield an image that will reproduce well in your newsletter.

Color originals lose details when converted to black and white. Dark colors that make up

7-14 SOURCES OF PHOTOGRAPHS

In addition to taking photos yourself or using a photographer, you can select from many collections.

Local sources of photos include historical societies; library archives; public agencies, such as port authorities and water bureaus; and corporations. And keep in mind your local commercial photographers, especially those with specialties, such as aerial or product photography. Most local newspapers, however, are not interested in sharing their files of photos.

Outside sources include state historical societies and departments of tourism, and huge collections, such as the Library of Congress.

For generic photos that you use similar to clip art, learn about stock photo services. Stock services provide digital images on floppy disks or compact discs. You select the image you want, then pay a royalty to use it. Costs and specific financial arrangements vary greatly among services.

To locate stock photo services, ask for suggestions from the art director at a local advertising agency.

shadow areas of the image move toward black; for example, blues and greens may all look black. Light colors, such as yellow, that make up highlights move toward white.

In addition to the tendency of colors to merge into darks and lights, color photos will lose their overall brightness when changed to black and white. As a result, images that seemed vivid turn flat.

Professional services can produce effective black-and-white versions of color photos.

There are two methods. First, a photofinishing company can use filters when making a black-and-white print from a color negative or slide. The filters enhance the differences among colors, therefore increasing details in both shadows and highlights.

The second method requires using image processing software, such as *Photoshop* or *PhotoStyler*. The software alters the relationships among colors in the same way as filters do, leading to a satisfactory black-and-white version.

Whether you have black-and-white prints made by a photo service or printouts made by a service bureau, you need to give clear instructions about the outcome. To get best results, follow these simple guidelines.

Photos for publication
Make it clear that you want prints or scans for publication. Verify that the service knows what kind of paper and printing process your newsletter uses—and that operators know how that information affects their work.

Start with the color
Verify that operators understand how relationships among colors affect results in black and white. If they say they'll make a black-and-white print first, then retouch it, look for another service.

Critical features
Describe the features of photos that you consider important. If details in faces are more important than those in surroundings, express your wishes clearly. Circle important features and write instructions on a photocopy of the image.

WORKING WITH PHOTOGRAPHERS
If you work with a photographer, make clear what kinds of images you want. Photographers give best results when they know the needs of your publication. Here are some things to explain.

Subject matter

Name the people and describe the scenes that interest you. Try to imagine some perfect images, then describe them. This helps the photographer think about what equipment and supplies to bring and the conditions under which the work will take place.

Editorial use

Tell the photographer the subject of the story, how long or important it is, who will read it, and what part photos play in carrying the message. State that images are for a newsletter and add a reminder to get some verticals as well as horizontals.

Presentation

Verify that prints will adhere to the quality standards outlined in Visual 7-13. Specify the paper surface and size for enlargements.

Details

Check that the photographer knows when and where to appear and when you need contact prints and enlargements. Make sure you both know who is responsible for getting caption information.

You do not need a model release for a photo in your newsletter unless the image might prove embarrassing to somebody in it. Using the photo elsewhere, however, such as in an ad or on the cover of a magazine, requires a release.

Photographers own copyrights to images they make. If you want to own copyrights, have exclusive use, or have access to images for future jobs without additional fees, negotiate the agreement while reviewing images, not after publishing them.

To learn more about working with photographers, consult books published by the American Society of Media Photographers. These guides give details about fees, copyrights, model releases, delivery memos and other business arrangements.

PHOTO LAYOUTS

Occasionally you might want a spread with many photos. When this happens, you may have to follow guidelines different from your usual design.

Start your spread by selecting an odd number of images. Five or seven work best. Pick one to feature at a large size. Use verticals as well as horizontals. Arrange the images flowing left to right and top to bottom to make sense the same way that people read.

Photo layouts look best when all images show the same quality. One bad one drags down good ones; one outstanding one makes others look feeble even if they would be individually acceptable. Images with dark backgrounds may make lighter ones seem washed out.

Dynamic photo spreads have plenty of white space. Use large margins to frame images, but don't trap white space between photos.

Photos in spreads need captions and credits. Try to write one caption per image and place it to the left or under its photo. Readers find clustered captions that refer to individual photos more difficult to comprehend.

Layouts need one large headline. The headline doesn't have to be at the top of the page, but it should be close to the upper left where reading begins.

Most photo spreads run across folds, so you need to anticipate where the crease falls. Try not to fold someone's face or staple an arm to a lectern.

If you work with a two-page spread, make one mechanical with one tissue overlay for the entire spread. Keylining and other pasteup techniques stay the same, but working two-up helps keep every element orderly.

The following six pages show a variety of successful uses of photos.

7-15 Piedmonitor *uses angled shadow boxes printed in brown to highlight photos, which are also twisted off-center. The same brown ink forms the wide band at the left of page one and appears in the nameplate. The captions for photos featuring children include quotations from the kids that reflect the image of the organization that they get from their parents.*

DOUBLE YOUR FUN
March/April programs offer something for everyone

Did you know that in the past year the Atlanta History Center has nearly doubled the number of programs it offers? Take advantage of your membership and choose from our wide variety of events, many of which are free. In addition to the programs listed here, please see features throughout this issue on other events.

The popular Books and Bob Hale series returns in March for two special programs. On Monday, March 1, at 7:00 p.m., bookstore owner and author Bob Hale moderates a panel discussion on the writing process. Noted participants include columnist and author Celestine Sibley; Emory medical doctor Neil Shulman, who wrote *What, Dead Again?*, on which the movie *Doc Hollywood* was based; and Turner Broadcasting's Xernona Clayton, author of *I've Been Marching All the Time*. The group will discuss researching, writing, editing, and publishing and take questions. A reception follows the program in Woodruff Auditorium.

On Tuesday, March 2, at 10:30 a.m., Hale reviews hot-off-the-press books. Audiences love his witty style and engaging conversation about books, their authors, and the world of publishing. A reception follows and books will be for sale (members enjoy a 10 percent discount).

At both events, you'll want to register for our free give-away: a copy of each book Hale reviews on Tuesday. You must be present at noon on Tuesday to claim your prize (one per person).

Overwhelmed with book choices? Let Bob guide you! Books and Bob Hale returns on March 1, when Celestine Sibley (l) and other authors join Hale. On March 2, Hale reviews new books.

Tickets (available at the door) for Books and Bob Hale are $8 for members, $10 for nonmembers.

Are you the family historian or do you enjoy researching your ancestors? Then sign up for the **Albert Perdue Boyklin Genealogy Workshop** for intermediate students. Rita Worthy leads the series designed to teach people how to organize their research materials. The class meets on Wednesdays, March 3, 10, 17, and 24, from 10:00 a.m. to noon in McElreath Hall. $40 for members, $45 nonmembers. Call the library/archives at 814-4040 for information or to register.

Calvin Trillin, March 15

The **Livingston Lecture series** continues on March 15 when author, columnist, and humorist Calvin Trillin speaks on "American Stories." Trillin will comment on the state of America—and everything from politics to education to food is fair game.

Called "perhaps the finest reporter in America" who writes "simply the funniest regular column in journalism," Trillin has written for *Time*, *The New Yorker*, and *The Nation*. The best of his nationally syndicated newspaper column, "Uncivil Liberties," is collected in *Uncivil Liberties*, *With All Disrespect*, *If You Can't Say Something Nice*, and *Enough's Enough (And Other Rules of Life)*. His other books include *An Education in Georgia* and *American Stories*.

For entertainment and a good challenge, Stump Franklin ranks right up there with "Jeopardy." On Sunday, March 7, bring your questions on Atlanta trivia and see if you can "stump" Franklin, official historian of the Atlanta Historical Society, the city of Atlanta, and Fulton County. Trustee Jim Landon moderates the fun. Stump Franklin, at 2:00 p.m. in Woodruff Auditorium, will be followed by a reception. Free for members; free with regular admission for nonmembers.

Stump Franklin, March 7

4

(cont'd on p. 5)

March/April programs (cont'd from p. 4)

The Livingston Lecture is at 8:00 p.m. in Woodruff Auditorium (doors open at 7:00 p.m.), and a reception and book signing follow. Funded by the Livingston Foundation, the lecture is free for members and nonmembers.

Upcoming speakers in the Decorative Arts Lecture series include Sumpter T. Priddy III on March 21 and William Nathaniel Banks on April 18.

A museum and furnishings consultant, Priddy will speak on "Recent Discoveries in Southern Neoclassic Furniture." Priddy's company specializes in the sale of American decorative and fine arts to museums and private collectors. His latest book, *American Fancy* (for sale in our Museum Shop), was published in conjunction with a 1992-93 exhibition of the same name at Colonial Williamsburg.

Nathaniel Banks will speak on "Life in a Period Setting." A contributor to *The Magazine Antiques* on early 19th-century American architecture, Banks has restored two early 19th-century houses, furnishing them with neoclassical pieces.

Both lectures begin at 3:30 p.m. Tickets (available at the door) are $8 for members, $10 for nonmembers, and $7 for students 18 + with I.D.

Celebrate spring training with "Southern Bases," the documentary film that inspired the Atlanta History Center Downtown's current exhibition by the same name. The one-hour film will be shown on Wednesday, March 24, at noon at the Georgia-Pacific Center Auditorium, 133 Peachtree Street.

Ted Ryan, Atlanta History Center visual arts archivist, and Connie Ward-Cameron, WPBA producer, created the documentary. Both will be on hand to answer questions.

WWII Remembered. The March 28 program focuses on women. Above, from the July 4, 1943, Atlanta Journal magazine, women from all branches of the military salute the red, white, and blue.

James Stewart, March 26

As a Page-One editor for the *Wall Street Journal*, Pulitzer Prize-winning journalist James Stewart covered the 1980s boom, bust, and scandals of Wall Street. Hear him speak on "Den of Thieves: Wall Street in America" at the Alston Lecture on Friday, March 26, at noon in the Georgia-Pacific Center Auditorium, 133 Peachtree Street.

The Alston Lectures, made possible by the Charles Loridans Foundation, Inc., and the Vasser Woolley Foundation, Inc., are free.

As the country commemorates World War II's 50th anniversary, the Atlanta History Center continues its World War II Remembered series with "What Did You Do in the War, Grandma?" On Sunday, March 28, at 2:00 p.m. in the Members Room, Dr. Evelyn Monahan and Rosemary Neidel Greenlee of the National Association of Women Veterans will present a slide show on women's World War II military involvement. Monahan will also lead a discussion in which the audience can share war recollections or hear others reminisce. Reception follows. Free for members; free with regular admission for nonmembers.

Martin Luther King, Jr., subject of March 30 lecture

April 4 marks the 25th anniversary of the assassination of civil rights leader Martin Luther King, Jr. In observance of that date, Dr. Ronald Quincy, executive director of the Martin Luther King, Jr., Center for Nonviolent Social Change, will speak on "The King Legacy" on Tuesday, March 30, at 8:00 p.m. Quincy will reflect on the King Center's impact on Atlanta and the nation. A reception follows the free lecture in Woodruff Auditorium.

(cont'd on p. 6)

5

7-16 *The Atlanta History* Center uses photos as well as words to tell readers about forthcoming events. Each photo reinforces a short article. Scalloped columns enhance the informal placement of the photos.

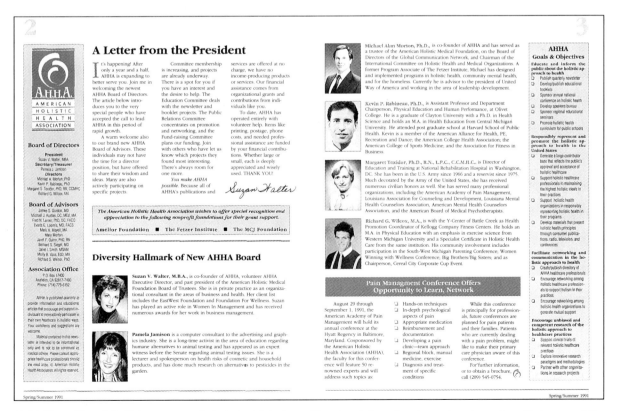

7-17 *The editor of* Ah Ha! uses mug shots to lead into the written description of each new board member. Photos are all the same size and define the maximum length of copy. The masthead at the left and goals statement at the right, each in a screen tint box, frame the two pages of photo stories about new board members.

7-18 *The internal newsletter* for a large company such as CUNA Mutual Insurance features employees in a wide range of situations and activities. The front page always features one large image associated with the lead article. Most photos show people doing or holding something, not merely looking at the camera. Printed on 80# gloss coated paper, Mutual Matters *uses top-quality photography, design and production to make every photo count.*

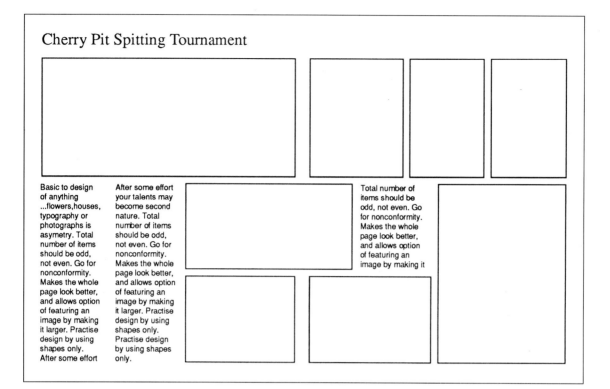

7-19 Grids for photo spreads *Use a grid to make your photo-layout job easier. Start by arranging your best images in a pattern that keeps eye flow moving around the page, but not off it. Make your arrangement look dynamic by keeping words and images slightly out of balance. Symmetrical layouts look lifeless. The image of teacher and students above works well for a crossover because the fold doesn't run through a critical part of the picture.*

Here are the winners...

Winners in the 9th annual *Mutual Matters* Photo Contest are:
People—color: 1st Place, **Ken McDonough**, Life Tele-Marketing; 2nd Place, **Mary Siedlecki**, Financial Management Services; 3rd Place, **Michael Meyer**, ISD
People—black & white: 1st Place, **Linda Speen**, Southfield; 2nd Place, **Susan Ice**, Typesetting
Places—color: 1st Place, **Timothy Eisele**, NARCUP; 2nd Place, **Donna Benson**, Pomona; 3rd Place, **Debra Hildebrandt**, Century Companies
Places—black & white: 1st Place, **Kris Rougier**, Pomona; 2nd Place, **Linda Speen**, Southfield
Things—color: 1st Place, **Susan Ice**, Typesetting; 2nd Place, **Steve Allen**, High Technology; 3rd Place, **Sonserae Schiebel**, Audio/Visual
Things—black & white: 1st Place, **Susan Maund**, ISD; 2nd Place, **Linda Speen**, Southfield
Animals—color: 1st Place, **Rick Feldkamp**, Century Companies; 2nd Place, **Penny Simms**, Tax/Travel Policy; 3rd Place, **Daniel Ciske**, North West District
Animals—black & white: **Kris Rougier**, Pomona
Honorable Mention: **Colleen Fraser**, Government & Industry Relations

more photos on page 8 . . .

Above: 1st—Things . . . "Back at Koinonia" by Susan Ice, Typesetting, taken at Koinonia Partners, Americus, Georgia.

1st—People . . . "Dreaming" by Linda Speen, Southfield, taken at Crossroad Village.

1st—Places . . . "Old Mill" by Timothy Eisele, NARCUP, taken in Augusta, Wisconsin.

2nd—Animals . . . "Hello World" by Penny Simms, Tax/Travel Policy, taken in her backyard.

1st—Animals . . . "Right at Home" by Kris Rougier, Pomona, taken at home.

2nd—People . . . "Wall of Water" by Mary Siedlecki, Financial Management Services, taken in Orlando, Florida.

1st—People . . . "Cooling Off" by Ken McDonough, Life Tele-Marketing, taken at home.

ART FOR KIDS' SAKE

District has designs on expanding student appreciation

Port Chester Middle School, through a unique relationship with the Port Chester Council for the Arts, has instituted an Artist-in-Residency program. Areas of instruction include watercolor/painting, mural design, storytelling and pottery/clay. Four artists will work in grades 5 and 6, providing an eight-week residency, for a total of 32 weeks. The first eight weeks is a pilot program, allowing time for improvement before the remaining sessions begin.

"The kids will get an incredible experience with all different disciplines," says Camille Linen, Board of Education president and Director of the Port Chester Council for the Arts.

Students will not only study art for art's sake, but come to understand the relationship between art forms and other areas of instruction.

For example, watercolor/painting relates to science through the blending of colors to create different colors, and examining the components of paint. Mural design can be traced back to ancient Egyptian pictographs and hieroglyphics. Storytelling goes hand-in-hand with history and writing. Pottery/clay utilizes math for measurement, design and the recipe for components.

The Middle School program has its roots in Port Chester's Arts in Education program, which is celebrating its fifth birthday. It all began in the fall of 1987, when grant money was used to fund Kinderart, a multicultural, multidisciplinary arts program introduced in kindergarten classes district wide. Visiting artists and teachers designed the program, which united visual arts, storytelling and participatory singing and music around a cultural theme. For example, if a storyteller chose a work from Africa, the visual artist might concentrate on mask-making and the classroom teacher would provide follow-up with additional literature and discussion.

The program was later expanded to include all elementary grades under the title Artist-in-Residency. One to two artists per

grade will be spending 10-15 weeks in each of the elementary schools this year.

Teachers are given a list of art forms from which to choose.

"For instance, a lot of them will choose a mural because all the children can contribute to part of it," says Mrs. Linen. A past project focused on a mural of the Village of Port Chester and highlighted key buildings, giving youngsters an introduction to architecture.

A major reason for the program's success is inviting artists into schools who love their work enough to want to share it with children.

"My theory is this," says Mrs. Linen. "If you love what you're doing and you really have a soul connection to it, you can teach it to anybody, any age."

It's interesting to note, says Mrs. Linen, that this year's 5th grade class attended the first full-day kindergarten, was the first Kinderart class, is the first 5th grade at the Middle School, the first to experience the expanded arts program and will be the first to graduate from high school in the new century, the year 2000!

Two of the artists returning to the program this year are Brigitte Loritz, a painter, and Lou Del Bianco, an actor, singer and storyteller. Both taught the first Kinderart program five years ago to the current 5th graders and will be working with them again this year.

Artists are not only in residence in the Port Chester Schools, but students are given the opportunity to visit performing artists in their natural setting – the theater. One program in support of this concept is offered to the John F. Kennedy Magnet School in conjunction with Lincoln Center in New York City. These expanded programs are evidence of the district's commitment to making study of the arts a priority in Port Chester.

PORT CHESTER PUBLIC SCHOOLS
1993-94
BUDGET CALENDAR

Nov. 4 – Dec. 1 - Administrators with planning and budgeting responsibilities meet with staff and generate input into decision-making and budget building.

Dec. 16 - Presentation of 1993-94 assumption budget to the Board of Education. Public invited to give input.

Dec. 18 - Completed budget materials returned in duplicate to the Assistant Superintendent for Business.

Jan. 12 - Citizens Advisory Committee meeting to review budget status and make initial recommendations. Sub-committee reports.

Feb. 10 - Draft 1 of Superintendent's Budget completed and available for review by the Board of Education. Public invited to give input.

Feb. 11 - Citizens Advisory Committee meeting to provide input for recommended revisions for Draft 1.

Feb. 24 - Board further discusses Draft 1. Public invited to give input.

March 10 - Update to the Board of Education on the 1993-94 budget development process. Public invited to give input.

March 15 - Citizens Advisory Committee meets to discuss further possible revision for the budget.

March 24 - Update to the Board of Education on 1993-94 budget development process. Public invited to give input.

April 14 - Board adopts 1993-94 budget. Public invited to give input.

April 19 - Proposed budget available in school offices and public library.

May 3 - Budget brochure mailed to residents.

May 19 - Budget vote and School Board election.

7-20 The structure of a grid *may take a back seat when photos themselves tell the whole story. Give strong images the space they need to make an impact. Use an odd number of photos and let one or two large images dominate the rest. Images presented at different sizes put action into the spread. When images are all the same size, your spread looks static.*

8. DESIGN

Graphic design determines how type and other visual elements appear on the page. Good design means that elements appear organized to make reading pleasant and efficient. Poor design means elements appear jumbled—tossed onto the page without care for the needs of readers.

Newsletter design includes format, type specifications and rendering of items, such as the nameplate and masthead, that appear in every issue. Layout is the way design is carried out for a specific issue. Design is the plan, layout its fulfillment.

Intelligent design makes content accessible. Design's secondary purpose, following at a great distance, is to represent personality or image. Style is not substance. Design can stimulate interest and make reading efficient, but design cannot camouflage thoughtless content or careless writing.

Every newsletter has a design, but some designs are better than others. Good design has standards. This chapter presents design standards and includes many visuals that demonstrate their application.

FORMAT

In effective design, form follows function. Format is the form that you give your newsletter consistent with its goals, objectives and audience. It includes page size, number of columns, and the dimensions of each column.

Think of format as the framework of your publication. Type, graphics and photos fit into the framework. Layout uses the framework to create a specific issue.

Format influences image and efficiency. It shapes how each issue looks, how hard you work to produce it, and how easily readers learn from it.

Choose the most simple format consistent with your goals. A complicated format makes unnecessary work and makes your newsletter less effective.

Keep format consistent throughout each issue and from one issue to the next. Consistency makes content most accessible. Equally important, consistency lets you concentrate on content and layout for each issue, knowing that you have the basic structure.

Express your format on paper, even if it also exists in some other form, such as computer memory. Make a dummy that shows column widths, alleys, margins and borders. Your newsletter is a paper product and only a representation on paper fully reveals how you want it to look.

A written format helps others do their part. If someone else produces type or substitutes for you as editor, format instructions help ensure efficient, accurate work. If others write articles for you, format tells them how much space a story and its headline might require.

Page size

Most newsletters in North America are 8$\frac{1}{2}$" x 11"—letterhead size. Almost all the rest are 11" x 17"—tabloid size. Only a handful of publications deviate from these two basic sizes.

An 8$\frac{1}{2}$" x 11" newsletter coordinates with typewriters, laser printers, printing presses, envelopes, file folders, ring binders, and dozens of other processes and products based on the standard size.

Unless you are an experienced designer or have a strong reason for using another size, use an 8$\frac{1}{2}$" x 11" page size. That size lets you pro-duce your best possible newsletter quickly and at the least cost.

If you have a four-page publication, have it printed on an 11" x 17" sheet that folds once to become 8$\frac{1}{2}$" x 11". Produce an eight-page publication from two 11" x 17" sheets or one 17" x 22" sheet folded and trimmed.

Letterhead size outside of North America is 8$\frac{1}{4}$" x 11$\frac{3}{4}$" (210mm x 297mm), also known as A4 size. If you have a four-page publication, have it printed on A3 sheets that fold once to become A4. Produce an eight-page publication from two A3 sheets or one A2 sheet.

Tabloid size newsletters are 11" x 17" in North America and A3 (11$\frac{3}{4}$" x 16$\frac{1}{2}$"; 297mm x 420mm) in other parts of the world. Unless you have lots of training and experience in newsletter design, stick with letterhead size. Tabloid pages are much harder to design.

Columns

Your format for letterhead size could have either one, two or three columns. Format for tabloid size could have either four or five columns.

The width and height of columns determines the alley between them and the margin around the outside of the page. Visual 8-1 shows appropriate dimensions. The white space created by generous margins and alleys helps make type legible.

Before deciding your format, experiment with several mock-ups. Consider whether your information will appear in charts and graphs as well as text and whether you will use drawing or photos. Think about how many articles you might have in a typical issue and how they might look when arranged on a page.

LAYOUT

Good newsletter layout ensures that articles, illustrations, photos, and other elements for each issue fit together for efficient reading.

Layout begins with knowing what articles and graphics you want in an issue and how important each one is. Priority is the key.

ONE- AND TWO-COLUMN LAYOUTS

8-1 Numbers News *Subscribers pay for data, presented via tables and graphs as well as in segments of one-column text. The designer keeps character counts within limits in the wide columns by leaving generous margins for contents lists, subheads and pull quotes. Subheads function as short summary decks, complete with arrows pointing at relevant text. Tables use reverses, overprints and screen tint percentages consistently throughout each issue.*

8-2 Dick Davis Digest *Readers pay for investment news and advice in paragraphs that look technical and authoritative. Dark blue type within the body copy highlights companies and investments. At twelve pages per issue, the publishers keep mailing costs low by printing on 40# opaque offset stock. The lightweight paper provides the additional benefit of making the newsletter feel similar to a stock prospectus.*

8-3 The Public Pulse *The frame of screen tint bleeding off all four sides confines text and graphics to the page, helping readers feel that information has been documented... "buttoned down"...certified believable. Justified type and centered headlines add to formality.*

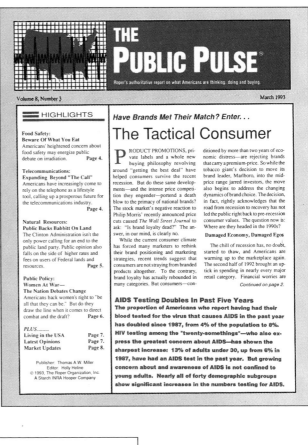

8-4 Random Lengths *News about the timber and lumber industry arrives in three newsletters from the same publisher. Each uses the same format and text type, but slightly different headline type. The weekly report is conveniently trimmed and folded off-center to feature separate color coded price guides. Two-page spreads in the monthly Yardstick allow infographics to tell the whole story without text.*

THREE-COLUMN LAYOUTS

8-5 HeartHealth *Four-color printing gives graphics and illustrations extra vitality. Note also summary decks, the small version of an illustration used in the contents box, and the heart icon used as a bullet.*

8-6 Focus *Generous white space lends a classic uncluttered look to the entire publication while it draws the eye to headlines and pull quotes. Three columns blend well with large illustrations, which by themselves are strong enough to bring us into the story on the two-page spread. This banker's publication stays true to its "news" format and doesn't try to become an advertising piece.*

HeartHealth

The HeartHealth Newsletter™   Vol. 3, No. 2, Spring 1993

IN THIS ISSUE

Heart-Smart Fitness
Ready for a lean machine?
Page 3

LightHearted Eating
Your guide to the Guide
Page 5

Questions for HeartHealth
Page 8

**Published Quarterly by the
Heart and Stroke Foundation**

EDITORIAL BOARD

Mary Jane Ashley, M.D.
Professor, Department of
Preventive Medicine and Biostatistics,
University of Toronto

Anthony F. Graham, M.D.
President, Heart and Stroke
Foundation of Canada,
Chief, Cardiology Division,
The Wellesley Hospital,
Associate Professor,
University of Toronto

Bretta Maloff, M.Ed., R.D.
Director of Nutrition Division,
Calgary Health Services

Yves Morin, O.C., M.D.
Professor of Medicine, Laval University,
Chief, Cardiology Services,
Hôtel-Dieu, Quebec

Kenneth M. Prkachin, Ph.D.
Associate Professor, Department of
Health Studies, University of Waterloo,
Associate Clinical Professor,
Department of Psychiatry,
McMaster University

HEART
AND STROKE
FOUNDATION

Making great strides in treating strokes

Every year, some 50,000 Canadians suffer a stroke. The best advice for most people hasn't changed — be sure to know the signals of stroke (see Page 2), and be prepared to act immediately. But there is lots of change when it comes to *treating* strokes, and the news is good.

Thanks largely to the diligent work of medical researchers, the odds in favour of stroke survivors making a full recovery are getting better all the time.

Stroke remains the third leading cause of death, and the leading cause of adult disability related to the nervous system. But significant strides have been made — and continue to be made — on three fronts: diagnosis, medication, and surgery. Here's a quick look at the key developments over the past few years.

New strides in diagnosis

Is a stroke taking place? How serious is it? Exactly where in the brain is there damage? These are critical questions, and the diagnostic techniques available to answer them are getting better all the time.

For instance, refinements are constantly being made in the field of magnetic resonance imaging (MRI). MRI is a technique that allows doctors to see what's going on inside the body without subjecting the patient to X-rays

| **Preventing strokes** |
| *Medical science is not only learning more about treating strokes. We're also learning more about preventing them. See Page 6.* |

or other potentially harmful radiation. The technique is pain-free for the patient, with no known risks or side effects. As equipment becomes more sophisticated over time, the images produced become more detailed.

In a similar procedure, doctors use what's called the colour-Doppler technique to create maps of the body in which blood velocity (motion) shows up in colour.

Doctors at J.P. Robarts Research Institute in London, Ont., in affiliation with University Hospital, are working on a clinical prototype that will take the colour-Doppler technique another step forward.

They've come up with a way to collect hundreds of these images at different stages in the cardiac cycle, and assemble them in a computer. In this way, they can produce a three-dimensional, colour image of blood flowing through an artery.

Dr. Aaron Fenster, the leader of the research team, points out the technique's potential advantages: "The physician can sit down in front of the computer screen and examine the blood flow without the patient being present.

To Page 2

FOURTH DISTRICT

FOCUS

Federal Reserve Bank of Cleveland

Fourth Quarter 1992

First VP Hendricks Retires From Cleveland Fed

William H. Hendricks, first vice president of the Federal Reserve Bank of Cleveland, will retire from the Bank, effective January 1, 1993.

Under his leadership as first vice president for the past 10 years, the Fourth District became one of the top-ranked Districts in the Federal Reserve System in terms of operating efficiency. Hendricks also played a significant role in creating the Federal Reserve's automated clearinghouse system and in upgrading its electronic funds transfer network. Over the last few years, he spearheaded the development of the Federal Reserve's new currency processing equipment.

According to Federal Reserve Bank of Cleveland President Jerry L. Jordan,

"Bill has made invaluable contributions to this Bank, the Federal Reserve System, and the Fourth District. Throughout his career, he has brought a very high level of dedication and integrity to his varied responsibilities - we will miss him."

Hendricks joined the Federal Reserve as an assistant economist in 1958 and held various positions throughout the Bank in his 34-year career. He will be succeeded by Sandra Pianalto, who is currently vice president and secretary of the board. In addition to her nearly 10 years with the Federal Reserve Bank of Cleveland, Pianalto has worked as an economist at the Board of Governors in Washington, D.C., and on the staff of the Budget Committee of the U.S. House of Representatives.

William H. Hendricks

'CRA Can Be Opportunity For Banks,' Says Jordan

Calling the requirements of the Community Reinvestment Act (CRA) a potential business opportunity, Federal Reserve Bank of Cleveland President Jerry L. Jordan recently urged Cincinnati-area bankers to consider using a CRA program to develop better customer relations.

"Regulated industries tend to forget how to be responsive to customers," he told the 100 bank and community representatives attending the Fourth District's annual Community Reinvestment Forum, "and bankers may need to develop the

same relationships with small customers as they have had with large corporate customers."

According to Jordan, the evolution of the financial system over the past two decades, with its increasingly competitive markets, has forced many banks to reexamine how they loan money in general, and how they have reacted to CRA in particular. "A narrow interpretation of CRA," comments Jordan, "is that is, the refusal to make loans in disadvantaged neighborhoods.

"A broader interpretation would be that CRA is a mechanism to ensure equal credit access to low- and moderate-income neighborhoods," he says. "The law mandates that financial institutions search for good loans in disadvantaged neighborhoods, but does not outlaw rationing of credit, nor does it require banks to make riskier loans."

In Jordan's view, the law imposes on banks and thrifts the costs of seeking out borrowers in areas that are perceived to be more risky. "It gives regulators the ability to impose penalties if the financial

(continued on page 2)

10

Corporate Tax Reform Would Lower Costs, Boost Investment

The corporate tax system is an expensive way to raise revenue, say economists Jeffrey Hallman, of the Federal Reserve Board of Governors, and Joseph Haubrich, of the Federal Reserve Bank of Cleveland. "Beyond its direct costs," they explain in a recent *Economic Commentary,* "which include collection and enforcement, the corporate tax

DOUBLE TAXATION

system also has high indirect costs that affect not only how corporations raise investment funds, but also how they distribute the proceeds."

According to Hallman and Haubrich, some of the disadvantages of the corporate tax include:

Double taxation - The federal government taxes corporate income at a 34 percent marginal rate, then taxes shareholders 15, 28, or 31 percent on dividends received, and on any appreciation of their shares at the point of sale. Some of these taxes are then passed on to workers and customers.

Paperwork - U.S. companies devote more than 500 million hours a year to filling out tax forms.

Tax avoidance - Harder to quantify, but just as damaging, are the indirect costs of tax avoidance, including

PAPERWORK

lawyers and accountants hired to exploit the existing law and lobbyists hired to change the law.

"In effect, current law favors noncorporate enterprises over corporations, debt over equity, and retained earnings over dividends," explain Hallman and Haubrich. "The effects of these tax policies can undercut the health and productivity of the entire economy."

Treasury Studies

Earlier this year, in a study of several tax reform proposals, the Treasury Department found that integrating business and personal income taxes would shift capital to the corporate sector, reduce corporate borrowing, boost dividend payments, and increase GDP by $3 billion to $30 billion.

Hallman and Haubrich describe the five reform proposals examined by the Treasury and note that all of them would reduce the financial distortions caused by the current corporate tax system. However, Hallman and Haubrich prefer the modified conduit approach, where net income is allocated to shareholders, but net losses are not. Under

TAX AVOIDANCE

this approach, corporations would still pay taxes, but shareholders would receive a nonrefundable tax credit for their share of the tax paid. Capital gains would be adjusted on a share basis.

Hallman and Haubrich suggest modifying this proposal to have taxes paid at the shareholder, rather than the corporate level. This would do the best job of minimizing distortions and would also preclude the untenable situation in which wealthy individuals pay no personal income tax at all.

"Many Americans cling to the belief that higher corporate taxes mean lower personal taxes," conclude Hallman and Haubrich. "But just the opposite is true: As business taxes go up, individuals ultimately pay more. Integrating corporate and personal income taxes would not only boost investment, but would also reduce financial distortions caused by the current corporate tax system." For a copy of their study, "Integrating Business and Personal Income Taxes" (*Economic Commentary,* October 1, 1992), call 1-800-543-3489.

The HeartHealth Newsletter™ is published quarterly by the Heart and Stroke Foundation as an educational service.

Articles on diet, fitness, research, medical treatment, and related topics are based on information from reliable sources. However, articles in *HeartHealth* are not intended to substitute for professional medical advice. Readers should consult their own physician or other health professional, as appropriate, for individual diagnosis and treatment.

Contents copyright © 1993, the Heart and Stroke Foundation. Articles may be quoted, or reproduced in their entirety, provided that full credit is given to: *The HeartHealth Newsletter™*, published by the Heart and Stroke Foundation."

Produced for the Foundation by Ariad Custom Publishing Limited. Editorial research and writing services provided by The Pepler Group Communications.

ISSN: 1183-1340.

For further information, contact: Heart and Stroke Foundation of Canada, Suite 200, 160 George St., Ottawa, ON K1N 9M2.
Telephone: (613) 237-4361.
Fax: (613) 234-3278.
Moving? Send your new address to *The HeartHealth Newsletter*, P.O. Box 8114, Station A, Toronto, ON M5W 1S8. If possible, please enclose your current mailing label.

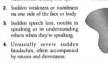

Treating strokes
From Page 1

It gives the viewer a very precise picture of the patient's vascular function."

Another diagnostic technique, called trans-esophageal echocardiography, enables doctors to see defects in the septum, the "wall" in the heart which separates the left side from the right side. Such heart defects appear to be the cause of some strokes.

Strides in medication

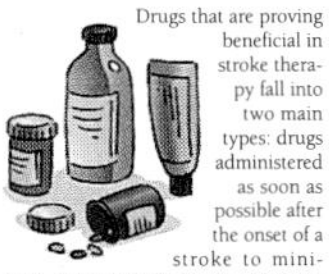

Drugs that are proving beneficial in stroke therapy fall into two main types: drugs administered as soon as possible after the onset of a stroke to minimize damage to the brain; and drugs used on a long-term basis to prevent a second, more serious stroke.

Among the former is NBQX. When administered soon after a stroke hits, it binds to individual brain cells to protect them from damage.

The development of new drugs that work in a similar fashion is especially important, since some studies suggest that brain cells don't die as rapidly from lack of oxygen as had been thought. In fact, there may be a seven-hour or eight-hour "window of opportunity" for therapy that can prevent or even reverse the damage.

Foremost among the drugs used to protect patients from suffering a second stroke are anti-clotting agents. These range from simple ASA (as prescribed by a physician), to the more exotic *avrin* and *hirudin* (derived respectively from pit vipers and leeches). Another well known anticoagulant is *warfarin*, a compound used in insecticides.

Recently approved for general use after about three years of clinical trials is the anti-clotting drug *ticlopidine*. In a study conducted at the Hamilton Civic Hospital Research Centre in Ontario, it reduced the likelihood of stroke by 30% among patients who had previously experienced warning signs or an actual stroke.

WHAT SIGNALS A STROKE?

A stroke can strike anyone, anywhere, anytime. Regardless of your age or general state of health, if you experience any of the following symptoms — even for a few minutes — seek medical attention immediately. Fast intervention could save your life.

Here are the four main warning signals:

1. Sudden blurring or loss of vision, often in only one eye.

2. Sudden weakness or numbness on one side of the face or body.

3. Sudden speech loss, trouble in speaking or in understanding others when they're speaking.

4. Unusually severe sudden headaches, often accompanied by nausea and drowsiness.

Some *other* early warning symptoms may include:

1. Sudden dizziness, vertigo, or loss of balance.

2. A sudden tingling sensation in one arm or leg, or on one side of the face or body.

3. A sudden difficulty in swallowing.

4. Sudden unexplained falls or loss of consciousness.

According to Dr. Vladimir Hachinski, Chairman of the Department of Clinical Neurological Sciences at the University of Western Ontario and one of Canada's foremost stroke experts, ticlopidine is about 18% more effective than ASA in preventing blood clots.

New strides in surgery

Treating strokes with various surgical procedures is becoming more successful too.

One new technique worked so well in clinical trials that part of the study was discontinued — so that patients not participating in the studies could also benefit from the surgery. In this technique, called carotid endarterectomy, plaque buildup is scraped away from the lining of severely blocked carotid arteries (leading up to the brain through the neck), thus improving blood flow.

Some cerebral aneurysms (blood-filled "bubbles" that form at the weak point of an artery at a tiny platinum coil that's threaded through the arteries to reinforce the weak point in the artery. Because it requires no general anesthetic and no operation on the brain, this technique is especially beneficial to high-risk patients who can't undergo traditional surgery.

Thanks to ongoing improvements in anesthesiology and surgical techniques, even delicate brain surgery is not nearly as risky as it once was.

The outlook

For stroke patients, the outlook gets brighter every day. Researchers around the world are constantly breaking new ground. With improvements in treatment, more people are surviving strokes. As well, more people who *do* have them are making fuller recoveries.

HEART-SMART FITNESS

Software ahead of hardware

From treadmills to ski machines, the technology is right for in-home physical activity. But first, think about it.

Looking to improve your heart health through physical activity, but tired of wet or cold Canadian weather and put off by health clubs? You now have your pick of in-home equipment, from treadmills to stair-climbers and ski machines. But before you spend money on the hardware, spend time on the software. In other words, think.

Which type of machine is best? "They're all good," says Dr. Bob Faulkner of the University of Saskatchewan's College of Physical Education.

But like all experts in physical activity and health, he says that you first have to understand why you want in-home equipment, and how to use it. One study found that 85% of all fitness equipment purchased for private use was no longer used after the first *week*!

"It becomes a question of motivation. It's a very individual thing," says Dr. Faulkner. "The best activity is the one that a particular person likes to do. What's right for one person isn't necessarily right for someone else."

Physical activity plays an important role in heart health. When we are active, we not only feel better, but we give our heart muscle a useful, strengthening workout. In fact, researchers have now added physical inactivity to the list of major risk factors for cardiovascular disease over which you have some control (the others are smoking, high blood pressure, and high blood cholesterol).

Research also shows that even a moderate amount of activity can help control weight, cholesterol levels, blood pressure, and stress.

Before you rush out to buy some equipment, however, consider the general advice of fitness and health experts:

▶ **Know yourself.** Don't spend a lot of money on equipment you won't use. Take time to decide why you want a stationary bicycle in your bedroom or den. Will you really use it when it's rainy or snowing outside?

▶ **Have a program.** It's important to have goals, and a plan. How often should you have physical activity? How can you measure your progress? If you're recovering from a heart attack or surgery, be sure you have a program from your doctor.

▶ **Weigh the costs and benefits.** Exercise equipment can be quite costly — but the benefits can be great too. Many models will help you time your exercise, and let you set the level of effort quite precisely.

▶ **Try the equipment first.** If possible, visit several retail outlets that have equipment for sale, and try

To Page 4

Environmental Sins of Borrowers May Be Laid on Lenders, Say Experts

Several bankers, lawyers, and community planners participating in a recent Federal Reserve Bank of Cleveland research conference urged caution to those who would finance urban redevelopment projects. "Fifteen years ago," says James B. Witkin, partner at the Washington, D.C., law firm of Content, Tatusko, and Patterson, "environmental issues were

"Lenders have become aware of the impact of environmental matters on their loans, and have modified their lending practices accordingly."

not a concern to those involved in real estate development and redevelopment projects.

"In the intervening years, however, laws have been enacted that dramatically changed the liabilities of the parties involved in such transactions."

Witkin, along with Nicholas E. Darrow, vice president of the Middle Market Group of Mellon Bank, N.A., and Robert B. Jaquay, manager of Program Planning for the Cuyahoga (Ohio) County Planning Commission, discussed lender liability at the Cleveland Fed's recent conference on "The Environment and Economic Development in the Great Lakes."

Superfund Liability

According to Witkin, current environmental liability problems began for lenders with the enactment of the Comprehensive Environmental Response, Compensation, and Liability Act of 1980, which is known as CERCLA or Superfund. "Superfund established a program to identify and clean up sites where hazardous substances have been discharged, and to allocate the costs of cleanups to responsible parties," says

Witkin. "Responsible parties could include current owners, owners or operators at the time of a hazardous dumping, any person who arranged for the disposal or treatment of the waste, or any person who transported the waste."

Because the law imposes liability regardless of fault, and because the liability under Superfund is legally "joint and several" - that is, a company or an individual may be held liable for the entire cleanup of a site, not just its proportionate share - Witkin says Superfund has developed a draconian reputation. He cites a recent survey by the Independent Bankers Association of America (IBAA) in which 86 percent of those bankers surveyed said Superfund affected their lending policies and 21 percent said that their bank had experienced a loss or default due to environmental impact.

"About the only protection provided to lenders affected by Superfund is the secured creditor exemption," says Witkin. "Several cases appear to hold that a secured creditor could be held liable under Superfund only if it had actual and active involvement in the debtor's day-to-day operations of a Superfund site." This protection, however, holds only against certain legal liabilities associated with Superfund, but

Lenders' Concerns

Darrow of Mellon Bank agrees with Witkin's assessment of how seriously bankers are taking their potential environmental liability. "Given the industrial heritage of much of the Great Lakes region," he comments, "the growth of this liability has been a major concern to lenders."

not against other federal or state environmental laws, and not against the risk of a decline in the value of lenders' collateral due to environmental impairment.

"Lenders have become aware of the impact of environmental matters on their loans, and have modified their lending practices accordingly," comments Witkin. "Certain types of businesses, such as service stations and convenience stores with underground gasoline tanks, have reported that it has become extremely difficult for them to obtain loans, regardless of their creditworthiness, solely due to lenders' concerns over environmental liabilities."

Darrow says the risks for lenders include:

- Potential liability of the lender itself as an owner/occupier of contaminated property;

- Cash flow impact of enforcement actions on the borrower, because that may affect repayment;

- Potential deterioration of collateral values; and

- Potential establishment of a prior lien position on the borrower's assets by an administrative agency such as the state, which would place the lender in a secondary position on collateral assets pledged to back the credit.

Darrow notes that lenders have responded to these risks by adopting more conservative lending practices. These practices may include doing environmental assessments, establishing guidelines for the minimum qualifications of those who perform these assessments, requiring internal responses depending on the outcome of the assessments, and outlining the steps that should be taken prior to foreclosure on real property.

"In addition to the due diligence steps taken in a real-estate-backed

transaction, lenders are now requesting other assurances," says Darrow. "These may include the use of environmental covenants and representations and warranties in the underlying loan documents. Lenders may obligate borrowers to notify them about environmental contamination or to submit to periodic environmental audits."

Darrow says if lenders cannot accept the potential risks and costs in a project, and if those risks cannot be allocated elsewhere, financing might be unlikely. "In the Great Lakes region, where contaminates may have reached the groundwater, for instance, arranging financing will be very difficult, unless the lender is satisfied that it is not put at undue risk."

For more information on lender liability for environmental problems, call the Public Affairs and Bank Relations Department at 1-800-543-3489 to order "Reducing Lender Risks to Environmental Liability," a packet of information prepared by Jeffrey A. Lange, policy advisor in the Banking Supervision and Regulation Department of the Federal Reserve Bank of Cleveland.

THREE-COLUMN LAYOUTS

8-7 **Mayo Clinic Health Letter** *Mayo designers use Optima, a modified serif typeface, for all type, including headlines. They add variety by changing size, weight and style, keeping the typeface consistent throughout. Four-color illustrations and photos present information in useful detail.*

8-8 **Wildflower** *Soft pastel colors printed on pale green paper unite readers in their affection for native flora. Notice the rules created reversing out of a screen tint of green and outlined by fine red lines and the overprints of green on lilac. Each issue contains a full color brochure on gloss coated stock to contrast with the newsletter itself.*

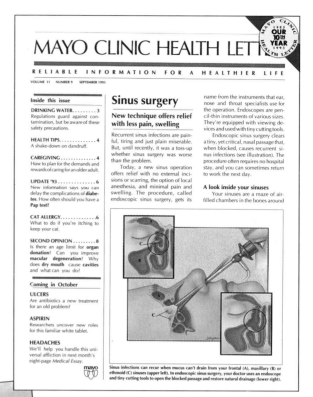

Update '93

News and our views

Diabetes: Can tight control of blood sugar delay complications?

For decades the answer was, "Maybe." Now, new information from the National Institutes of Health (NIH) says, "Yes."

Diabetes means your body doesn't make or respond properly to insulin, a hormone needed to metabolize food. The result is an elevation of sugar (glucose) in your blood. This disruption in metabolism can damage your heart, blood vessels, kidneys, eyes and nerves. (See *Medical Essay*, June 1992.)

An NIH-sponsored study shows tight blood-glucose control reduces, by about 60 percent, the risk for development and progression of eye, nerve and kidney complications, as compared with less precise control of blood sugar.

If you have insulin-dependent (Type I) diabetes, tight control means:

- checking your blood sugar more often using finger pricks,
- adjusting insulin more frequently and
- keeping good records.

If you don't take insulin for diabetes, carefully control blood sugar with diet, regular exercise and, if prescribed, oral medication.

The bottom line: The closer to normal you keep your blood sugar, the lower your risk of complications. ❐

How often should you have a Pap test?

You may have read about new studies suggesting that some older women can reduce frequency or even stop having Pap tests to screen for cervical cancer. A study in the *Annals of Internal Medicine* (September 15, 1992) proposes that women with a history of normal Pap tests probably won't benefit from continued testing after age 65.

But other physicians say more study is needed to establish a safe level of screening frequency. And there is still considerable doubt among experts about the advisability of stopping regular screening altogether.

Our advice is consistent with recommendations from the American College of Obstetrics and Gynecology: Ask your physician to assess your risk status and recommend appropriate screening for you. If you're at increased risk for developing cervical cancer, have an annual exam and Pap test. You're at increased risk if you've had sexual intercourse before age 18 or more than one sexual partner.

If you've had three or more consecutive annual exams with normal findings, you may need less frequent Pap tests. But ask your doctor for advice.

No matter what your age, do have annual breast and periodic pelvic exams. ❐

Cat allergy

What to do if you're itching to keep the cat that makes you scratch and sneeze

Cats are clean, independent and companionable. They also make more people scratch and sneeze than any other pet.

This is because, despite their ability to cause allergies, they remain popular pets.

Of the 6 million Americans who are allergic to cats, about one-third of them keep a cat in their home.

If you or someone you live with is allergic to cats, you have two options: Put the cat out of your house for good. Or follow our simple suggestions to help you and your cat live together comfortably.

What is a cat allergy?

An allergy is a sort of mistaken activation of your immune system. Your immune system makes antibodies that protect your body from dangerous invaders such as bacteria and viruses.

But, in the case of an allergy, your immune system identifies a normally harmless substance (allergen) as a menace and produces specific antibodies against it.

If you're allergic to cats, entering a home where cats live brings you into contact with cat allergen. In turn, allergen reacts with your antibodies, triggering an allergic reaction, including release of histamines. Histamines can cause the sneezing, itching, wheezing and puffy eyes common in allergies.

Scientists now know that cat allergen comes from a cat's oil-producing (sebaceous) glands in its skin and from its saliva. However, some researchers believe cat dander also plays a role — allergen piggybacks on tiny dander particles to become airborne.

Allergy test is simple skin prick

One of the telltale signs of cat allergy is rapid onset of symptoms when you're exposed to cat allergen. This quick reaction is probably due to the large amount of cat allergen that remains airborne. Other allergens such as dust-mite allergen don't stay in the air as easily as cat allergen.

Cat allergies tend to run in families. If you think you may be allergic to cats, consider having a simple skin test (see photo).

During the test, a small amount of cat allergen is placed on the skin of either your arm or back. Your skin is then pricked or scratched to introduce allergen beneath your skin's surface. A tiny amount of allergen may also be injected directly into your upper arm. If swelling and redness appear after about 20 minutes, you have a cat allergy.

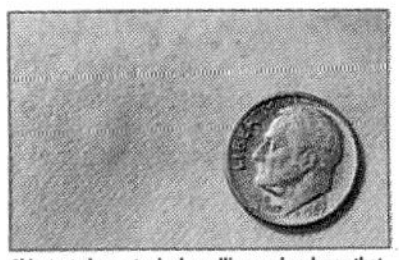

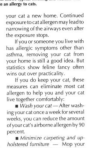

Skin test shows typical swelling and redness that indicate an allergy to cats.

Combating cat allergy: Get rid of the cat?

The best way to make your allergic symptoms disappear is to avoid cats completely. If this means finding a new home for your cat, thoroughly clean your house after your cat is gone. But remember, it can take weeks — even months — for allergens to disappear from your carpeting and upholstered furniture.

If you or someone in your home has asthma due to cat allergy, find your cat a new home. Continued exposure to cat allergen may lead to narrowing of the airways even after the exposure stops.

If you or someone you live with has allergic symptoms other than asthma, removing your cat from your home is still a good idea. But statistics show feline fancy often wins out over practicality.

If you do keep your cat, these measures can eliminate most cat allergen to help you and your cat live together comfortably:

- *Wash your cat* — After washing your cat once a week for several weeks, you can reduce the amount of your cat's airborne allergen by 90 percent.
- *Minimize carpeting and upholstered furniture* — Mop your floor frequently and vacuum using a high-efficiency filter attachment.
- *Use an effective air cleaner* — High Efficiency Particulate Arresting (HEPA) air cleaners remove more than 99 percent of dust particles that pass through the filter. The dust that's filtered includes cat allergen.
- *Control your cat's access* — Keep your cat outside as much as possible. Don't let your cat on your bed — or even in your bedroom. Make other rooms you spend a lot of time in also off-limits.
- *Increase ventilation* — Super-insulated, tightly sealed homes have higher allergen levels. ❐

Treatment: Today and tomorrow

The basic drug treatment for most allergies is use of antihistamines. These medications stop your body's reaction to histamine.

Other medications such as cromolyn sodium actually block your production of allergy-causing chemicals, including histamine.

Allergy shots (immunotherapy) involve injecting tiny amounts of known allergens into your system. After several injections, usually weekly, you may build up tolerance to the allergen. Then you may need monthly injections for up to several years.

Not only are allergy shots inconvenient, but people also occasionally react severely to the injections. If you have a cat allergy severe enough to require shots, some doctors recommend that you simply stay away from cats.

Research on future treatments centers on "turning off" your body's immune response to cat allergen. In a first-of-its-kind approach, researchers are injecting people who are alllergic to cats with synthetic versions of cat-allergen peptides (portions of the cat allergen molecule).

By injecting increasing amounts of these peptides, researchers hope the immune cells that mount an allergic response to cat allergen will "turn off." This treatment is still experimental.

ildflower Center offers educational materials

One of the National Wildflower
earch Center's primary goals is to
vide vital and reliable information
ut conserving and using native
its in traditional landscape and
dening designs. To respond to the
lic's increasing awareness,
usiasm, and interest in wildflow-
and native plants, the Wildflower
ter offers a number of programs
resources.

• **Fact Sheets.** The Wildflower
ter offers more than 250 indi-
al fact sheets including recom-
ded species lists for each state
cies information is still being
arched for Alaska, Hawaii,
ada, and Utah), regional lists of
ve plant nurseries, and regional
iographies. Basic information
ut gardening and landscaping
natives, wildflower meadow
dening, creating a prairie, and
tat gardening also are available.

• A special **Education Packet** for
hers is available and includes
flower fun facts, alternatives to
flower collection, how-tos on
cting and pressing wildflowers
seed collecting, an education
iography, a bibliography of native
t uses, and parts of the flower.

• **Regional Slide Programs.**
e shows featuring wildflowers
d in six regions of the United
es are available for lease or

Fact Sheet Order Form

Members receive this special Education Packet free. The packet is available to non-members for $4. Send this form (or a copy!) to: Educator's Packet, Clearinghouse, 2600 FM 973 N, Austin TX 78725-4201. The Educator's Packet includes:

- Fun facts
- Alternatives to wildflower collecting
- Bibliography of educational references
- Bibliography of native plant uses
- Slide program order form

Name ________________
Address ________________
City, State, Zip ________________

purchase from the Center's Clearinghouse. Each program consists of 35 to 40 slides of a particular region's most common native wildflowers and is accompanied by a script that lists each species' botanical and common names, bloom period, and habitat preference.

• **Publications.** The Center publishes a bimonthly newsletter and a biannual journal. The newsletter is geared toward home gardeners who want to incorporate native flora into their landscape and garden designs, while the journal targets an audience that includes members of the academic and scientific communities, as well as the layperson who wants more in-depth information on native flora.

Fact sheets are free to members and $4 per packet for non-members. For more information on the materials and resources available at the Wildflower Center, contact the Clearinghouse at the address listed on the back page or use the order form above.

As it enters its second decade, the Wildflower Center will continue to respond to America's growing interest in wildflowers and native plants. Through our educational programs and materials, our members can help us teach others about the economic, aesthetic, and ecological importance of our native flora.

Plant now for spring beauty!

continued from page 1

vell to severe pruning in the fall or
te winter.

Because native plants are
dapted to their environments,
ttle or no chemical maintenance is
quired. Native plants come with
eir own "built-in" pesticides and
ngicides. Once established,
ative plants will crowd out all but
e most noxious weedy invaders,
iminating the need for herbi-
ides.

Native plants usually do not
quire fertilizers. Many natives
rive in very poor soils and
applying fertilizers could chemically burn them or stimulate lush foliage growth with few flowers. Fertilizers also stimulate the growth of unwanted species.

Mow only at the end of the bloom season. Mowing after the flowers have set seed will help reseed your wildflowers and produce a strong display next year.

By planting native species, you provide habitat and food resources for wildlife and encourage the presence of native insects and microorganisms that benefit plants and keep them healthy. With a little care, thought, and patience, your landscape can become an interacting, changing entity that offers a unique look into the complex interactions of the natural world — right in your own backyard.

F. M. Oxley
Resource Botanist
National Wildflower Research Center

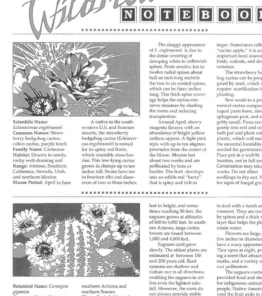

Wildflower NOTEBOOK

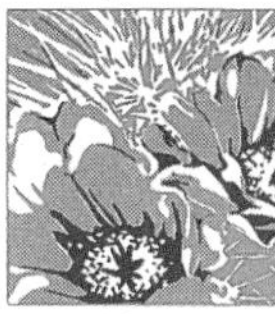

Scientific Name: *Echinocereus engelmannii*
Common Names: Strawberry hedgehog cactus, calico cactus, purple torch
Family Name: Cactaceae
Habitat: Deserts in sandy, rocky well-draining soil
Range: Arizona, Southern California, Nevada, Utah, and northern Mexico
Bloom Period: April to June

A native to the southwestern U.S. and Sonoran deserts, the strawberry hedgehog cactus (*Echinocereus engelmannii*) is named for its spiny red fruits, which resemble strawberries. This low-lying cactus grows in clumps up to ten inches tall. Stems have ten to fourteen ribs and diameters of two to three inches.

The shaggy appearance of *E. englemannii* is due to the dense covering of drooping white to yellowish spines. From areoles, ten to twelve radial spines about half an inch long encircle the two to six central spines, which can be three inches long. This thick spine coverage helps the cactus conserve moisture by shading the stems and reducing transpiration.

Around April, showy magenta flowers with an abundance of bright yellow anthers appear. A light pink style with up to ten stigmas protrudes from the center of the bloom. Blooms last about two weeks and are pollinated by bees or beetles. The fruit develops into an edible red "berry" that is spiny and rich in sugar. Sometimes called "cactus apple," it is an important food source for birds, rodents, and desert tortoises.

The strawberry hedgehog cactus can be propagated by seed, which may require scarification before planting.

Sow seeds in a pot of normal cactus compost (equal parts loam, shredded sphagnum peat, and sharp gritty sand). Press seeds gently into soil and cover both pot and plant with plastic, which will maintain the essential humidity needed for germination. Place pot in a well-lit location, not in full sun. Germination may take two weeks. Do not allow seedlings to dry out. Watch for signs of fungal growth.

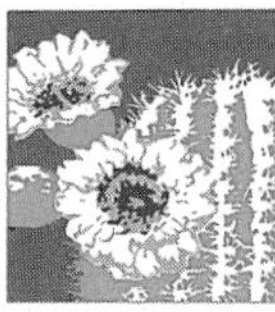

Botanical Name: *Carnegiea gigantea*
Common Name: Saguaro
Family Name: Cactaceae
Habitat: Rocky and sandy desert slopes and flats
Range: Extreme southeastern portions of California to southern Arizona and northern Sonora
Bloom Period: May to June

The state flower of Arizona, the saguaro cactus is a prominent desert landscape feature. Averaging 30 to 40 feet in height, and sometimes reaching 50 feet, the saguaro grows at altitudes of 600 to 4,000 feet. In southern Arizona, large cactus forests are found between 1,000 and 4,000 feet.

Saguaro cacti grow slowly. The oldest plants are estimated at between 150 and 200 years old. Root systems are shallow and radiate out in all directions, enabling the saguaro to utilize even the lightest rainfall. However, the roots do not always provide stable anchorage; high winds can blow these huge cacti over.

The main stems can have a diameter of two and one-half feet and are a good example of nature's ability to deal with a harsh environment. They are covered by spines and a thick waxy layer that helps the plant retain water.

Flowers are large, up to five inches in diameter, and have a waxy appearance. They open at night, producing a scent that attracts bats, moths, and a variety of insect pollinators.

The saguaro cactus has provided food and shelter for indigenous animals and people. Native Americans used the fruit pulp to make cactus jelly, oil extracted from the seeds was used in cooking, the seeds could be ground into a butter, and the fermented juice made an intoxicating drink.

THREE-COLUMN LAYOUTS

8-9 **Ships and Shipwrecks** *A second color of watery blue on flecked recycled paper enhances the theme of this newsletter about ancient treasures under the seas. Inside, the second ink color appears as a screen tint representing water in the illustration. The simple three-column format moves the news along with its flexibility of illustration and photo arrangement.*

8-10 **Syvamonitor** *Heavy flecked paper and a different combination of two colors plus black throughout each issue help make this marketing newsletter effective for Syva customers. The colors transform large "woodcut" illustrations into memorable art, a signature style consistent issue after issue. Extra leading for ragged-right body type makes text seem both elegant and friendly.*

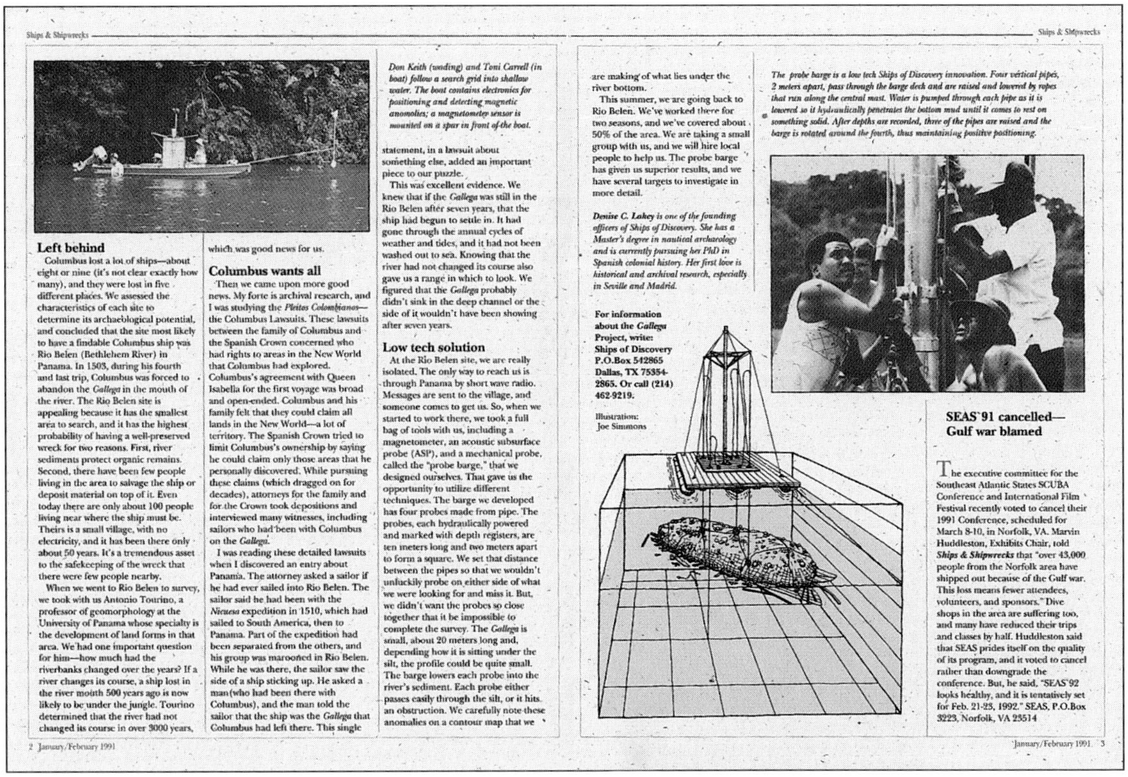

Ships & Shipwrecks

Don Keith (wading) and Toni Carrell (in boat) follow a search grid into shallow water. The boat contains electronics for positioning and detecting magnetic anomolies; a magnetometer sensor is mounted on a spar in front of the boat.

Left behind

Columbus lost a lot of ships—about eight or nine (it's not clear exactly how many), and they were lost in five different places. We assessed the characteristics of each site to determine its archaeological potential, and concluded that the site most likely to have a findable Columbus ship was Rio Belen (Bethlehem River) in Panama. In 1503, during his fourth and last trip, Columbus was forced to abandon the *Gallega* in the mouth of the river. The Rio Belen site is appealing because it has the smallest area to search, and it has the highest probability of having a well-preserved wreck for two reasons. First, river sediments protect organic remains. Second, there have been few people living in the area to salvage the ship or deposit material on top of it. Even today there are only about 100 people living near where the ship must be. Theirs is a small village, with no electricity, and it has been there only about 50 years. It's a tremendous asset to the safekeeping of the wreck that there were few people nearby.

When we went to Rio Belen to survey, we took with us Antonio Tourino, a professor of geomorphology at the University of Panama whose specialty is the development of land forms in that area. We had one important question for him—how much had the riverbanks changed over the years? If a river changes its course, a ship lost in the river mouth 500 years ago is now likely to be under the jungle. Tourino determined that the river had not changed its course in over 3000 years, which was good news for us.

Columbus wants all

Then we came upon more good news. My forte is archival research, and I was studying the *Pleitos Colombianos*—the Columbus Lawsuits. These lawsuits between the family of Columbus and the Spanish Crown concerned who had rights to areas in the New World that Columbus had explored. Columbus's agreement with Queen Isabella for the first voyage was broad and open-ended. Columbus and his family felt that they could claim all lands in the New World—a lot of territory. The Spanish Crown tried to limit Columbus's ownership by saying he could claim only those areas that he personally discovered. While pursuing these claims (which dragged on for decades), attorneys for the family and for the Crown took depositions and interviewed many witnesses, including sailors who had been with Columbus on the *Gallega*.

I was reading these detailed lawsuits when I discovered an entry about Panama. The attorney asked a sailor if he had ever sailed into Rio Belen. The sailor said he had been with the *Nicuesa* expedition in 1510, which had sailed to South America, then to Panama. Part of the expedition had been separated from the others, and his group was marooned in Rio Belen. While he was there, the sailor saw the side of a ship sticking up. He asked a man (who had been there with Columbus), and the man told the sailor that the ship was the *Gallega* that Columbus had left there. This single statement, in a lawsuit about something else, added an important piece to our puzzle.

This was excellent evidence. We knew that if the *Gallega* was still in the Rio Belen after seven years, that the ship had begun to settle in. It had gone through the annual cycles of weather and tides, and it had not been washed out to sea. Knowing that the river had not changed its course also gave us a range in which to look. We figured that the *Gallega* probably didn't sink in the deep channel or the side of it wouldn't have been showing after seven years.

Low tech solution

At the Rio Belen site, we are really isolated. The only way to reach us is through Panama by short wave radio. Messages are sent to the village, and someone comes to get us. So, when we started to work there, we took a full bag of tools with us, including a magnetometer, an acoustic subsurface probe (ASP), and a mechanical probe, called the "probe barge," that we designed ourselves. That gave us the opportunity to utilize different techniques. The barge we developed has four probes made from pipe. The probes, each hydraulically powered and marked with depth registers, are ten meters long and two meters apart to form a square. We set that distance between the pipes so that we wouldn't unluckily probe on either side of what we were looking for and miss it. But, we didn't want the probes so close together that it be impossible to complete the survey. The *Gallega* is small, about 20 meters long and, depending how it is sitting under the silt, the profile could be quite small. The barge lowers each probe into the river's sediment. Each probe either passes easily through the silt, or it hits an obstruction. We carefully note these anomalies on a contour map that we are making of what lies under the river bottom.

This summer, we are going back to Rio Belen. We've worked there for two seasons, and we've covered about 50% of the area. We are taking a small group with us, and we will hire local people to help us. The probe barge has given us superior results, and we have several targets to investigate in more detail.

Denise C. Lakey is one of the founding officers of Ships of Discovery. She has a Master's degree in nautical archaeology and is currently pursuing her PhD in Spanish colonial history. Her first love is historical and archival research, especially in Seville and Madrid.

For information about the *Gallega* Project, write: Ships of Discovery P.O.Box 542865 Dallas, TX 75354-2865. Or call (214) 462-9219.

Illustration: Joe Simmons

The probe barge is a low tech Ships of Discovery innovation. Four vertical pipes, 2 meters apart, pass through the barge deck and are raised and lowered by ropes that run along the central mast. Water is pumped through each pipe as it is lowered so it hydraulically penetrates the bottom mud until it comes to rest on something solid. After depths are recorded, three of the pipes are raised and the barge is rotated around the fourth, thus maintaining positive positioning.

SEAS'91 cancelled—Gulf war blamed

The executive committee for the Southeast Atlantic States SCUBA Conference and International Film Festival recently voted to cancel their 1991 Conference, scheduled for March 8-10, in Norfolk, VA. Marvin Huddleston, Exhibits Chair, told ***Ships & Shipwrecks*** that "over 43,000 people from the Norfolk area have shipped out because of the Gulf war. This loss means fewer attendees, volunteers, and sponsors." Dive shops in the area are suffering too, and many have reduced their trips and classes by half. Huddleston said that SEAS prides itself on the quality of its program, and it voted to cancel rather than downgrade the conference. But, he said, "SEAS'92 looks healthy, and it is tentatively set for Feb. 21-23, 1992." SEAS, P.O.Box 3223, Norfolk, VA 23514

2 January/February 1991

January/February 1991 3

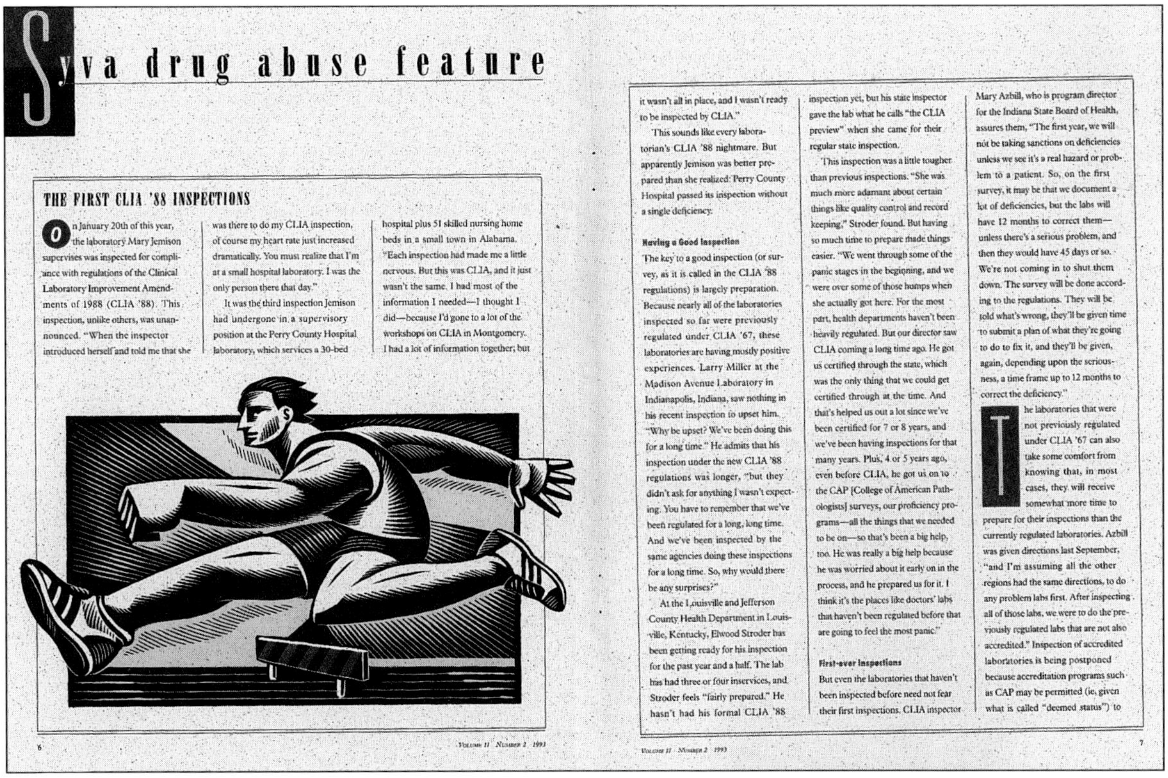

Syva drug abuse feature

THE FIRST CLIA '88 INSPECTIONS

On January 20th of this year, the laboratory Mary Jemison supervises was inspected for compliance with regulations of the Clinical Laboratory Improvement Amendments of 1988 (CLIA '88). This inspection, unlike others, was unannounced. "When the inspector introduced herself and told me that she was there to do my CLIA inspection, of course my heart rate just increased dramatically. You must realize that I'm at a small hospital laboratory. I was the only person there that day."

It was the third inspection Jemison had undergone in a supervisory position at the Perry County Hospital laboratory, which services a 30-bed hospital plus 51 skilled nursing home beds in a small town in Alabama. "Each inspection had made me a little nervous. But this was CLIA, and it just wasn't the same. I had most of the information I needed—I thought I did—because I'd gone to a lot of the workshops on CLIA in Montgomery. I had a lot of information together; but it wasn't all in place, and I wasn't ready to be inspected by CLIA."

This sounds like every laboratorian's CLIA '88 nightmare. But apparently Jemison was better prepared than she realized: Perry County Hospital passed its inspection without a single deficiency.

Having a Good Inspection

The key to a good inspection (or survey, as it is called in the CLIA '88 regulations) is largely preparation. Because nearly all of the laboratories inspected so far were previously regulated under CLIA '67, these laboratories are having mostly positive experiences. Larry Miller at the Madison Avenue Laboratory in Indianapolis, Indiana, saw nothing in his recent inspection to upset him. "Why be upset? We've been doing this for a long time." He admits that his inspection under the new CLIA '88 regulations was longer, "but they didn't ask for anything I wasn't expecting. You have to remember that we've been regulated for a long, long time. And we've been inspected by the same agencies doing these inspections for a long time. So, why would there be any surprises?"

At the Louisville and Jefferson County Health Department in Louisville, Kentucky, Elwood Stroder has been getting ready for his inspection for the past year and a half. The lab has had three or four inservices, and Stroder feels "fairly prepared." He hasn't had his formal CLIA '88 inspection yet, but his state inspector gave the lab what he calls "the CLIA preview" when she came for their regular state inspection.

This inspection was a little tougher than previous inspections. "She was much more adamant about certain things like quality control and record keeping," Stroder found. But having so much time to prepare made things easier. "We went through some of the panic stages in the beginning, and we were over some of those humps when she actually got here. For the most part, health departments haven't been heavily regulated. But our director saw CLIA coming a long time ago. He got us certified through the state, which was the only thing that we could get certified through at the time. And that's helped us out a lot since we've been certified for 7 or 8 years, and we've been having inspections for that many years. Plus, 4 or 5 years ago, even before CLIA, he got us on to the CAP [College of American Pathologists] surveys, our proficiency programs—all the things that we needed to be on—so that's been a big help, too. He was really a big help because he was worried about it early on in the process, and he prepared us for it. I think it's the places like doctors' labs that haven't been regulated before that are going to feel the most panic."

First-ever Inspections

But even the laboratories that haven't been inspected before need not fear their first inspections. CLIA inspector Mary Azbill, who is program director for the Indiana State Board of Health, assures them, "The first year, we will not be taking sanctions on deficiencies unless we see it's a real hazard or problem to a patient. So, on the first survey, it may be that we document a lot of deficiencies, but the labs will have 12 months to correct them—unless there's a serious problem, and then they would have 45 days or so. We're not coming in to shut them down. The survey will be done according to the regulations. They will be told what's wrong, they'll be given time to submit a plan of what they're going to do to fix it, and they'll be given, again, depending upon the seriousness, a time frame up to 12 months to correct the deficiency."

The laboratories that were not previously regulated under CLIA '67 can also take some comfort from knowing that, in most cases, they will receive somewhat more time to prepare for their inspections than the currently regulated laboratories. Azbill was given directions last September, "and I'm assuming all the other regions had the same directions, to do any problem labs first. After inspecting all of those labs, we were to do the previously regulated labs that are not also accredited." Inspection of accredited laboratories is being postponed because accreditation programs such as CAP may be permitted (ie, given what is called "deemed status") to

6 Volume II Number 2 1993

Volume II Number 2 1993 7

FOUR-COLUMN LAYOUTS

8-11 Ah Ha! *You can use the fourth column of a four-column grid for a contents box, masthead or sidebar as well as for more text type. Make sure that narrow columns of ragged type do not result in awkward gaps and trapped white space. Here the turquoise second color shows as the bold rule bleeding off the top of each page and as screen tints with keylines. Note also the miniature logo that becomes a dingbat to show that the story has ended.*

8-12 Currents *In Ah Ha! above, the four columns have equal widths. In Currents, the fourth column, kept at the outside edge of the page, is half the width of the other three columns. The designer uses the narrow column for author mug shots and bios, pull quotes and editorial notes. Centered headlines add to the elegant combination of dark red and black.*

THE QUARTERLY NEWSLETTER OF THE AMERICAN HOLISTIC HEALTH ASSOCIATION

Ah Ha!

FURTHERING THE UNDERSTANDING OF HOLISTIC HEALTH

WINTER 1992

Contents

Did You Know...
New information on patient rights and more. **2**

AHHA's Goals and Objectives
New and improved. **3**

Communicating Wellness
A simplified explanation of holistic health. **4**

Can What You Eat Cause You Problems?
Find out how to determine which foods might make you feel bad. **5**

The "Science of Life"
Fourth article in modality series explores Maharishi Ayur-Veda. **6**

AHMA Conference
Washington, D.C. site of American Holistic Medical Association conference. **7**

Washington Report
Election-year politics likely to delay reform of national health policy. **8**

EVERY DAY MIRACLES

Harnessing attitudes as a powerful resource for optimum health

Excerpted from Happiness Is A Choice by Barry Neil Kaufman

When a young boy in a wheelchair, suffering from a progressive and fatal neuromuscular disease, began to entertain the idea that he could help himself improve despite the prognosis of experts, he began to regain the use of his hands. After a thirty-five year old woman discarded her beliefs about the burdens of adulthood, she experienced dramatic relief from years of chronic back pain. Once a business executive forgave his dishonest partner, a bleeding stomach ulcer began to heal.

These amazing and inspiring stories open us to questioning what might be possible for you, for me, for any of us. Perhaps the most useful way to explore such a question would be to look at how we see the world and the limits that can come from our perceptions.

"I can't help it, that's the way I am." This familiar idiom, which many of us use casually to explain feelings, behaviors, and physical states, suggests an out-of-control relationship between us (the thinking/decision-making self) and our emotions, actions, and bodies. In essence, we become victims rather than initiators, responders rather than creators, adapters rather than masters.

What if all of these notions were simply cultural myths rather than facts? What if who we are, what we have become, and how we can change are arenas under our complete personal jurisdiction? What if we are in charge, and have always been so, but have never found a useful way to understand, acknowledge, and harness that power?

The Option Process acknowledges our beliefs as the key to taking charge of our lives. To be happy, and to foster physical well-being, becomes more than a debatable philosophical construct for some distant time, but an actual living possibility, a choice that we can make right now. We become happier and healthier by exploring and changing our beliefs.

The impact of the beliefs we hold is profound. The ramifications can be empowering and liberating, but they can also be devastating. If I think something is wrong with me or that I am unlovable, I will probably have corresponding feelings associated with such beliefs—sadness, isolation, and impotence. My actions will follow from such beliefs. For example, I might leave a relationship or bury myself in work to find meaning or a sense of self-worth. Ultimately, my body process (sluggishness, suppressed immune system, vulnerability to disease and viruses) will reflect my mind-set. Without implying that I am to blame, it becomes clear that I precipitate my susceptibility to illness. I can divert my body, with my beliefs, from working properly. The realization that we are responsible for our health

Continued on page 3...

From the book *Happiness Is a Choice*, by Barry Neil Kaufman. Copyright © 1991 by Barry Neil Kaufman. Reprinted by permission of Ballantine Books, a division of Random House Books.

Instructors invited to speak out! See page 3.

Currents

in Emergency Cardiac Care

Official Newsletter of

American Heart Association   Citizen CPR Foundation, Inc.

Is school-site CPR at recess?

For years, CPR training advocates in the U.S. have encouraged schools to teach not only the fundamental "three Rs," Reading, 'Riting, and 'Rithmetic, but also the "fourth R," Resuscitation. From the time Peter Safar, MD, and colleagues confirmed the feasibility of teaching CPR to the lay public in the late '50s and early '60s, and began calling for training of the masses, school-site CPR training has been an integral part of this vision.[1-3]

Now, more than 30 years later, public health education advocates are *still* working to incorporate CPR into school curricula. Continued interest in school-site CPR training is evident in the recent introduction of new programs in numerous communities from Excelsior Springs, Missouri, to Kingston, New York, to Webster County, Mississippi. It is evident in the Houston Independent School District plan to train all 15,000 eighth grade students citywide in CPR. It is evident in communities like Leadville, Colorado, where CPR has become a required component of physical education in grades six through twelve. It is evident in the establishment of the country's first "CPR Explorer Post," which aims to train high school students as CPR instructors so that they, in turn, can train their peers. And it is evident in the work of the newly formed Save-A-Life Foundation, which is lobbying for mandatory CPR and first aid training for teachers in Illinois, and plans to bring the cause to national levels.

These developments give us a glimpse at local efforts, but how far have we come as a nation? In 1982, more than half (55%) of American secondary (junior and senior high) schools offered CPR training to their students, according to a nationwide survey conducted by the ACT (Advanced Coronary Treatment) Foundation. At that time, school-site CPR training was typically offered in ninth or tenth grade health classes by school faculty, and was funded through the general school budget. The American public was all for the idea—a 1983 Gallup poll found that eight out of ten adults believed that CPR should be a prerequisite for graduation from high school.

By 1986, several national organizations, such as the American School Health Association, the National Education Association, and the National Parent-Teacher Association (PTA), had endorsed school-site CPR training for students, teachers, and school employees alike. In addition, six states and the District of Columbia *required* CPR training in secondary schools, 16 states had legisla-

See RECESS page 8

Volume 4
Number 3
Fall 1993

INSIDE

3 New instructor column

4 AHA ECC report

5 Changes in drug therapy

7 Australians ignite Spark of Life

10 Current science

11 Arming police with AEDs

12 AEDs go to the hospital

A bookbag, a lunch, and an AED

Each day, Cindy Johns drives her two sons, Brandin, 11, and Bryan, 7, to Poulsbo Elementary School in Poulsbo, Washington. Each day, they pack their bookbags, their lunches—and an automated external defibrillator (AED). Brandin, a sixth grader, has congenital heart disease and is subject to periodic episodes of pulseless ventricular tachycardia. But Brandin is confident that if anything goes wrong, he will have the best and quickest emergency medical care possible, not only because 15 to 20 teachers and two school staff members have been trained to use the AED, but also because his younger brother is skilled in its use.

The arrangement is the brainchild of Judy Graves, RN, of the Center for Evaluation of Emergency Medical Services in Seattle, who learned about Brandin's situation through colleague, Jim Pierce, EMT-P,

See BOOKBAG page 9

© CURRENTS AHA 1993

---

84 EDITING YOUR NEWSLETTER

COMMUNICATING WELLNESS

A Simplified Explanation of Holistic Health

by Greg Anderson

If we hope to integrate the belief in and practice of holistic health on a wide-scale basis, we must first "unmuddle" our communication of the principles.

Through the Cancer Conquerors Foundation, we have attempted to do this. The context is our work with cancer patients and their families. The format is a combination of lecture and small group discussions. Participants attend a weekly session which lasts two hours.

Although we were certainly helping people, it became clear we were missing the mark when it came to putting the program into meaningful use. Participants would get a bit here, a piece there. Confusion on what to do or when to do it was often the biggest problem.

We needed a simple-to-understand and easy-to-implement model that brought all the plan's elements together. In response, we developed the following eight-point wellness plan and graphic. This simple tool has been credited with making holistic health understandable and workable for thousands of people who had vague or negative perceptions of the principles.

We first teach the fundamental principle that wellness is much more than the lack of physical symptoms. Total well-being and the interdependence of body/mind/spirit is new to nearly all our participants. We emphasize that our minds and spirits are ill only if we allow it. This issue of personal responsibility for our choices is a theme that is carried throughout the program.

Each of the eight points of the Cancer Conquerors wellness program cover basic holistic beliefs and practices. One point in the plan is typically emphasized each session.

Treatment

We teach participants to practice these techniques in addition to, not in place of, appropriate qualified physical, emotional, and spiritual guidance.

People are encouraged to hold a strong belief in their wellness team both as people and as to the practices they recommend.

Beliefs and attitudes

Most of our time is spent challenging the myths about illness. There are widely-held beliefs that cancer means death. Similar beliefs of suffering, incapacitation, or one's imminent demise are also held for other illnesses. We teach that each person's experience is different and that there is much we can do to influence our personal encounter with disease.

Exercise

Cancer Conquerors teaches a simple program

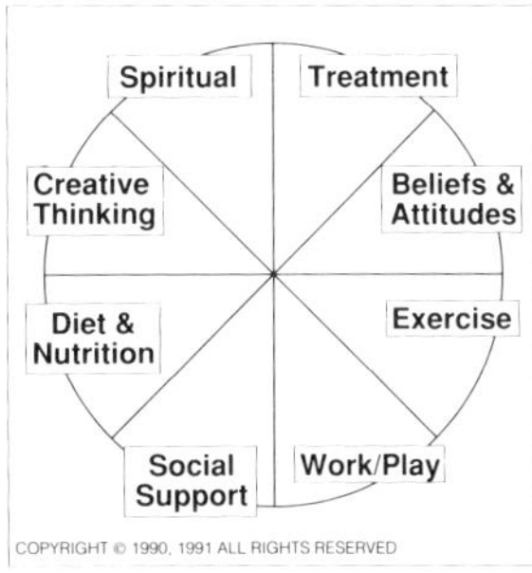
Spiritual
Treatment
Creative Thinking
Beliefs & Attitudes
Diet & Nutrition
Exercise
Social Support
Work/Play
COPYRIGHT © 1990, 1991 ALL RIGHTS RESERVED

The above graphic, designed by The Cancer Conquerors Foundation, serves as a tool for making holistic health more easily understood by newcomers to the concept.

of "comfort zone" physical exercise. Full-body stretches that can be done whether one is confined to bed or is mobile are possible for everyone. For those who are able, we encourage a walking routine working up to a maximum of 30 minutes per day.

Work/Play

We give people permission to play. For many, it is one of our most important teachings. For others, we encourage a new look at their life's purpose, helping them explore and find a work that brings fulfillment on many levels. We strive for a work/play balance.

Social support

We ask people to make an appraisal of the relationships in their lives, both personal and professional. Participants are encouraged to give minimal time and emotional energy to those relationships that are toxic. This frequently means some relationships need to be put "on hold" for a time. Social support also means participation in the weekly support groups.

Diet and nutrition

We recommend a "modified" vegetarian plan

Continued on page 7...

Can What You Eat Cause You Problems?

by William D. Manahan, MD

The answer is yes! How you feel, some symptoms, and certain diseases are linked to what you eat.

For example, John was a patient of mine who experienced intermittent headaches over a period of three years. They suddenly vanished after he quit drinking coffee.

Robert, another patient of mine, was amazed when he discovered that the four glasses of milk he was drinking each day to help his duodenal ulcer were actually making it worse. Robert's heartburn, abdominal pain, and stomach gurgling went away completely, following a two-week dairy elimination diet.

Melinda's seven-year old son, Sean, had been hyper a large share of the time and was prone to recurrent ear infections. When sugar was eliminated from Sean's diet, he began to act like a more normal child. When Melinda was told by a trusted friend that the change in Sean's behavior couldn't be due to eliminating sugar, she restarted the sugar and Sean began to display hyperactive behavior again and got another ear infection.

There are six major culprits in the modern diet that can cause medical problems. They are caffeine, salt, milk, processed foods, sugar, and fats. At least 150 different symptoms, complaints, and problems can be caused from eating foods that fall into those categories.

Those of you who wish to actively participate in your own health can begin to observe how what you eat affects how you feel.

There are at least 150 different symptoms, complaints, and problems that can be caused from eating such foods as caffeine, salt, processed foods, sugar, and fats.

First, are there any foods that you know tend to cause you some problems? Second, are there foods that you tend to crave? And third, are there foods that would be hard for you to give up entirely or at least go without for two or three weeks?

If two or three different foods come to mind as you ask yourself these questions (such as chocolate, bread, cheese, or ice cream), try going on a two-week elimination diet, completely avoiding those foods. If you feel any different at the end of these two weeks, it could be one of those foods causing the problem. If you are unsure, do a rechallenge test. On the fifteenth day eat a large amount of one of the suspect foods and then monitor how you feel in the next 24-48 hours.

When John drank several cups of coffee after going without it for two weeks, he got a very severe headache again. When Robert tried four glasses of milk after going two weeks without dairy, his heartburn returned. Like Melinda, John and Robert learned that elimination of the food improved symptoms and reintroduction of the food stimulated the symptom or disease. In other words, they learned that they had control over at least part of how they were feeling each day.

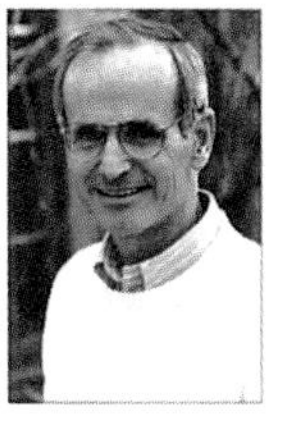

Dr. Bill Manahan director of the Wellness Center of Minnesota. He earned his medical degree from the University of Minnesota. Besides a part-time family medicine practice, he also has a preventive medicine/community health practice, and he serves as Medical Director of Quality Assurance at Immanuel-St. Joseph's Hospital in Mankato.

A proponent of holistic medicine, Dr. Manahan is author of *Eat for Health: A Do-It-Yourself Nutrition Guide for Solving Common Medical Problems*. He is president of the American Holistic Medical Association, is a member of the Mankato Health Action Council, and from 1977 to 1986 was an assistant professor of Family Medicine with Mayo Medical School in Rochester.

ADVICE

• *continued from page 4*

about half of the patients regardless of whether lidocaine was given. Fortunately, reperfusion arrhythmias in most patients are short-lived and often tend to be clinically rather benign.

[1] *Latocha, G, Bernauer H. Effect of antiarrhythmic drugs on the postischemic metabolic recovery of isolated rat hearts. Arch Int Phartmacodyn Ther 1991;312: 39-54.*

[2] *Gao, R. Reperfusion arrhythmias in acute myocardial infarction. Chung Hua Hsin Hsueh Kuan Ping Tsa Chih 1992;20:84-6.*

Joseph P. Ornato, MD, FACC
Chairman
AHA Committee on ECC
Richmond, Virginia

EDITOR'S NOTE: In addition to the sequence cited to the right, several readers have inquired about the omission of the recovery position from the new BLS skillsheets. Originally, the BLS subcommittee believed it was unnecessary to include the recovery position on the skillsheets, since the recovery position was addressed elsewhere in the guidelines and could be used at any time during a rescue if the victim resumes breathing. In response to reader input, the subcommittee decided to add a reference to the recovery position in future published versions of the skillsheets, including those that appear in the new BLS Heartsaver Guide.

Q. In the new BLS skillsheets published in the Summer 1993 issue of *Currents*, the sequence for management of the infant with a foreign body airway obstruction who initially is conscious but becomes unconscious is inconsistent with the sequence suggested for management of the adult and the child in the same condition. What is the rationale for this difference?

Dorrie Effron
Tulsa, Oklahoma

A. While all sequences for foreign body airway management recommended in the BLS skillsheets published in *Currents* are scientifically sound, you are correct in noting this inconsistency. In the interest of educational consistency, the infant sequence for foreign body airway obstruction will be modified slightly in future published versions of the skillsheets to make it more consistent with the adult and child sequences. However, it is scientifically valid and acceptable to follow the present published sequence.

Mary Fran Hazinski, RN, MSN
Co-chairman
AHA Subcommittee on Pediatric Resuscitation
Nashville, Tennessee

IN BRIEF

• **At least seven states—** Arizona, Colorado, Florida, Montana, New York, Rhode Island, and Virginia—have enacted prehospital do-not-resuscitate (DNR) laws. Several counties or health districts have similar policies, including Orange and Napa Counties, California; Hennepin County, Minnesota; Kansas City, Missouri; and Johnson County, Kansas. In some instances, only patients with terminal or irreversible conditions are eligible for DNR orders; in others, no restrictions apply.

• **What do New Jersey's state** health commissioner, Bruce Siegel, MD; AHA Affiliate president, Henry Waxman, MD; and Rep. Richard Zimmer (R-12th Dist.) have in common? All lost their fathers to cardiac arrest and all are actively promoting the state's new EMT-Defibrillation legislation. The goal is to have 650 rescue, police, and firefighter teams across the state trained to defibrillate. To date, 135 rescue squads have been trained and three lives have been saved. Siegel has urged state residents to support volunteer rescue squads in their efforts to raise funds for the equipment.

• **The failure of communities** in the U.S. to equip ambulances with defibrillators is "inexcusable," and may be costing many lives, according to Richard Cummins, MD, vice-chairman of the AHA Committee on Emergency Cardiac Care, who spoke recently at the annual meeting of the North American Society of Pacing and Electrophysiology in San Diego. AHA recommendations have established early defibrillation as a standard of care that should be available to all citizens in need. This means that all first-responding vehicles should be equipped with the devices, and all personnel who are trained and expected to provide CPR should also be trained to defibrillate. Rapid defibrillation should also be more readily available in sections of hospitals where unacceptable delays to defibrillation can occur.

• **By June 1994, all 1,500** driving schools in Japan will have implemented mandatory CPR training programs, in compliance with a newly approved amendment to the Road Traffic Act. It is anticipated that one million students will be trained each year.

• **More than a thousand Houston**, Texas, residents spent two and a half hours on Mother's Day learning how to save a child's life with CPR. The mass infant CPR training event, believed to be the first of its kind in the world, drew not only mothers, but also fathers, grandparents, older siblings, and child care workers. It was a "great way to spend Mother's Day," according to participant Lillian Harris, mother of a 14-month-old daughter.

The mass training event was organized by the City of Houston and the Gulf Coast Division of the AHA in less than two months, and was made possible through the help of 75 volunteer instructors. An indirect benefit was that the event resulted in the best media coverage on CPR in Houston to date, according to Paul Pepe, MD, director of emergency medical services. Due to the success of the effort, organizers are considering repeating the event next year—this time on Father's Day. "Every parent should learn CPR," declared Pepe, who recently became a parent himself. ■

Spark of Life conference highlights multidisciplinary CPR issues in Australia

On April 30 and May 1, the Australian Resuscitation Council held the "Spark of Life" conference in Melbourne, under the leadership of Professor Gordon A. Harrison, Council chairman, and Professor John Pearce, conference chairman. The opening ceremony of the conference was regal and featured vibrant two-time heart transplant patient, Fiona Coote.

The objective of the conference was to analyze critical CPR issues. The satisfaction of this objective was facilitated by 14 pre-conference workshops on topics including advanced life support, expired air resuscitation (EAR) with adjuncts, casualty simulation, rescue and resuscitation in or around water, and practical anatomy and physiology for lay teachers of CPR.

The workshops and conference proved enormously attractive to the CPR community. It was necessary to close registration at over 1,000 registrants weeks before the conference, turning hundreds of potential participants away. Attendees came from across the spectrum of those involved in the teaching and practice of CPR and other aspects of emergency care, including physicians, nurses, paramedics, ambulance officers, lifesavers, police, armed services, and lay teachers.

Initial focus was provided by invited speakers, Allan Braslow, PhD, on "CPR: A Skill for Everyone?," William Montgomery, MD, on "CPR— State of the Art," and Colin Robertson, MD, on "Guidelines of the European Resuscitation Council in Basic and Advanced Life Support." In addition, 120 papers from Australian and overseas speakers presented the broad picture. Abstract sessions included: teaching basic life support, emergency life support in hospitals, protocols and assessment in BLS, teaching ACLS, special considerations in resuscitation and first aid, early defibrillation, teaching CPR and ECC to health professionals, BLS teaching and practice, ethical issues, pediatric resuscitation, pharmacologic aspects of resuscitation, and teaching and practice of CPR in different clinical settings.

> *"I was very impressed by the degree of enthusiasm among participants and how well the Australian Resuscitation Council coordinates the training activities of its 15-member organization."*
>
> *William Montgomery, MD*

By the end of the conference, it was clear that many key issues in Australia are similar to those in North America and Europe, but modified by Australia's relative geographical isolation in the world, by concentration of more than 80 percent of its 15 million population in fewer than ten predominantly coastal major cities, by an enormously long coastline, and by the vast distance between country towns. Australia has well-developed professional emergency response systems in its large cities and a very enthusiastic base of volun tary lay teaching bodies.

The major issues identified during the conference were: 1) the need for international guidelines; 2) strategies to investigate the cost effectiveness of more widespread availability of automated external defibrillators in urban and rural settings; 3) the impact of the fear of AIDS on the teaching and practice of CPR; 4) potential targeting of CPR teaching; 5) the need for quality control of CPR adjunct equipment; 6) the development of a national database on CPR and emergency care teaching, and practice to evaluate the Australian Chain of Survival; 7) monitoring standards of CPR in hospitals; and 8) strategies for dealing with sudden (sometimes unusual) emergencies in remote or difficult environments. There were also a number of issues raised in the field of ethics, such as aftercare of victims, counseling of those affected by death or significant disability after emergencies, and debriefing of participants in CPR or emergency care attempts. These and other issues will be considered by the Council during its next several meetings.

The conference also provided a useful opportunity to initiate discussion with some colleagues from the Asian-Pacific region on the value of regional cooperation in the teaching and practice of CPR and related activities.

Overall, the Spark of Life was judged an overwhelming success. It is likely another international conference will be mounted in three years time. ■

Professor G. A. Harrison

The Australian Resuscitation Council is a multidisciplinary decision-making group comprised of the following members: Australian and New Zealand College of Anaesthetists; Australasian College for Emergency Medicine; Australian Defence Force; Australian New Zealand Intensive Care Society; Australian Red Cross Society; Cardiac Society of Australia and New Zealand; Confederation of Australian Critical Care Nurses, Inc.; Institute of Ambulance Officers; National Heart Foundation of Australia; Royal Australasian College of Surgeons; Royal Australian College of General Practitioners; Royal College of Nursing, Australia; Royal Life Saving Society, Australia; St. John Ambulance, Australia; Surf Life Saving Australia, Ltd.

Layout requires that some elements appear earlier, longer or larger than others. Priority tells you what goes on page one, what takes the largest headline, and what gets bumped to the pile labeled "maybe-in-another-issue."

The following guidelines help you create successful layouts.

Simplicity

The layout easiest to make is probably easiest to read, too. Simplicity and efficiency go hand in hand.

Sticking to one format and just a few typefaces and sizes keeps your publication simple. Remember, too, that clip art and other graphics are just clutter if they don't contribute to a specific objective.

Every strong element on a page competes for attention with every other. Headlines, photos, charts, areas of color and screen tints all shout, "Look at me!" When you put an element on the page, make sure it deserves attention.

Structure

Readers want your help. Use headlines to signal importance of stories. Make the most important headlines also the biggest. Place them near the top of the page. Don't make two headlines look like one by positioning them across from each other, an error commonly known as tombstoning. To review guidelines concerning headline writing and placement, consult Visual 5-9.

Use rules and screen tints to organize information that is not text or captions. Rules are especially important to box tables and other data graphics.

White space on the outside frames a layout, but on the inside steals its harmony. Push white space out toward the margins so it encloses elements.

Eye flow

Readers enter a layout at the upper left and exit at the lower right. Put a headline where eye flow begins. Use a strong visual, such as a photo, to anchor the weakest point of the page at the lower left.

Keep in mind that readers look first at headlines, photos, captions, and other strong visual elements throughout the entire newsletter. Thoughtful layout makes it easy to skim, then return to specific material.

Proportion

Perfectly balanced pages are as dull as perfect people. Compose pages using the same guidelines that lead to interesting photos: Divide pages in thirds rather than halves. Use an odd, not even, number of major elements. Build interest with asymmetry.

Size, weight and placement of elements determines contrast. Use text to divide a large headline from a dark photo. Make captions long enough so a diagram at the end of a column doesn't seem to fall off the bottom of the page.

Spreads

Readers see only your first and last pages by themselves. Other pages are usually seen two at a time as part of a spread. Layout must take the spread into account, not just the single page.

NAMEPLATES

Your nameplate belongs at the top of the front page, where it sets the tone for your entire publication.

Imagine your newsletter on a table or desk with other publications. Your nameplate should help readers identify your newsletter in the pile and invite them to reach for it first. Try to make your nameplate pass this test of visual competition.

Except for date and issue number, keep your nameplate the same issue after issue. Consistent design trains readers to identify your publication. More important, consistency lets you focus exclusively on content for each issue.

To get maximum value from your nameplate, design it to follow these simple guidelines.

Useful facts

Let your name and subtitle tell who you are and why readers should pay attention. Make sure readers can immediately identify your purpose and organization.

Full information

Certify the required information—name of newsletter, subtitle, date—and optional information, such as logo, issue number, publisher or editor.

Impact

Ensure that design helps readers focus on your message. Use bold type, color, placement and other graphic techniques to highlight your most important words.

Simplicity

Verify that you have an uncluttered design that readers can understand at a glance. Delete every word and image that doesn't contribute to your message.

Depend on words

Avoid logos and other flourishes unless you know that readers recognize them instantly.

Image

Evaluate whether your design fits the image of your organization. Is it too formal or informal? Too classical or modern? If typefaces or colors don't feel right, change them.

Avoid "newsletter"

Your readers know that you produce a newsletter, so put a more precise communications term in your nameplate. Consult Visual 1-4 for ideas.

If you feel uncertain about creating a nameplate yourself, get help from a graphic designer. Review the suggestions about working with designers given in chapter two.

USING COLOR

If you want color in your newsletter, consider how it relates to your purposes and readers. Don't let the ease of adding color tempt you to use it without thinking about why. Make color help achieve your communication goals, not just decorate your pages.

When used well, a second color builds contrast, makes elements more vivid, and helps you organize information; it does not, however, make type more legible or reading easier. On the contrary, headlines in a color different from text type actually slow readers down. Forcing readers to switch from color to color makes your message harder to understand and remember.

NAMEPLATE REDESIGNS

8-14 Dispatcher *The Outline map in the old nameplate appears flat compared to the three-dimensional new version. Colors in the "before" are hidden within the type, but become much more bold in the "after." Key word in the redesign is much easier to read at a glance. (Redsign by Rose Ann Froberg.)*

8-15 Outreach *The editors of Outreach redesigned their entire newsletter, not just the nameplate. The new nameplate drops the world-and-cross logo, creating space to expand the name in dramatic script. Headlines, pull quotes, and everything else about the front page become more contemporary and professional. (Redesign by Dave Gustafson.)*

Think of color as a language as potent as words. Here are a few tips to make the language earn its place in your newsletter:

• Use color to put information into categories by assigning each category the same hue. For example, put the calendar inside a red box every issue. Don't switch to a blue box for winter and a yellow box for summer.

• Make big items and backgrounds pale, small items and foregrounds bright.

• Add variety by using tints of one color and overlapping tints of two colors, not by adding a third or fourth color.

If you print in only one color and don't want black, use dark blue or brown to ensure best legibility. Before selecting any color other than black, test how well it reproduces photos and screen tints on the specific paper used for your newsletter.

Preprinting

You can have an inexpensive second color in elements that stay the same by using the technique of preprinting. Preprinting means having color printed on enough paper at one time to last for many issues. For example, if you make five hundred four-page newsletters on a monthly schedule, you need six thousand 11" x 17" sheets per year. You could have the color portion of your nameplate printed on all six thousand sheets, then print black on five hundred as needed. The cost of preprinting adds little to overall yearly costs.

Using the technique of preprinting means that the date, issue number, headlines, and other elements unique to one issue appear in black, not color. You need to estimate preprinting quantities generously to take into account spoilage during each print run and changing needs from issue to issue.

Overlapping tints

Using one color in addition to black can yield many useful color combinations. You can have black and the color each at 100 percent and at several other percentages of screen tints. You can print black type at 100 percent over a tint of the color or, if it's dark enough, 100 percent of the color over a tint of black. You can reverse from both black and the color. Visual 8-23 shows some examples.

When thinking about what colors to use, consult a book of ink samples available at a print shop, design studio or art supply store. Ink sample books give customers and printers numbers by which to identify colors. The most commonly used books are PANTONE guides. If you wonder how a specific color would look when screened, consult a color tint chart as well as ink samples.

You can design almost any newsletter by selecting from a handful of colors whose effectiveness you know well and that readers find attractive. While it's tempting to follow trends, the colors listed below prove most popular year after year:

• violet — PANTONE Violet or Trumatch 39-b4
• warm red — PANTONE 032 or 185, or Trumatch 6-a
• cool red — PANTONE 199 or Trumatch 2-a
• burgundy — PANTONE 201 or Trumatch 2-b6
• blue — PANTONE 286 or 300, or Trumatch 36-b1 or 34-a
• green — PANTONE 347 or Trumatch 19-a
• brown — PANTONE 469 or Trumatch 49-a6

In addition to facilitating design, working with just a few colors controls costs and speeds production. You limit the risk of errors in electronic files and make it easier to work with printer and prepress services. Furthermore, these hues are so popular that many ink companies keep a premixed supply so they will cost less for printers to buy.

MASTHEADS

Every issue of your newsletter needs a masthead, the area with business information. Your

8-16 Preprinting color *The blue type and rule are preprinted on a large number of sheets. Some of those sheets become stock for a monthly issue printed in black only. The result is a two-color newsletter that costs little more than printing one-color. Note that preprinting requires a format that stays the same from issue to issue.*

8-17 Overlapping screen tints *The five blocks at the left show black in 100 percent and a tint, blue at 100 percent and a tint, and, in the middle, overlapping tints of blue and black. The same colors and their tints are used to create the nameplate at the right. Screen tints can be preprinted at the same time or instead of 100 percent of a color.*

Overlapped tints simulate a third color. The exact hue of that color depends on the original ink colors, the percents at which they are screened, the color and surface of paper being printed and several other factors. Many art supply stores, design studios and printers have charts that show common combinations.

8-18 Impact of color *The examples above, all produced by professional graphic designers, reveal how color influences image. Deciding to use color and selecting a specific hue should involve your publisher. Moreover, using color in design takes more skill than using black only. If you feel even a little unsure, consult with a graphic designer whose portfolio includes newsletters that use color.*

8-19 COLOR DO'S AND DON'TS TO CONTROL COSTS

Stick with black. Don't use color for

- body copy
- decks
- captions
- subtitles
- headlines
- sidebars
- photos
- infographics

It's OK to use a dark ink color for

- screen tints, rules and boxes
- illustrations and clip art
- nameplate and logo
- headers and footers

Stick with white or very light paper, such as ivory, cream or natural.

8-20 Chateau Montelena *Tabloids typically have 11" x 17" or A3 pages that provide a large canvas for visuals and creative typography. Chateau Montelena's marketing newsletter uses four-color printing on ivory matte-coated paper to convey a sense of sophisticated quality. The five-column grid accommodates maps and large photos on the inside spread. The issue folds into a self-mailer size of 5¹/₂" x 8¹/₂" with an address panel as one-fourth of the back page.*

8-21 Samaritan Today *Most of* Samaritan Today *appears in black ink only, but uses almost every design technique possible to create dramatic pages. Tints appear in ovals and circles, type and illustrations break up long lines, and columns run around oval pull quotes. On the two pages per issue where a second color is available, bold art bleeding off the pages lets the designer get away with departing from the three-column grid used in the rest of the publication.*

Garden Tools
A monthly report to the members of the South Coast Rose Society
Issue Number/Date

Issue Number / Date

Maintainance
MATTERS   News from Fairfield Public Works about service, repairs, and construction

PREMIE
PRIMER
Resources for parents of premature babies

Issue Number/Date

Date/Issue Number

Gales Creek Perspectives
A quarterly forum for the residents and friends of Upper Gales Development District

West Hills Wildlife Alert
Monitoring flora and fauna in Fairfield western ecosystems

Issue Number/Date

LastCall
Issue Number/Date
Trends in Square Dancing from Anchorage to Miami

HoodviewHorizons
Issue Number/Date
Recreational opportunities throughout the Mt. Hood National Forest

HEADLINER HIGHLIGHTS
Tracking the hottest bands in the hippest clubs
Issue Number/Date

masthead should have the same design and stay in the same location from one issue to the next.

The masthead tells
- name and address of your sponsoring organization,
- your name as editor,
- how readers can reach you.

You could also tell frequency of publication and subscription costs, if any, and give names of key officers and contributors. Potential contributors look in your masthead to learn if you solicit articles and photographs and what you pay for them.

If your newsletter is copyrighted, the notice belongs in your masthead. If you want librarians to catalog your publication, you should include an International Standard Serial Number (ISSN). The National Serials Data Program of the Library of Congress, Washington DC 20540, will assign ISSNs at no expense.

Newsletters that are mailed second class must display either an ISSN or a Post Office identification number in their nameplate, masthead or return address.

CALENDARS

Some people read a newsletter mainly for its schedule of events. No other publication has such a specialized listing.

A calendar is one of the most difficult design tasks. It should be easy to assemble and proofread, efficient to read and conservative of space. It should appear in the same place each issue and not have other important items to be clipped out from its opposing side.

Newspaper designers have ingenious ways of presenting schedules. Study the organization and use of type in a major newspaper, especially in its Friday and Sunday issues, for ideas. For additional ideas, look at inexpensive computer programs that keep track of forthcoming activities and show various approaches to calendar design.

Begin designing a schedule for your newsletter by asking what readers want to know. Try to make design help answer their questions. Here are some possibilities.

Location

If you're announcing activities at branch libraries or a series of public hearings, readers probably want to know only about locations they find convenient. Put the place first or in bold type, then tell dates and details.

Activity

If you're listing a variety of events, group them into categories that make sense to your readers. Don't make people who care only about one kind of event fight their way through the list of everything else.

Date

If you're presenting a variety of dates for the same event, such as a stage play, let your design highlight dates instead of program or performers. You don't need to repeat the name of the event next to the date for each performance.

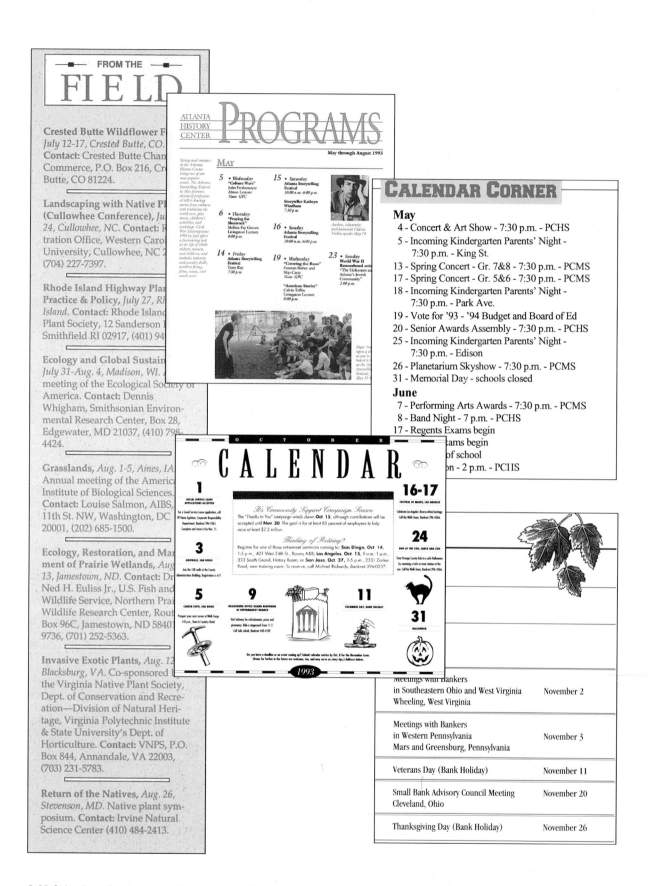

FROM THE
FIELD

Crested Butte Wildflower F...
July 12-17, Crested Butte, CO. ...
Contact: Crested Butte Cham...
Commerce, P.O. Box 216, Cre...
Butte, CO 81224.

Landscaping with Native Pl...
(Cullowhee Conference), Ju...
24, Cullowhee, NC. **Contact:** R...
tration Office, Western Caro...
University, Cullowhee, NC 2...
(704) 227-7397.

Rhode Island Highway Plan...
Practice & Policy, *July 27, Rh...*
Island. **Contact:** Rhode Island...
Plant Society, 12 Sanderson ...
Smithfield RI 02917, (401) 94...

Ecology and Global Sustain...
July 31-Aug. 4, Madison, WI. ...
meeting of the Ecological Society of
America. **Contact:** Dennis
Whigham, Smithsonian Environ-
mental Research Center, Box 28,
Edgewater, MD 21037, (410) 798-
4424.

Grasslands, *Aug. 1-5, Ames, IA...*
Annual meeting of the America...
Institute of Biological Sciences...
Contact: Louise Salmon, AIBS,
11th St. NW, Washington, DC ...
20001, (202) 685-1500.

Ecology, Restoration, and Ma...
ment of Prairie Wetlands, *Aug...*
13, Jamestown, ND. **Contact:** Dr...
Ned H. Euliss Jr., U.S. Fish and...
Wildlife Service, Northern Prai...
Wildlife Research Center, Rout...
Box 96C, Jamestown, ND 5840...
9736, (701) 252-5363.

Invasive Exotic Plants, *Aug. 12...*
Blacksburg, VA. Co-sponsored ...
the Virginia Native Plant Society,
Dept. of Conservation and Recre-
ation—Division of Natural Heri-
tage, Virginia Polytechnic Institute
& State University's Dept. of
Horticulture. **Contact:** VNPS, P.O.
Box 844, Annandale, VA 22003,
(703) 231-5783.

Return of the Natives, *Aug. 26,*
Stevenson, MD. Native plant sym-
posium. **Contact:** Irvine Natural
Science Center (410) 484-2413.

8-30 Calendars *Good calendar design begins with clear knowledge of what readers want to know. Keep typography well orga-*
nized and complete. Notice how much information the above examples include and how they help readers by anticipating ques-
tions. When properly designed, calendars advertise, not merely notify.

8-31 Contents *A table of contents advertises the information inside and can add a useful design element to the front page. Most newsletters have one, but many don't need one. If your newsletter has no more than eight pages, readers may ignore a contents panel. If it's more than eight pages, they may welcome it, depending on your design and their interest.*

9. PRODUCTION

Graphic design considers production as well as appearance. While planning your newsletter, you calculate printing method and paper as well as type, graphics and photos.

Whether you print using a photocopy machine or offset press, you need an original to start with. The original might be as simple as one sheet from a desktop printer or as complex as an imagesetter printout complete with halftones.

The process of preparing the original for printing is called pasteup when done by hand and desktop publishing when done using a computer. In either case the process, if carried out properly, results in camera-ready copy.

Whether you prepare camera-ready copy yourself or have someone else do it, you need to know how it should look. You keep control over the cost, quality and schedule when you can verify that copy is truly camera-ready. In this chapter, you learn how to establish that control.

This chapter describes camera-ready copy and how it relates to printing. You learn about halftones and scaling and how to work with service bureaus and printers. You discover the essential techniques for pasting up and guidelines for judging whether your copy is ready to print.

TYPE AND GRAPHICS

Printers think about the visual elements of your newsletter as either line copy or continuous-tone copy. Line copy has high contrast, usually black on white. It includes type, rules and clip art. Continuous-tone copy has dark and light areas, but also has many intermediate shades of gray. It includes all photos and some illustrations.

Printers divide their world into line and continuous copy because copy machines and printing presses operate on an all-or-nothing principle. An image is reproduced 100 percent or not at all. There is no middle ground.

An offset press either places ink on paper or not; it doesn't place just a little bit of ink. Photocopy machines, using toner instead of ink, work the same way. An area of paper to receive toner or ink could be as large as a 72-point bold letter or as small as a dot in a 100-line screen, but the coverage within the area must be 100 percent.

To ensure legibility, keep type sharp and consistent. For the best possible quality, use fresh ribbons or toner cartridges in your computer printers. Streaks, faded characters, or uneven densities across the page create distractions that make your newsletter more difficult to read.

Type and graphics from an imagesetter are sharper and more consistent than type from a laser printer. Imagesetters are machines found at printers and services bureaus and at some advertising agencies and design studios. Their lasers place images on photo paper, not plain paper as in laser printers. Imagesetters can also print out on film ready for commercial printers to make plates.

Imagesetters print out computer files the same as desktop printers, but with higher resolutions. Desktop printers have 300 or 600 dots per inch (dpi) resolutions, whereas imagesetters have 1,200 or 2,400 dpi. Regarding line copy, higher resolution means sharper focus and greater density.

PHOTOGRAPHS

Continuous-tone copy must be changed to line copy before a printer can reproduce it. The change requires breaking the images into thousands of tiny dots. Dot patterns create illusions of original images, tricking the eye into thinking it sees continuous tones. You can see the dot patterns in Visual 9-2.

9-1 INSPECTING TYPE

Sharp, dense type in high contrast with its background yields legible copy. Use this list as a guide when you examine type from a desktop printer or imagesetter.

Specifications Confirm correct point sizes, styles, leading and line measure.

Dark characters Check characters for adequate density and uniform blackness. Inspect type for holes or breaks.

Straight lines Put a ruler under a few sample lines to ensure they have no hills or valleys.

Parallel lines Study lines to make sure they look parallel to each other.

Even justification Lay a ruler down the left edge and, if set flush right, down the right edge to verify proper alignment.

Sensible hyphenation Certify that words are divided correctly. With ragged-right copy, divisions should avoid awkward gaps.

White paper Note whether paper looks bright white and free from stains or flaws that might reproduce.

Consistency Check that features such as density, point sizes and line measures stay identical with type set on different days, by different machines, or originating in different software.

9-2 Continuous tones to halftones *The ball and background are screened at forty lines per inch to make individual dots easy to see. Even these large dots create the illusion of the original continuous-tone image.*

9-3 Halftone and line reproductions *The top version of the portrait is a halftone. The bottom version shows the high-contrast results of reproducing a photo that has not been halftoned.*

In areas of the image with small dots, more paper shows through, creating highlights; portions of the image with large dots show less paper, thus representing shadow areas. Illustrations made with soft pencil lines or brush strokes have continuous tones the same as photographs, thus requiring halftoning.

A halftone on paper is a halftone positive. On film, it's a halftone negative.

Photocopy and quick printing require halftone positives as part of pasteup. Commercial printing using metal plates uses halftone negatives. When your newsletter is printed using metal plates, you provide the printer with photos prepared according to instructions given later in this chapter.

Halftones may be made using a scanner or process camera. If your halftones will be photocopied, screen rulings should be 85-line. For quick printing, get 100-line. For commercial printing, use 133-line.

Scanner

Using a scanner to make a halftone means that the image may be seen on a computer screen, manipulated with regard to size and shape, and assembled along with type and graphics into a completed page. The ruling of halftones originating in scanners depends on the quality of the scanner and the output device.

Working with scanned images on a computer screen requires desktop publishing software. Even then, the pace may be slow and, depending on size, you may be limited to one image per page.

If you scan photos into your computer, you get better output from an imagesetter than a desktop laser printer. The higher resolution of the imagesetter means that it can produce halftones with more subtle tone variations. Halftones from imagesetters look closer to the original than halftones that come from laser printers.

Process camera

Process cameras are made specifically for graphic arts photography. Small ones, sometimes called stat cameras, may be found at many design studios, blue print companies, and advertising or public relations agencies. Larger machines are used by commercial printers and trade camera services.

Halftone positives made using a process camera are known as stats or photomechanical transfers (PMTs). Stats or PMTs are not the same as Veloxes, which are higher quality and cost more because they require making negatives first.

When you buy halftones, you are charged by the size of paper or film used, not the size of original copy. You can save money by grouping images all scaled to the same percentage. Grouping, usually called ganging, may result in some loss of quality if originals differ in contrast or density. Ganged images are all scanned or shot at a common exposure rather than at

exposures determined for the needs of individual images.

While making halftones, service bureaus and printers can improve the images in the ways described in chapter eight. When you specify or inspect halftones, verify that the results are what you want.

The paper on which halftones are reproduced affects choice of screen ruling. Uncoated paper absorbs ink quickly: Dots may soak in, spread out, become fuzzy at their edges and touch each other. A somewhat coarse screen helps shadow areas retain detail on uncoated paper. Coated paper holds the ink on its surface, so a finer screen may be used.

To get the most out of photos in your newsletter, print on coated paper.

To learn more about how screen ruling and paper affect reproduction of halftones, ask a printer to show you demonstration materials from paper manufacturers. Companies such as Warren and Hammermill publish booklets and

Kathleen Ryan

85-line screen for photocopy   *100-line screen for quick printing*   *133-line screen
for commercial printing*

9-4 Halftones in three screen rulings *The halftones above show the three screen rulings most appropriate for newsletters. As rulings become finer, details in the image become clearer.*

charts showing photographs in many screen rulings and colors, with special effects, and on a variety of papers. These materials are free and make good visual aids for learning about halftones.

SCALING

Frequently a drawing or photo is the wrong size or shape for a layout. It can easily be reduced or enlarged to fit. You must, however, identify the new size that you need.

Scaling is the process of determining the new size at which you want an image.

New size is expressed as a percent of original size. If you want the image 10 percent smaller, specify it at 90 percent; if you want it 10 percent larger, specify it at 110 percent. With no instructions, operators reproduce at 100 percent. Writing "same size" or "SS" makes it clear that you want copy reproduced without changing its size.

Determine sizes using a scaling wheel, also called a proportion scale. Scaling wheels show the new height and width. With this knowledge, you know how the image at its new size will fit into your layout.

Because the arithmetic of scaling involves only one dimension (width or height), it's easy to forget that copy shrinks or grows in two directions. A block of type enlarged to 120 percent may appear much bigger than you expected; a photograph reduced to 50 percent may

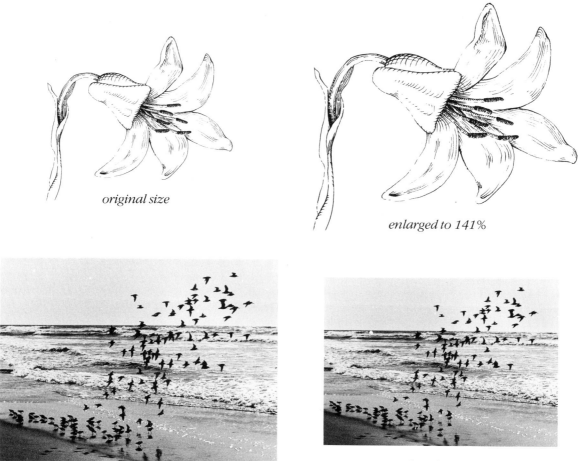

original size

enlarged to 141%

original size

reduced to 83%

9-5 Enlarging and reducing You can change the size of line and continuous-tone copy to fit your layout. Keep in mind, however, that enlarging copy magnifies flaws. And reducing shrinks every feature. Fine lines or dot patterns may end up too thin to print.

lose too many details. Shooting at 200 percent means the new copy will occupy four times the area of the original: twice as high and twice as wide.

Assembling pages on a computer screen means you can change the size of line art, and perhaps of photos, to fit your layout. Laser printing assembled pages as camera-ready copy avoids the need to scale. If you use the software only for doing layout, however, you must still give scaling specifications to a printer. In that case, use the ruler on the screen to determine new sizes and a scaling wheel to compute percentages.

ELECTRONIC COPY

You can assemble elements for printing on a computer screen or use adhesives and mounting boards. When you assemble type and graphics in final form on a computer screen, the process is desktop publishing.

When you use a computer to lay out your newsletter, you can provide the results to your printing company as hard copy or electronic copy. Hard copy includes printouts from a laser printer or imagesetter; art, such as logos; and photos and illustrations for halftoning. Electronic copy means anything transmitted via a digital medium such as a disk or modem.

Many editors blend hard and electronic copy, using a digital medium for type and graphics and hard copy for photos.

You can use a wide variety of software to create electronic copy. For newsletters, the most common software is word processing programs such as *WordPerfect* and *Microsoft Word*. These applications include an ample selection of fonts and graphics and let you import drawings and infographics created in other applications, such as spreadsheets. Advanced versions of some word processing programs include newsletter templates.

Newsletters requiring complex design use art and desktop publishing software. These applications, with brand names such as *PageMaker*, *QuarkXPress* and *Ventura Publisher*, let you create pages composed from many complex graphic elements.

If you send electronic copy to your printing company, supply the following information:
- name, version and platform of all software used to create the files
- name, manufacturer and style of all fonts
- list of special effects, such as graduated screens or color builds

When you send electronic files, make sure to send low resolution printouts of the same version of files. Don't count on prepress staff to understand your newsletter by examining it only on a computer screen. And don't expect your printer or imaging service to print out files that you couldn't print out on your own desktop equipment.

HARD COPY

When you prepare copy for printing by hand, the process is called pasting up. Many newsletters involve a blend of electronic copy and pasteup. Pasteup requires just a few simple supplies, tools and techniques.

Mounting boards

These are sheets of paper that are backing for your mechanical. They should be about half an inch bigger all the way around than the page size of your newsletter. For 8½" x 11" pages, use at least 9" x 12" boards. The extra margin is for space to write instructions and for handling without touching the image area.

Use sturdy, coated paper for mounting boards. The coating is very important because it allows you to reposition elements with minimum damage to the paper or the element itself. Coated-one-side (C1S) cover stock works fine and costs much less than paper packaged as mounting sheets. C1S cover is the inexpensive stock used for paperback books and technical manuals.

Tissue overlays

Use any thin translucent paper that can be taped as a flap to protect the mechanical. Even photocopy bond works OK. The overlay is the correct place on which to write instructions about screen tints, photos and color breaks. Visual 9-7 shows an example.

You can make almost any mechanical for two-color printing using tissue overlays. You only need acetate when you want copy in the second color to touch or overlap copy in the first color. In the typical situation of making headlines, drawings, rules or screens in a second color, the printer can make color breaks using photo techniques faster and more accurately than you can while pasting up.

Adhesives

Choose between wax, glue sticks, rubber cement or artists spray. All have editors who swear by them; all have editors who swear at them.

Halftones

When your newsletter includes photos, you can arrange halftones either by producing keylines showing a printer where to put the images or by placing the images yourself. Using the keyline approach, you provide photos separately from mechanicals. You identify each image, mark it for cropping and scaling, and relate it to the correct position on your mechanical.

Identify every photograph with your name, name of your newsletter and a number. For best results, mount each print on a backing sheet similar to that used for pasteup. Write instructions and crop marks on the mount board or tissue overlay. With unmounted prints, write in the narrow margin on the image side of the print.

To indicate the portion of the photo you want printed, draw crop marks in black on the white margins or on a tissue overlay. Photographs can also be photocopied and cropping instructions drawn on the copies.

When you scale a photograph, specify dimensions that allow it to overlap the keylines by at least one-sixteenth inch on each edge. This extra one-sixteenth inch gives printers plenty of room to ensure that photos fit properly.

Relate photographs to your mechanical using the keyline method shown in Visual 9-7. The print shop will not reproduce the keylines unless you specify that you want them to appear as borders along the edges of photos. For keylines that don't print, make them using your computer software or a high-quality ballpoint pen. For keylines to print, use your computer or $1/2$-point border tape.

When you deliver copy for printing, compare it to specifications. Your printer should agree that copy represents the work that specifications describe. If not, determine differences, decide on how they affect production and costs, and write the new information on the specifications sheet. This is the surest way to prevent surprises, such as alteration charges on the final invoice.

PROOFS

A proof is any test sheet made to reveal errors or flaws, predict results on press, and record how you intend your newsletter to appear when finished.

Notice the word "sheet." The outcome of printing is images on paper. Don't proof your newsletter on a computer screen.

Proof every issue of your newsletter before going to press. Checking proofs is the only way to assure that mechanicals, negatives and plates are accurate and complete. Proofs also help determine who is responsible for mistakes and should pay for corrections. Visual 9-8 tells how to check a proof.

Typically, your newsletter passes through either three or four principal stages before it's actually printed: as an electronic file created using word processing or page layout software, as mechanicals, as film (either output by an imagesetter or exposed from mechanicals) and as printing plates. At each stage you can examine features you consider important.

Type

Use a photocopy or desktop printout to check for accuracy and placement.

Graphics

Use a photocopy or desktop printout to check rules, reverses, screen tints, clip art and infographics. If you have large areas of screen tints or graduated tints, examine printout from an imagesetter or a blueline (also known by the brand name Dylux).

Photos

Use a photocopy or desktop printout to check keylines. Also check cropping, scaling and position of halftones. Use an imagesetter printout or blueline to examine sharpness and contrast.

Guidelines

Use a photocopy or desktop printout to check corner marks and register guides.

Color

Use a digital color printout or a laminate proof of film when color match is critical.

Finishing

Stick photocopies or laser printouts together back to back and collate, bind and trim pages to look as close as possible to the finished newsletter. Leave nothing to imagination.

When examining printouts, follow the strict guideline that the printout represents the latest version of the file. Even one keystroke or mouse click can change the file to make the proof irrelevant.

9-6 CHECKING CAMERA-READY COPY

Camera-ready copy represents precisely how you want your publication to look. Make the message accurate and complete, leaving no doubts about what you expect.

Use the following list to verify that printouts are ready for prepress. Also remember an important intangible: Truly camera-ready copy tells printers how professionally you approach your work. Clean, complete files and printouts with clear instructions get the respect they deserve.

Identification Mark every disk, printout and loose photo with a name and phone number and the name and date of this issue.

Correctness Verify that words say what they are supposed to and that photos and art are what you want.

Completeness Check that each file, board and overlay includes all the type, art and graphics it is supposed to have. Give all materials to the printer at one time.

Accuracy Verify marks for cropping, corners, folding, trimming, scoring and perforating. Register and trim marks must align correctly on printouts and overlays.

Security Confirm that you have backups and proofs for every page. Protect printouts with tissue overlays during handling, transit and storage.

Cleanliness Verify that electronic files have no unintended paragraph returns or fonts. Inspect boards, overlays and tissues to ensure they have no smudges, fingerprints, bits of glue or toner, or stray guidelines.

Coordination Examine separate copy, such as photos, graphs, maps and illustrations, to be sure they are clean, cropped, scaled and keyed according to a system agreed on with the printer.

Communication Look at each board and overlay to ensure it includes specifications about ink colors, screen rulings and reverses.

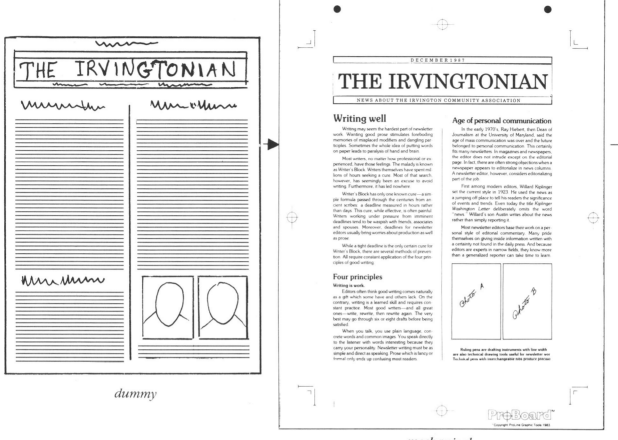

dummy

mechanical

9-7 From layout to newsletter page

Pasteup by hand or on a computer screen can begin with a mock-up as shown above. The mounting board for the mechanical in this example has preprinted corner and register marks. Mount photos separately, with instructions written on their mounting boards.

The mechanical needs a tissue overlay for protection and instructions before going to the print shop.

This example is pasteup for commercial printing. If the pasteup were for photocopy or quick printing, the screen tint and halftone positives would be on the mounting board so all contents of the page are reproduced at once.

mounted photograph

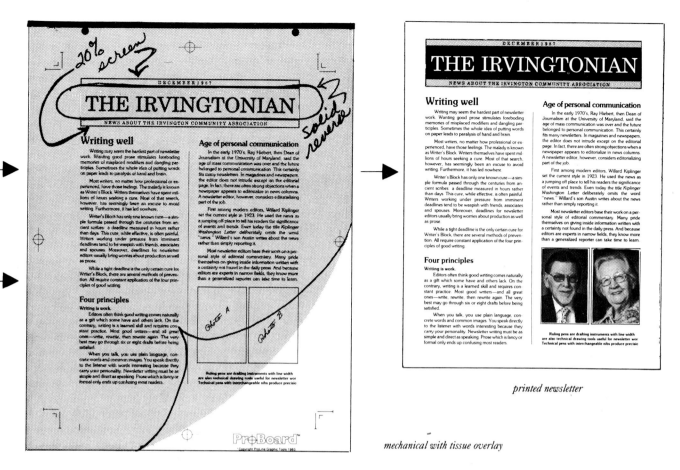

mechanical with tissue overlay

printed newsletter

9-8 HOW TO CHECK A PROOF

Use a proof to help control quality and cost and ensure good service. When examining a proof, keep these items in mind.

Slow pace Take your time. Don't let a deadline make you careless.

Individual features Make a list, then check each feature throughout the entire proof. For example, go through once just to check borders and rules. Continue to examine headlines and display type. Finish by studying areas of critical register and color.

Photos Check every photograph to verify that the correct image is in the correct space, is scaled and cropped properly, and faces the proper direction. Look for sharp focus, especially in portions of the image farthest from the center.

Flaws Boldly circle every blemish, flaw, spot, broken letter, and anything else that seems wrong.

Previous corrections Double-check any corrections that were made on the previous set of proofs.

Instructions Write directly on the proof in a clear, vivid color. Be very explicit.

Finishing Anticipate bindery problems. Measure trim size. Check that folds are in the correct direction and relate to copy as planned.

Colors Confirm that your proof shows color with sufficient fidelity to make you feel confident about the printed newsletter.

Questions Ask about anything that seems wrong. Asking questions that seem stupid is a lot smarter than printing mistakes.

Costs Discuss the cost of changes and agree about who pays for what.

10. PRINTING

Newsletters are printed using either offset presses or photocopy machines. This chapter explains how to get the best quality and price from either process, but concentrates on offset. It explains differences among printing companies and tells how to write specifications, check proofs, and analyze jobs for payment.

Regardless of your method of printing, paper is a major cost. In this chapter, you learn how to select paper for best results while keeping costs down.

Although this chapter helps you buy printing as a more sophisticated customer, it emphasizes working with, not against, your printer. Cooperation keeps your schedule intact, quality up, costs down and ulcers away. For more information about printing and print buying, consult my book *Getting It Printed*.

QUICK VS. COMMERCIAL PRINTING

The world of printing companies includes two categories appropriate for newsletters: quick printers and commercial printers. Which you choose depends on your press run, page count, quality needs, schedule and several other factors.

Quick printers are appropriate for press runs up to about 2,000 copies. From about 2,000 to 4,000 copies, it's uncertain which shop would give the best price. After 4,000, it would be unusual for a quick printer's price to be lower than a commercial printer's. For print runs under 1,000, your printer may use a commercial photocopy machine.

All printers have employees who convert camera-ready copy to printing plates. Printers refer to the process as prepress. At a quick print shop, prepress requires only one step from copy to plate. At a commercial printer, prepress may require several steps to prepare and assemble copy, make negatives and then make plates.

Distinctions between quick and commercial printing businesses apply to in-plant print shops as well. The standards of quality, schedule and service discussed in this chapter apply to company-owned printers as well as outside shops.

If you use a lettershop to prepare your newsletter for mailing, check whether it offers printing as well. Lettershops often print using a web press especially suited for relatively long runs of publications with modest quality requirements.

Plain paper photocopiers handle any grade, surface or weight of paper with the exception of gloss coated. If you want to use the technique of preprinting, you can load a photocopy machine with paper previously offset printed with color. Keep in mind, however, that photocopy machines do not register nearly as well as printing presses; avoid register closer than one-eighth inch.

PAPER

The cost of paper represents 20 to 40 percent of the cost of printing your newsletter. The exact percentage depends on the quality of paper, number of copies and many other complex factors.

Upgrading paper is an easy and relatively inexpensive way to improve your entire publication. The price difference between routine and outstanding paper is insignificant compared to the overall cost of producing your newsletter. Upgrading paper adds to the value of writing, design and printing without adding any time to those tasks.

Although quality paper can improve your image with little effort, remember that paper is a variable cost. Dollars to raise quality might work much harder if spent instead on a fixed cost, such as professional design, computer software or training.

Three grades of paper are suitable for newsletters: offset, coated and bond.

Offset

Also called uncoated book paper, offset is for general printing of all kinds. Offset paper comes in several shades of white plus half a dozen light colors useful for newsletters. It's available in a variety of finishes and weights. Quality #1 is smoothest and brightest; quality #3 is most commonly used. Avoid #4 and #5 paper altogether.

Halftones on #1 paper look satisfactory, whereas photos on #3 may look flat. Uncoated paper, especially less than #1 quality, absorbs ink quickly, resulting in fuzzy dots and halftones that don't look sharp.

Offset paper costs about the same as bond of comparable quality, but works better for newsletters. Mills make bond for printing on one side; offset paper for printing on both sides. If your newsletter is printed both sides, ask the printer to use offset paper.

Coated

Sometimes called enamel paper, coated gives better ink holdout than offset or bond. Ink holdout refers to the extent to which ink dries on the surface instead of soaking in. It is especially important when printing halftones because dots stay crisp. Holdout also enhances ink gloss, making colors look brighter.

Coated paper comes in several finishes, such as matte, dull and gloss, and a variety of shades of white, such as cream and ivory. It costs about 20 percent more than comparable quality offset.

Bond

Mills make bond for one-page correspondence, such as letters and forms, thus it lacks the opacity of offset or coated paper. For newsletters, bond works best in photocopy machines rather than printing presses.

PAPER CHARACTERISTICS

Understanding traits that grades of paper have in common helps clarify differences among the grades and how they will affect your newsletter.

Size

The graphic arts industry in North America is coordinated to 8¹/₂" x 11" and multiples of that size. Small presses, photocopy machines, computer printers and typewriters use 8¹/₂" x 11" as the most common size, as do binders, envelopes, file folders, and other products related to paper. Because 8¹/₂" x 11" is so standard, it is the most economical page size for newsletters.

Don't confuse page size, however, with sheet size. Quick printers use 8¹/₂" x 11" or 11" x 17" sheets. Commercial printers have larger presses, so they use 19" x 25" or 23" x 35" sheets.

Most newsletters are printed on 11" x 17" sheets. If your publication is four or eight pages, try to have it printed on 11" x 17" stock that is folded once to 8¹/₂" x 11", not printed on 8¹/₂" x 11" sheets that must be stapled.

If you need more than about 2,000 copies of one issue, printing on larger sheets probably is more cost effective than printing on paper already cut to 11" x 17". Don't decide, however, without getting quotes. Many factors in addition to press size influence printing costs.

Weight

Printers express the weight of paper as the weight of five hundred sheets cut to a standard size. With bond papers, the weight is known as substance weight (Sub); with offset and coated papers, as basis weight (BS). Higher numbers mean heavier paper, thus more opacity and higher cost.

Bond paper that is sub 20# is the same weight as 60# book; sub 24# bond is the same as 70# book. (I *know* it doesn't make any sense. Trust me!)

Understanding paper weight helps control costs. Paper that is 70# costs about 15 percent more than 60#. If you print twenty-five thousand copies per year of an 8¹/₂" x 11", eight-page newsletter, the cost difference of the paper might be several hundred dollars.

If you mail first class, weight of paper may affect postage. An eight-page newsletter on 70# paper weighs slightly more than one ounce, meaning it qualifies for the 2-ounce rate. The same publication on 60# paper weighs about .9 ounce, so it goes for one stamp.

Opacity

Type on one side of the paper should not show through to interfere with type on the other. Opacity restricts show-through. It is affected by coatings, colors, chemicals, ink color and coverage, and impurities. Heavy papers are more opaque than lighter ones.

Bond paper is not as opaque as offset or coated. If you must print on bond, use 24#, not the 20# most commonly provided for photocopy machines and quick print jobs, and use bond with a slight color.

Some uncoated book papers are made in regular and opaque versions. For best opacity when specifying uncoated book, make sure that the word "opaque" is part of the description.

Surface

As mills turn pulp into paper, they can adjust surface to affect look, feel and printability. Paper can be smooth or have a pattern, such as laid or linen. Coatings may be glossy or dull.

Paper with surface patterns or coating costs a little more, but not as much more as you may think. Don't hesitate to compare costs.

Color

Mills add dyes and pigments to pulp. Colors vary from mill to mill and there is no standard for naming them. What one mill calls ivory may be called buff, cream or sand at another.

White is the least expensive paper because it's in greatest demand and is easiest to make. Light colors cost slightly more.

Color in paper increases opacity but decreases legibility because of the loss of contrast between type and background.

Print your newsletter on white; on shades of white, such as cream or ivory; or on a very light tone of gray, blue or brown. Avoid dark colors and tones of red, even for holiday issues. And don't print different issues on paper of different colors. Using a variety of colors increases costs and may confuse readers.

To become more familiar with papers, examine sample books at a print shop, paper distributor or retail outlet. To learn details about papers and compare printing on a variety of common papers, consult my book *Papers For Printing*.

ENSURING QUALITY

A printer should closely reproduce your original. If your newsletter doesn't look as good as your copy and almost as good as your photos, something is wrong.

Even skilled printing buyers sometimes overlook lapses in quality. Before selecting a printer, ask for names of other newsletter editors who have used that shop. Call one or two to verify satisfaction.

Regardless of the kind of printer you use and how often you have relied on the specific shop, inspect printing for features described in the following paragraphs.

Register

When an image appears on the page precisely where intended, it is correctly registered.

Register with photocopy machines can vary ± $1/8$ inch, with quick printing ± $1/16$ inch, and with commercial printing ± $1/100$ inch. The vari-

ations apply to each color of ink or pass through the press. Larger variations are easily prevented and should not be considered acceptable work.

Density

Printing should result in dark body copy and headline type to ensure legibility. Large solids may appear faded or mottled when quick printed.

Commercial printers use a densitometer to measure density. A densitometer reading approximately 150 for black ink meets quality needs for most newsletters. Density should not vary more than 5 percent across the page, from page to page or throughout the run.

Halftones

Quick printed halftones don't have very good contrast or sharpness. Commercially printed halftones should have good contrast and some shadow detail and appear sharp, although they will still not look as good as originals.

Flaws

Sheets with smudges, dirt, streaks or fingerprints don't belong in your job. An occasional bad newsletter will slip through the best quality control, but printing with consistent problems, such as blurred type, should be rejected.

Bindery work

Printers refer to folding, trimming, drilling, and other postpress operations as bindery work.

Machines for folding are less accurate than presses. Folds should always be correctly aligned, but the fold line can vary ± $1/8$ inch from a quick printer and ± $1/16$ inch from a commercial shop.

Most newsletters are printed on paper already cut to size, so do not need trims. If yours needs trimming, the cuts should be square and conform to corner marks. Trims from quick printers may vary ± $1/16$ inch, from commercial printers ± $1/32$ inch.

Approximate newsletter printing costs

Newsletter type	Number of copies	on 60# offset house sheet	on 70# matte house sheet	on #1 offset 60# uncoated	on #1 dull 70#
4 pages, 1 ink color	500	$274/.55¢ ea	$337/.67¢ ea	$293/.59¢ ea	$417/.83¢ ea
	1,000	300/.30	376/.38	327/.33	475/.48
	2,000	368/.18	470/.24	410/.21	607/.30
	5,000	458/.09	561/.11	506/.10	743/.15
	10,000	685/.07	847/.08	772/.08	1,149/.11
4 pages, 2 ink colors	500	$422/.84¢ ea	$491/.98¢ ea	$444/.89¢ ea	$578/$1.16 ea
	1,000	457/.46	538/.54	487/.49	644/.64
	2,000	544/.27	651/.36	589/.29	795/.40
	5,000	721/.14	823/.16	763/.15	1,002/.20
	10,000	942/.09	1,106/.11	1,030/.10	1,414/.14
4 pages, 1 ink color preprinted 2nd color	500	$264/.53¢ ea	$305/.61¢ ea	$272/.54¢ ea	$376/.75¢ ea
	1,000	291/.29	338/.34	302/.30	439/.44
	2,000	351/.18	410/.21	370/.19	572/.29
	5,000	508/.10	602/.12	550/.11	940/.19
	10,000	779/.08	931/.09	859/.09	1,549/ 16
8 pages, 1 ink color	500	$415/.83¢ ea	$511/$1.02 ea	$442/.88¢ ea	$630/$1.26 ea
	1,000	473/.47	595/.60	515/.52	752/.75
	2,000	528/.26	651/.33	576/.29	853/.43
	5,000	741/.15	932/.19	834/.17	1,276/.26
	10,000	1,159/.12	1,472/.15	1,333/.13	2,069/.21
8 pages, 2 ink colors	500	$623/$1.25 ea	$750/$1.50 ea	$668/$1.34 ea	$914/$1.83 ea
	1,000	693/.69	846/.85	753/.75	1,048/1.05
	2,000	713/.36	835/.42	755/.38	1,034/.52
	5,000	994/.20	1,190/.24	1,090/.22	1,543/.31
	10,000	1,392/.14	1,710/.17	1,569/.16	2,316/.23
8 pages, 1 ink color preprinted 2nd color	500	$405/.81¢ ea	$472/.94¢ ea	$416/.83¢ ea	$575/$1.15 ea
	1,000	459/.46	539/.54	479/.48	702/.70
	2,000	535/.27	636/.32	569/.28	907/.45
	5,000	817/.16	988/.20	897/.18	1,609/.32
	10,000	1,305/.13	1,586/.16	1,458/.15	2,754/.28

10-1 Approximate newsletter printing costs When using the above chart to estimate printing costs, keep in mind that it only shows approximate dollar amounts. Use the figures as guidelines for comparisons, not predictions.

Definitions "1 ink color" means black; "2 ink colors" means black plus another flat color; "preprinting" means printing a second ink color on enough stock to last one year.

Assumptions One- and two-ink color costs assume that you pay for paper as part of issue-by-issue print costs. Preprinting costs (slightly lower than one-color costs) assume paying for a yearly supply of paper and dividing costs among issues throughout the year. Printing on coated stock assumes an average of six halftones for four pages and ten halftones for eight pages.

Regional variations For the following areas, add 10 percent: Anchorage, Boston, Hartford, Honolulu, Los Angeles, New York, Philadelphia, San Diego, San Francisco, San Jose, Washington DC. For the following areas, subtract 10 percent: Memphis, New Orleans, Omaha, Salt Lake City. If you live in Canada, adjust for the current exchange rate.

CONTROLLING COSTS

You can avoid paying more than you should to produce your newsletter by following simple guidelines about finding and working with printing companies.

Go shopping

Printing prices depend on the complexity of the job, paper and inks used, quantity needed, and number of other jobs in the shop. A 20 percent variation among four or five printers using the same specifications is normal; 50 percent is not unusual.

If your printer has a standard price list, ignore it. Menu prices apply to walk-in jobs needing instant attention. Planning ahead and contracts for periods of a year or longer should get you prices at least 15 percent below those considered standard. You don't get the discount, however, unless you ask.

Work long-term

Write specifications and ask for price quotations for even the most simple and routine newsletter every two or three years. Long contracts save money because they assure the printer regular work.

Written specifications do not prevent printers from making suggestions. In fact, they encourage you to think about options. Even though you welcome alternatives, insist on knowing a price based on original specs. That dollar figure is an important basis for comparing printers.

Use house sheets

Paper for newsletters is best purchased as part of the cost of printing. Printers buy lots of paper, so they get better prices than you can.

Printers have "house sheets," paper kept in inventory and suitable for a wide range of jobs. A 60# offset and 70# coated, each white, would be typical house sheets. Using the house sheet usually gives satisfactory quality at the best price.

If you don't want the house sheet, you may select a stock from swatch books or by matching another printed product. Your printer will help you decide by telling you how each possibility would affect price. Do not, however, expect printers to suggest using Olde Antique Cream instead of Modern Mauve. Design is not their job.

Reduce quantities

If your organization is typical, you print too many copies of every issue. You send newsletters to people who don't want them or who no longer live or work at the address.

Every wasted newsletter costs you paper, press time and, most important, postage. You may measure your costs in pennies, but they can add up to thousands of dollars in just a few months. Chapter ten includes a simple way to estimate savings by reducing quantities.

To learn more about controlling print costs, consult the booklet *90 Ways to Save Money Producing Your Newsletter*, by Polly Pattison, or the list of cost-cutting tips in my manual *Newsletter Sourcebook*.

WORKING WITH PRINTERS

You can ensure a good relationship with your printer by having reasonable expectations and understanding the printer's point of view.

Most printers deliver more copies than you specified, but they have a loophole if spoilage resulted in delivering too few. Business practices in the graphic arts include tolerance for an overrun or underrun of 10 percent. If you absolutely must have a certain number of newsletters, tell your printer that number is the minimum acceptable quantity.

Printers can meet the tight deadlines, but they are not magicians. You must deliver mechanicals when you promise if you expect newsletters when they promise.

Whether you pay on delivery, invoice or statement, check every aspect of the printing before authorizing payment. Compare your

10-2 WRITING SPECIFICATIONS

Printing specifications spell out the requirements of your newsletter. They are normally written as part of a request for price quotation on a form such as Visual 10-3.

Good specifications are complete, accurate, and written in language printers understand. They are important for the following reasons:

Assure accurate comparisons When each printer quotes on the same specifications, you can compare prices accurately and fairly.

Look professional Clear specifications convey to printers that you expect appropriate quality, attentive service and reasonable price.

Provide a checklist Specifications help you review the entire production sequence

and save you time in getting quotes. They make it obvious if you forgot an important detail.

Keep costs down Specifications on your standard form notify printers that you are soliciting competitive bids.

Reduce guesswork With good specifications, printers can figure costs exactly, identify ways to save money and spot potential problems.

Help monitor changes Almost every set of specifications changes as the job proceeds. With the original specifications as a guide, you can keep track of alterations.

Make payment easier By comparing the final bill to the specifications, you can see exactly what you called for, what the printer did, and how alterations affected the invoice.

newsletter to its specifications to verify receiving what the printer wants you to pay for.

If you question an invoice, discuss the matter candidly with the printer. Try to show that you are correct. The evidence is obvious if the specifications and invoice both called for printing on Wonder Gloss, but the press operator used Wonder Dull.

Final costs are often different from quotes because customers make changes. If your copy was late, your printer may have paid overtime to meet your deadline. The extra charge is justified, but should be clearly identified on the invoice.

Quality is more subjective. You are responsible to match your expectations to a printer's ability to produce and to explain your needs clearly. If you feel unhappy with quality, tell your printer exactly what you think is wrong.

You should not have to pay for poor quality work, but might feel stuck if there is not time to reprint. If the errors or flaws don't make your newsletter useless, you can negotiate the price and distribute the poorly printed issue.

Too often newsletter customers are in such a rush that they forget to say, "Thanks. Nice work." When you like your printing, say so.

Request for Quotation

Newsletter name _____ Date _____ PO# _____

Contact person _____ Phone _____ / _____ Fax _____ / _____

Business/organization _____

Address _____

Specifications ▬▬▬▬▬▬▬▬▬▬▬▬▬▬

Number of pages _____

    page size _____ X _____ inches

    folded size _____ X _____ inches

Quantity per issue _____ copies

Issues per year _____

Date(s) mechanicals to printer _____

_____

_____

Date(s) newsletters needed _____

_____

_____

_____

Art as 1-up pages supplied
- ❏ camera-ready
- ❏ electronic file
- ❏ composite film

■ screen tints
- ❏ printer adds
- ❏ supplied

■ halftones
- ❏ printer adds
- ❏ supplied

■ Paper

    weight _____

    color _____

    finish _____

    brand name _____

■ Ink colors

    side one _____

    side two _____

Proofs ▬▬▬▬▬▬▬▬▬▬▬▬▬▬

❏ galley   ❏ page

❏ photocopy   ❏ blueline

❏ overlay color   ❏ press check

❏ dummy included with these specifications

Miscellaneous instructions _____

_____

_____

_____

10-3 Request for quotation *Accurate, complete specifications for printing your newsletter help you control quality, schedule and cost. Use this form so service bureaus and printers know exactly what you expect.*

11. DISTRIBUTION

How your newsletter gets to its audience affects decisions about schedule, content and budget.

Most newsletters reach readers by mail. Controlling costs of postage and speed of delivery requires thorough knowledge of both your mailing list and Post Office regulations.

This chapter tells how to maintain your address list and explains the major options offered by the Postal Service. It describes lists and labels, classes of mail, presorting, and how to work with mailing services.

Postal regulations are too long, complicated and changeable for presentation here. If you're starting a newsletter, get a copy of regulations before deciding about schedule and design. If you have experience, read the regulations to discover cost-saving opportunities you may be missing.

Although they seem very specific, postal regulations are subject to interpretation by local officials. Learn from the same people who might check your mailings how they view regulations.

In addition to publications of the Postal Service itself, many private organizations produce guides that summarize and interpret regulations. The best handbooks come from the Direct Marketing Association and Pitney Bowes Corporation.

Local postal officials in larger cities offer

frequent workshops. There is a USPS Mailer Education Center in New York City with a regular schedule of classes. And, of course, you can read a newsletter. *Memo to Mailers* comes free from USPS, Springfield VA 22150-0999.

ADDRESS LISTS

The list of addresses to which you send your newsletter offers potential savings of hundreds and perhaps thousands of dollars per year. You can realize the savings by ensuring that your publication goes only to people who want it, that their addresses are correct and that you presort.

Many copies of the typical newsletter go to people who don't want them. It's not unusual for 15 percent or even 25 percent of copies to be thrown away immediately on delivery. Considering what you pay to print, fold and address those copies as well as mail them, you can cut costs substantially by never producing them in the first place.

Every year, without fail, study your address list one name at a time. Make sure that each name really belongs. Don't hesitate to spend money surveying readers to certify those who want to continue receiving your publication.

In addition to reducing your list to people whom you know want your newsletter, verify that you have correct addresses.

Postal officials estimate that 15 percent of mail is improperly addressed, so it can't be delivered or arrives later than it should. The figure may be 25 percent for third-class mail. The problems come from people who have moved and from incorrect numbers for suites, apartments, street addresses and ZIP codes.

After doing everything possible within your own system to correct addresses, consult with local postal authorities about how they can help. The Postal Service has several ways to help customers maintain accurate address files. They include printing "Address Correction Requested" on the newsletter itself and the computerized National Change of Address system (NCOA).

The Postal Service is so eager that mail have correct addresses and that machines can read addresses that it will even clean up your files and add ZIP+4 codes at no cost. You provide addresses in electronic files and they do the rest. Call the National Address Information Center at (800) 238-3150 for details.

Unless you mail just a handful of newsletters, your address list should be computerized. Keep names in a database or mailing program that you can sort by ZIP code, not in an ordinary word processing file.

If you're a large organization or part of a larger group such as United Way or a trade association, ask that headquarters subscribe to an address correction service on CD-ROM. Discs issued monthly or quarterly list every address in the country, correct misspellings, add suite and apartment numbers, add four-digit extensions to ZIP codes, and may add bar codes.

Most organizations have one database for names and addresses that can be used for a variety of purposes. The database should have fields, such as renewal dates, applicable to your publication. Ideally fields will include detailed information about readers so you can send special inserts to certain addresses or decide whether you will need to produce a second newsletter.

If you ever use someone else's mailing list, check very carefully how they keep it up-to-date. Old names, sloppy keyboarding and other errors can mean that half the addresses are undeliverable. Stick with lists of active subscribers to periodicals. Avoid lists of people who attended a trade show or appeared in a directory.

ADDRESS LABELS

Postal regulations prohibit mailing pieces that do not conform to requirements about size, color, indicia, return address and bar codes. Rules about the location and format of addresses affect how accurately and rapidly workers can deliver your mail.

The Post Office can sort mail most efficiently when addresses can be read by optical character recognition (OCR). To be OCR readable, the last line of the address must be one inch from the bottom of the envelope or address panel. You need good contrast between ink and paper and the address should align with edges of the paper, not be skewed.

Optical character recognition requires a common typeface and plenty of space between letters, words and lines, but does not require punctuation. Addresses using all capital letters make OCR reading easier. Put city, state and ZIP code all on the last line. Use standard two-letter abbreviations for states.

If you maintain your mailing list with ZIP+4 codes in a computer database, you may be able to bar code each newsletter as it's addressed, thus saving on first- or third-class postage. Ask for details at a mailing service.

MAIL CLASSIFICATIONS

Newsletters that arrive in the mail get off to a good start. The mail brings the most personal written messages. Whether you use first, second or third class depends on your budget and need for speedy delivery.

When considering what class of mail to use and how diligently to study the regulations, remember that postage is a variable cost. The percent of your budget for postage increases along with number of newsletters that you mail. If you send only a few hundred copies four times a year, postage amounts to very little when compared to the fixed costs of writing and preparation for printing. If you send several thousand copies twelve times a year, the cost of postage might be your largest single expense.

First class

When you need overnight delivery locally and two- or three-day service nationwide, mail first class. It's the fastest category—and, of course, the most expensive.

Subscription newsletter publishers use first class to convey important news arriving in timely fashion. Many organizations with tiny budgets and memberships also use first class to ensure that news arrives quickly.

Because you pay for first-class postage by the ounce, weight of paper affects costs. Weigh a dummy of your publication to avoid an expensive surprise when your first issue goes into the mail. Use a scale at the Post Office, not one in your back room. If you mail in an envelope, put it on the scale along with your dummy.

By using first class that must be returned if undeliverable, you can keep your mailing list up-to-date. It's cheaper and less hassle than some of the other address correction options, but doesn't always tell you a new address.

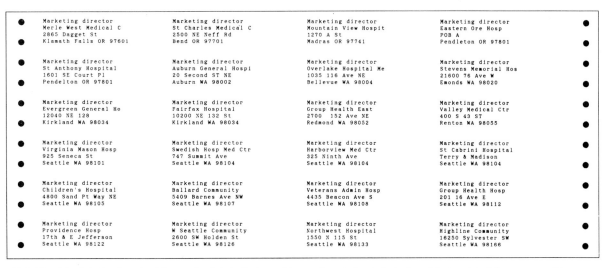

Marketing director Merle West Medical C 2865 Dagget St Klamath Falls OR 97601	Marketing director St Charles Medical C 2500 NE Neff Rd Bend OR 97701	Marketing director Mountain View Hospit 1270 A St Madras OR 97741	Marketing director Eastern Ore Hosp POB A Pendleton OR 97801
Marketing director St Anthony Hospital 1601 SE Court Pl Pendelton OR 97801	Marketing director Auburn General Hospi 20 Second ST NE Auburn WA 98002	Marketing director Overlake Hospital Me 1035 116 Ave NE Bellevue WA 98004	Marketing director Stevens Memorial Hos 21600 76 Ave W Emonds WA 98020
Marketing director Evergreen General Ho 12040 NE 128 Kirkland WA 98034	Marketing director Fairfax Hospital 10200 NE 132 St Kirkland WA 98034	Marketing director Group Health East 2700 152 Ave NE Redmond WA 98052	Marketing director Valley Medical Ctr 400 S 43 ST Renton WA 98055
Marketing director Virginia Mason Hosp 925 Seneca St Seattle WA 98101	Marketing director Swedish Hosp Med Ctr 747 Summit Ave Seattle WA 98104	Marketing director Harborview Med Ctr 325 Ninth Ave Seattle WA 98104	Marketing director St Cabrini Hospital Terry & Madison Seattle WA 98104
Marketing director Children's Hospital 4800 Sand Pt Way NE Seattle WA 98105	Marketing director Ballard Community 5409 Barnes Ave NW Seattle WA 98107	Marketing director Veterans Admin Hosp 4435 Beacon Ave S Seattle WA 98108	Marketing director Group Health Hosp 201 16 Ave E Seattle WA 98112
Marketing director Providence Hosp 17th & E Jefferson Seattle WA 98122	Marketing director W Seattle Community 2600 SW Holden St Seattle WA 98126	Marketing director Northwest Hospital 1550 N 115 St Seattle WA 98133	Marketing director Highline Community 16250 Sylvester SW Seattle WA 98166

11-2 Cheshire labels *Standard format for labels that machines cut and glue is forty-four labels printed four-up on wide, continuous form paper. Side-to-side measurements may vary, but vertical measurements must be one inch from the top of one address to the top of the next. ZIP code order starts with lowest zip at upper left and goes across lines, not down columns. Most lettershops have Cheshire labeling machines.*

Second class

Periodicals published at regular intervals at least four times per year may use second class. Publications must be presorted and go to people who pay to receive them. Payment can be via subscription or a membership fee that specifically includes the newsletter.

Second-class pieces receive the same handling as first-class pieces, but rates are much lower. Costs are based on complicated formulas that take into account percentages of advertising and editorial content, weight and other factors.

Most newsletters qualify for second-class rates and service; few take advantage of them. If you want first-class service at about half the cost, do what it takes to get classified for second class.

Third class

Also known as bulk rate, third class is the least expensive mail category. Per piece costs vary greatly depending on the level of presort and status (commercial or nonprofit) of the mailer. Generally speaking, third-class rates are approximately 60 percent of first class.

Each piece of third-class mail must be identical except for its address. There's a two hundred-piece minimum and all pieces must be presorted. Most newsletters easily qualify.

Third-class mail moves more slowly than first or second class. Postal officials claim local delivery takes two or three days and regional a few days longer. Experienced mailers double those figures.

If you use third class, mail in the middle of the month to avoid competition with large first-class mailings and in the middle of the week to avoid the Friday deluge of second-class magazines.

NONPROFIT STATUS

Organizations that are not for profit may send second- and third-class mail for about half of what commercial mailers pay.

Not every organization qualifies for nonprofit status. You must apply to the USPS, whose publications and officials tell you the information to provide. As a minimum, you need documents, such as bylaws, financial reports, and minutes of annual meetings. Already having nonprofit status with the Internal Revenue Service helps, but does not guarantee that USPS will think you equally deserving.

Once you have nonprofit status, protect it

carefully. Don't let anyone else mail under your permit, and diligently keep the records that postal officials may ask to examine.

PRESORTING

The Post Office pays customers to sort their own outgoing mail. Payment takes the form of discounts from standard rates.

In the case of first-class mail, presorting is optional and earns a 20 percent discount. You must send at least five hundred newsletters and you get a slightly higher discount for using ZIP+4 codes and/or bar codes. In the case of second- and third-class mail, presorting is required and earns discounts from 50 percent to 80 percent. You must send at least two hundred newsletters.

Mailers who presort must follow strict rules. Regulations govern how many pieces to put in categories, such as five-digit ZIP codes, and how to tie, sack and label each bundle. The rules are best learned from USPS publications and workshops.

Presort rules are worth learning. For example, if you send four thousand copies of a monthly newsletter by first class, presorting

---

11-3 FLATS VS. LETTERS

To keep postage costs low, send your newsletter as a "letter," not a "flat." The Postal Service charges less for delivering letters than flats.

A letter is any piece of mail no larger than $6^{1}/_{8}$" x $11^{1}/_{2}$", no thicker than $^{1}/_{4}$ inch, and no heavier than 3.3 ounces. A flat is larger, thicker or heavier.

A standard $8^{1}/_{2}$" x 11" newsletter folded once or twice qualifies as a letter. An $8^{1}/_{2}$" x 11" newsletter not folded is a flat. A tabloid folded only once (11" x 17" folded to $8^{1}/_{2}$" x 11") is a flat, but a tabloid folded twice (either $5^{1}/_{2}$" x $8^{1}/_{2}$" or $5^{2}/_{3}$" x 11") is a letter.

---

saves approximately $2,500 per year in postage (at 1995 rates).

If you lack just a few names to make the minimum for presort, calculate what you would save by sending a handful of newsletters to yourself.

When many copies of your newsletter go into just a few neighborhoods, consider carrier route sorting. Carrier route sorts require additional label codes, but can cut postage costs another 50 percent. You can get labels already sorted from most lettershops. Consult with people at your Post Office or lettershop for details.

Presorting does involve some costs. There is a small annual permit fee. In addition, someone must do the work that otherwise would be done at the Post Office. With large organizations, that someone would be a specialist at a lettershop. With smaller mailings, that someone might be you.

If your organization does not use a professional mailing service, someone should specialize in knowing postal rules and fees. Huge savings and efficiencies reward people who take the trouble to learn their way around the Postal Service.

MAILING SERVICES

Correctly preparing several thousand newsletters for mailing is so complex that it often makes sense to have professionals do it.

Mailing services, also known as lettershops, specialize in handling large mailings. They have machines to put glue on labels and affix them automatically. They have staff trained to presort newsletters into the most cost-efficient bundles, then get them sacked and tagged according to Post Office standards.

Once you use a good lettershop, you'll wonder why you ever spent one minute twisting the arms of family, friends or fellow workers to help you peel and stick labels and sort newsletters.

Lettershops charge by the service and the number of pieces handled. Their staff can

		1994 rates in cents		19__ rates in cents	
		Regular	Nonprofit	Regular	Nonprofit
First class	Basic unsorted	29	NA		
	ZIP + 4 unsorted	27.6	NA		
	Basic presorted	24.8	NA		
	ZIP + 4 presorted	24.2	NA		
	Carrier route	23	NA		

Second class
 	
In addition to piece rate, pay
  14.7 lb regular
  10.6 lb nonprofit
  11.6 lb in county
for total mailing
	Basic presorted	20.1	16.9		

	ZIP + 4 presorted	19.2	16.2		
	Bar code presorted	18.2	14.6		
	All in county	7.7	NA		
Third class	Basic presorted	19.8	11.1		
	ZIP + 4 presorted	18.9	10.4		
	Carrier route	14.2	7.4		

11-4 Postal rates chart *As the number of copies of your newsletter increases, postage becomes a larger percentage of overall costs. You can use presorts, bar codes and other techniques to qualify for discounted rates that produce substantial savings.*

The chart above shows single-piece rates applicable to the typical newsletter when mailed letter size (folded, not flat). Keep in mind that each class of mail has additional regulations about number of items, size, weight and advertising. Check with officials at your post office before making final decisions or planning your budget.

explain postal regulations and help you get permits.

Most lettershops have computers and high-speed printers to help you maintain and print your list. They can keep your list up-to-date and print as you need it or print only when you supply a disk. Their computer printer can probably produce labels faster than yours, and their ink jet printers may be able to apply bar codes in addition to character addresses.

Look under "Mailing Services" in a classified directory to find lettershops in your area. As with any other business, ask for references

to previous customers. Pay particular attention to how you might be treated as a small customer. You may feel impressed by your six or eight thousand newsletters, but they are peanuts compared to the mountains of monthly utility bills and retail offers that the lettershop also handles.

Many communities have sheltered workshops run by organizations such as Goodwill and United Cerebral Palsy, whose workers can label, sort and bundle newsletters. They take a little longer, but charge a little less than a commercial lettershop.

12. EVALUATION

Readers evaluate your newsletter every day as they respond—or don't respond—to your work. Every two or three years, however, you need a systematic appraisal to learn how readers benefit from your newsletter. You also need thorough evaluation whenever your organization makes a major change in mission or management.

Professional pollsters use many techniques to learn opinions, but a short, written survey works best for most newsletters. Surveys are easy to plan, fill out, analyze and report.

WRITING QUESTIONS

Skilled pollsters know that useful surveys meet the following criteria:

• Write as many questions as possible that readers can answer by checking a box.

• Questions easiest to answer get highest response. They are (1) yes or no; (2) multiple choice; and (3) rank by number.

• Limit each question to one idea. Don't ask, "Do you like receiving the newsletter weekly or would you prefer monthly?"

• Ask specific questions: "Do you like Smith's reports from the capital?" not "Do you like political news?"

• Make some questions fun. Offer choices that poke fun at yourself: most forgettable article; check "yawn" or "smile."

GETTING USEFUL ANSWERS

You can increase your chances of getting helpful information by preparing items for clearest response:

- Specify how many answers readers can check or rank. Make your instructions very clear. Tell your readers to "pick two" or "rank the top three."

- With multiple choice questions, offer four options. Readers who are faced with three or five choices will normally tend to pick the one in the middle.

- Offer choices in columns, not within sentences.

- Force readers to choose: top three of ten; best one of four; most useful article on the following list.

ARRANGING QUESTIONS

The sequence of questions affects the outcome of the survey as a whole:

- Start with easy-answer questions so readers learn how quickly they can proceed. Save open-ended questions for last.

- Reserve open-ended questions for optional answers, clarifications or suggestions. Don't ask for essays.

- Finish by asking if readers would pay $1 per issue to continue receiving your newsletter. If many say "no," listen up!

PREPARING FOR RESPONSE

Before you send your survey, follow a few simple steps to help make sure it achieves its goals:

- Test your survey on two or three typical readers. Ask them to spot questions they find confusing, awkward or useless.

- Tell readers to expect a survey and promise to publish results.

- Verify that your average reader can finish the survey in no more than five minutes.

- Consult people who will tabulate results for you.

ENSURING RESULTS

To get the information you need from your readers by the time you need it:

- Guarantee anonymity. Avoid questions that even hint at a reader's identity.

- Limit the survey to one page. If you need more space, use a better design or cut some questions.

- Design your survey as a loose insert, not as a page of the newsletter itself. Include a postage paid return envelope or pre-addressed envelope for interoffice delivery.

- Give a deadline for returning the survey about one week after readers receive it. Don't let your readers toss the survey onto the "to do" pile.

- Send your survey in October or February. Avoid months with vacations or popular holidays.

HOW MANY SURVEYS TO SEND

You can predict approximately what percent of your readers will return your questionnaire. Percents vary depending on your audience. Surveys for subscription newsletters and publications for internal relations (employees and members) get 30 percent to 40 percent response rates. Surveys for public relations and marketing newsletters get 10 percent to 20 percent response rates.

The percents in the previous paragraph assume that you have a clean mailing list. If you haven't used the techniques described in chapter eleven to remove bad addresses from your list, you can expect lower responses.

After making a rough prediction of response rate to your survey, you can plan how many surveys to send. If you have more than one thousand readers, you may decide to survey a sample instead of the entire list. Use response rate estimates to plan on receiving at least one hundred completed surveys. Less than one hundred returns won't yield sufficiently valid results.

CONTENT IDEAS THAT WORK

Some publishers believe newsletters should avoid topics more weighty than birth notices and bowling scores. On the contrary, readers want serious information to help them be more productive and feel more important to the organization.

Whether your organization is a small college or large factory, a rural hospital or urban neighborhood, a local business or international association, your readers want you to treat them as adults. They care about quality, productivity and economics. Certainly they want to know about retirements and the softball schedule, but their top priorities lie with data that affect their lives.

Effective editors take readers seriously. Newsletters from every type of organization and reflecting every level of budget all rely on vital news and analysis. Thousands of readers pay for subscription newsletters containing information that directly affects them.

Surveys of employees show that they rank information that they want from their employers in the following order:

Rank	Topic
1	Organization's status and plans
2	Personnel policies and practices
3	How to improve productivity and quality
4	Job-advancement opportunities

5	Effect of external events on jobs
6	How my job fits overall organization
7	Organization's stand on current issues
8	Organization's community involvement
9	Personnel changes and promotions
10	Organization's financial performance
11	Stories about other employees
12	Personal news (births, birthdays, etc.)

Use the ideas on the following pages to stimulate your thinking about newsletter articles. As you skim main headings, browse subheads and examine specific themes, you can turn words in this book into headlines, captions and lead sentences for your newsletter.

Accounting balance sheets; bookkeeping; income statements—What is your fiscal year and why? What accounting practices influence procedures elsewhere in your organization? How? What records/procedures do you need to maintain nonprofit status? • Compare organizational with personal accounting to make it easier to understand. Tell readers how to make the work of accounting easier/more accurate. Print some of the "you should have heard this one" excuses given to people in accounts receivable.

Achievements breakthroughs; feats; accomplishments; recognition for; motivation—What awards/incentives do you offer for specific accomplishments? How has your community/trade association recognized your accomplishments? What contests/competitions can readers enter?

Advertising campaigns; plans; promotions—How do you advertise and why? What new products or services are you promoting? • Explain where advertising ideas come from and how readers can influence future campaigns. Invite ideas from readers and print acknowledgments with descriptions of ideas.

Annual report prospectus; statement—Are you required to produce an annual report? When does it appear? To whom is it sent? • Summarize your annual report in a series of articles. Follow the production process from planning through printing.

Associations leagues; unions; societies; coalitions—What associations have you joined? Why? What benefits does membership bring you? What services/publications do associations offer that your readers can use? • Print a list of associations you belong to and tell readers who, within your organization, to contact for information. Describe an association accomplishment and your role in it.

Audiovisual services videos; films; overheads; slides; tapes—What audiovisual capabilities (video equipment, slide show production, presentation software) do you have? How can readers use existing resources? • Describe how audiovisual aids can strengthen presentations.

Awards scholarships; grants; prizes; honors; tributes—Who qualifies for awards given by your organization? By external sponsors? Who are contacts and what are the entry materials and deadlines? • Report about awards in plenty of time so readers can apply or recommend someone. Describe an award-winning project/idea/design and how it furthers your work.

Benefits insurance; unemployment; child care; maternity; paternity; vacation; counseling; retirement—What benefits do employees/members value most? Value least? What benefits do employees want added/improved? Are cash benefits taxable? What "hidden" benefits does management pay for (parking, family leave, fitness)? • Start a question-and-answer column about benefits. Publish names of people in charge of programs.

Bottom line factors affecting; growth of; meaning of; long/short term—Where does the term "bottom line" come from? What does "bottom line" mean to you and your readers? • Print a typical financial statement showing steps to computing your bottom line. Explain how internal/external factors affect your bottom line.

Break time day off; vacations—How do people spend work breaks? • Describe unusual break or vacation acitivities. Print photos of people taking advantage of breaks.

Budget factors affecting; development process; impact of; changes—What does your budget cover? What control do managers/departments have over how much they get and spend? When/to whom are requests submitted? What happens if income falls short of forecasts? • Spell out where the money comes from. Describe how funds are allocated to various departments/functions.

Buildings renovation; remodeling; history; moving; construction—What is the history of your buildings? How are people consulted during planning for building or renovation? Are there changes planned in the near future? What factors are considered when new buildings are designed?

Calendars agenda; schedules; events; holidays; festivals; meetings; conventions; presentations—What special events do you plan? How will they affect employees/members/the public? Are there special events or dates on the "outside world" calendar that affect you?

Certification credentials; accreditation; licenses/permits; programs—What jobs require certification? How can readers get certified? What programs do you sponsor to help people gain new certification/licenses/permits? • Explain what departments require as well as what your organization/industry requires. Highlight support you offer empoyees/members getting further training. List dates/times/requirements for certification classes/exams. Print a directory of credentials and abbreviations (example: ABC=Accredited Business Communicator) relevant to your industry.

Chapters branches; field offices; divisions—What work do groups outside the main office perform? How independent are branches/divisions? How connected are they? What are their achievements? How do they stay in touch with headquarters? • Report on special activities important to the entire organization. Print photos of people at work in distant settings.

Communication internal; external; policies; methods; technology—What systems do you have for internal/external communication? How do employees/members use them? • Describe policies governing internal/external communication. Explain where communication tends to break down in internal/external relations. Publish suggestions for solving problems.

Community relations involvement; image; responses to needs—What makes a desirable member of its community? Do you encourage/discourage involvement in the community? How? • Explain reasons for community relations policies. Write a case study of your policies in action. Clarify differences between community relations and advertising. Write a feature story about a "good citizen" award that you received.

Community service social; economic; political; charitable—What help does your community need? How have individuals/the community members benefited from your past efforts? What community activities have readers helped? What motivates people to get involved? How can readers get involved?

Compensation wages; bonuses; fees; royalties; stipends—What is your pay structure? How/when are changes made? What qualifies individuals for raises? What other forms of compensation does the company offer (bonuses, commissions, travel expenses)? What about overtime pay? How do taxes affect earnings? • Remind readers about nonmonetary compensation (working conditions, vacation time, recreation facilities).

Competition new products/services; other organizations—What does "competition" mean to your organization? Who are your competitors? What are the positive effects of competition? Negative effects? How do competitors' plans affect you? • Report trends that might bring new competition. Print results of internal competitions to achieve specific goals (safety, attendance, sales). Compare your product/services with those of your competition.

Computers capabilities; hardware; platform; peripherals; supplies; training—What do computers do for you? Who is in charge of purchasing/maintenance/training? What electronic communication do you have (bulletin boards, LANs, e-mail, modems)? Who should readers contact with questions/comments/problems? • Define jargon and explain new technology. Profile employees/members with special computer talents.

Consultants what they do; who they are; who uses them—What do consultants offer to help your organization? How do you decide which consultant to use? Where do you find the right one? What fees do consultants usually get? What are the most effective uses of consultants?

Controlling board directors; supervisors; trustees; regents; commissioners—What powers do the people who direct your organization have (set goals, make policy)? How do they relate to management/leadership? Who appoints/elects board members? When/where do they meet? • Compare responsibilities of Chair of Board and CEO. Profile key board members. Report on changes in membership.

Conventions assemblies; caucuses; councils; conferences; rallies; meetings—When/where is the next "must attend" convention? What should people look for at conventions? What conventions of interest to your organization come near to your city next year? • Write a special issue or report about a major convention. Compare pros/cons of attending conventions.

Cost cutting waste; efficiency—How do cost savings relate to profit or opportunities for growth/service? What incentives do you offer to find ways to cut costs? • Profile an employee/member who seems unusually cost conscious. Explain how to work with vendors or customers to cut their costs.

Customers buyers; clients; students; patients; shoppers; users—How can/do customers suggest additional products/services? How do you keep old customers and get new ones? How much business does the typical customer represent for one year? Five years? How about your best customer? • Write about new products/services/features your customers want. Feature a customer suggestion that worked. Interview some customers about how they perceive your organization.

Customer service programs; maintenance; policies; guarantees; contracts—How are compliments/complaints from customers handled? What complaints do you get? What about compliments? What training do customer service reps get? How do you keep track of customer satisfaction? • Describe how long it takes to get service at peak times and tell when peak times are. Specify what information service people need to help customers get better service. Explain warranties, guarantees and refunds.

Databases records; lists; files; directories—What databases do you maintain/have access to? How can these computer files help readers? Who can access them and under what conditions? • Explain how sales or services rely on database information.

Departments mergers; splits; functions; missions—How is your organization structured? What is each department/unit responsible for? Have any departments merged/split? Have specific departments organized programs (safety, productivity, attendance) that others might duplicate? • Follow a project through each department to show how they work together/communicate.

Development fund-raising; grants; proposal writing; bequests—What are your development goals? How do you solicit contributions? How does development affect day-to-day operations? Who manages development drives? What, other than money, do you need/receive? • Explain how fund-raising drives are conducted. Profile a typical contributor/volunteer.

Disabilities programs for; awareness of; special needs—Where are handicap-accessible buildings/facilities located? What changes do you need to become more accessible to people with disabilities? What programs are you considering? • Present information that increases your utility/accessibility. Describe how construction/remodeling meets accessibility standards.

Distributors warehousing; brokers; agents; catalogs; suppliers—Who distributes your products? How do distributors relate to your advertising/marketing? What guarantees/customer services do distributors offer? • Profile a typical distributor. Print a photo spread showing your products in catalogs and at trade shows. Explain how you market your products to distributors.

Donations given to community; to charities; programs for—Which community groups/charities do you support? Do you have a matching program for employees who contribute? What do you give other than money (time, food, equipment, space, skills)? • Describe local/national programs needing support and what readers could do for them.

Donations received money; time; space; materials; supplies—What kinds of donations do you receive? Do you advertise or print a "wish list"? How do donations help you reach your goals? • Interview major donors about their views on your goals/objectives. Report on how volunteers helped you reach a goal/make your work possible. Feature a volunteer who made an outstanding contribution.

Drugs policies; programs; issues; treatment—Do you have a drug policy? Are there treatment policies/programs? Where can readers get information? What resources does the community offer? • Write a question-and-answer column with facts, not rumors. Report on laws/liability. Review symptoms of drug abuse in a report on drug use/treatment options.

Economy local; regional; national; international—What economic factors affect you? Which changes/trends help and which threaten you? Who monitors changes and plans for how they affect you? • Tell readers what indicators (prime rate, housing starts, trade deficit) relate to you and where to find/how to interpret them. Interview top management/leadership about trends that affect you.

Education continuing; scholarships; internships; apprenticeships; training—What degrees/certificates do new employees have/need? Do any departments have special education programs? What help (scholarships, financing, time off) do you offer employees? • Describe educational opportunities especially suited to your readers.

Emergencies crises; catastrophes; disasters; accidents—What emergencies do you prepare for? How do you prepare? What are plans to keep you operating? Who speaks for your organization under emergency conditions? What are your fire/first aid programs? • Print details of emergency procedures. Describe some past emergency and how you responded to it.

Endorsements support; patronage; sponsorship—Who/what do you endorse (products, candidates, causes)? Why? How do you benefit from endorsing products/candidates/causes? Who endorses your products/services? How are endorsements obtained?

Endowment gifts/bequests; programs funded; grants awarded—Where does your endowment come from? How does your endowment provide funds for your programs? Who manages it and with what goals? • Announce achievements made possible only because of your endowment. Tell employees/members how they can help increase your endowment. Report on social events and business activities used to solicit or acknowledge gifts.

Energy electricity; gasoline; coal; oil; solar; nuclear—What are your energy needs? How are they met? How do you conserve energy/cut costs? What regulations apply to your energy use? • Write about machines/procedures that have special energy needs. Compare current and possible future energy sources and costs.

Environment air; water; noise; resources—How does your work affect the environment? Do you replenish resources that you use? • Describe environmental laws and regulations that affect your operation. Spell out your programs/policies that protect the environment.

Equal opportunity affirmative action—What positive changes have equal opportunity programs created inside your organization? What measures does federal compliance require? How can readers support equal opportunity programs?

Ethics values; code of conduct—Do you have an ethics policy? What does management/leadership consider unethical behavior? How do you deal with possible violations? What should readers do if they suspect an ethics violation? • Describe hypothetical situations in your industry/organization and explain ethical/unethical behavior.

Etiquette manners; protocol; customs—What does management consider good form? What standards/customs do you observe when dealing with customers/vendors from other countries? How about with fellow employees/members? • Tell readers how dress is important to your image.

Evaluation ratings; tests; surveys; reviews; qualification—How often are employees/members/programs evaluated? Who keeps records of performance reviews? How are possible new products and services evaluated? How are customers/clients evaluated? Does anyone (trade association, government) evaluate your organization as a whole? • Describe how your mission statement affects evaluation. Explain programs and encourage readers to participate.

Facilities rooms; equipment; areas; courses; courts—What education/food/health/fitness/training/recreation facilities do you maintain? Who can use them and when are they open? What does each of them provide? What are the most widely used facilities, who uses them and for what?

Financial services banks; advisors; indexes; databases; credit unions—What savings/pension/stock plans do you offer? Who gives advice/information? What choices do readers have? How do employees/members enroll in programs? • Give detailed but easy-to-understand lists of programs/requirements/ pros and cons of joining. Help program administrators write question/answer columns. Describe how programs affect taxes.

Food services cafeteria; catering; vending—What special problems does food service have because of the nature of your organization (storage conditions, working hours)? How does food service take into account employee/member health concerns? • Tell readers how to make suggestions about food service. Explain how to specify special menu items. Print a joint interview with the directors of food service and health/fitness programs.

Goals purposes; objectives; missions—What are current goals? How well are you meeting them? How are employees/members involved in setting goals and objectives? How is compensation related to meeting goals? • Describe programs that are especially relevant.

Government local; regional; state/province; federal—Which governmental bodies do you come in contact with and how? What changes will new regulations force you to make? What regulations protect your organization? • Explain how employees/members can help the organization comply with regulations.

Grants awards; bequests; foundations; agencies—What is a grant? How do grants fit into your financial structure? How do you qualify for specific grants? Who writes grant proposals for your organization? • Describe the granting agencies most related to your needs. Interview an evaluator from a granting agency about strengths and weaknesses of a grant request. Follow a grant proposal from inception to decision.

Grievances employees; members; customers—How do you receive/resolve grievances and complaints? Who serves as a hearing officer? What are your standards of confidentiality/fairness? • Profile a complaint (anonymously) that was resolved quickly and fairly. Summarize some generic complaints and report on steps taken to deal with them.

Growth expansion; additions; upsurges—What growth plans do you have? How do you measure growth (number of people, gross income, profits)? What do you consider the right rate of growth? How will growth affect readers? Will there be new jobs/chances for promotion?

Health and wellness exercise; athletics; nutrition—What health care/wellness education do you provide? • Write a health and fitness question-and-answer column. Feature one person who benefited from your health and fitness program. Interview an occupational therapist about simple exercises (stretching/eye rest) and work procedures (proper use of computer monitors, good reading conditions) for maintaining health.

History of organization; of buildings—What is your historical significance to the community/industry? How does your history relate to your present function? What traditions do you have? • Describe how past decisions and circumstances affect current events. Print old photos.

Human services family; social; personnel; community; jobs—What information/counseling do you offer for specific problems? How do your human services tie into those in the community? • Explain resources and encourage readers to use them.

Information services libraries; subscriptions; bulletin boards; reference services—What services does your library offer? What materials do employees/members have/sub-scribe to? How and when can readers use them? What outside sources are especially convenient/relevant to your readers (college library, trade association, business group)? • Review new publications that are especially relevant.

Insurance health; property; liability; accident; life; unemployment—What/whom do you insure? What coverage are you required to carry? Who decides what coverage to buy? Who files claims? Do you insure anything unusual (databases, physical skills)? Are volunteers insured against injury? In what circumstances? • Outline insurance coverage that affects readers or their families.

International developments; communication; travel—How do developments in other countries/regions affect your organization? What do you sell/buy from other countries? Who specializes in laws/languages/customs of countries you deal with? • Profile employees/members with special skills relating to international activities.

Inventory maintenance; checking; warehouse; valuation—What makes up your "inventory"? How often does it turn over? Who maintains the inventory? What are the implications of having too much or too little? Who has access to information about your inventory (customers, sales reps)? • Take readers on a photo tour of the warehouse. Describe what problems buyers have. Explain the type of inventory system your organization uses (LIFO, FIFO) and why.

Investments stocks; bonds; mutual funds; real estate—What are your investment goals (income, growth, tax benefits, liquidity)? Who decides how much to invest? Where/when?

Jargon technical vocabulary; buzz words; idioms—What special terminology do your employees/members and others in your industry/field use? What guide should readers use to learn appropriate jargon? • Tell why people use special language. Run a sidebar with definitions of commonly used special terms. Present a short piece that uses unnecessary jargon humorously and a rewrite in plain language. See also Computers, Information services.

Laws and legislation lobbying; compliance; benefits—What laws/legislation affect your daily operations? How do they affect long-range planning? What changes will new legislation force you to make? When? What will the changes cost? What can readers do to influence proposed legislation/changes in existing legislation? • Explain the benefits of recent or pending legislation.

Licenses permits; renewals; requirements—What operating licenses do you need? Who applies for them? Who issues them? What role does your trade association/union have in issuing/renewing licenses? • Describe step-by-step application for a vital permit. Profile a person/agency that reviews applications in your industry. Alert readers to activities/conditions that may threaten renewals.

Loans leverage; debt; borrowing; interest—What do you borrow money for? In what form is it borrowed (leases, mortgage, short-term, long-term)? What portion of your income goes for interest payments? • Explain your credit rating and tell readers how to protect/enhance it. Interview management/leadership about the relationship between growth and leverage.

Mail services internal, external; distribution; postage; bulk mail—What are your postage costs per month/year? How can you reduce them (bar coding, bulk mail, prune address lists)? Who sorts/distributes incoming mail? What policies/guidelines do they use? • Interview a postal official about trends/costs affecting your industry. Explain techniques to reduce postage costs.

Maintenance physical plant; work areas; equipment; outside spaces; preventive; janitorial—What maintenance schedules do you use? Which machines/buildings/facilities need the most maintenance? How much time/money does maintenance take each year? How can

readers help maintain work areas? • Profile those in charge of maintaining the various elements of your organization and how to contact them. Describe/photograph a day/night in the life of janitorial services.

Management selection; training; accessibility; goals; accomplishments; structure; responsibility—How does management establish/help reach goals for your organization? Who selects managers? What criteria are used? How can readers reach management with questions/concerns? • Feature the background/skills/goals of one top manager/leader every issue.

Market population; needs; trends—Who/what makes up your market? What specifics do you know about your market (location/size/age/preferences)? What changes in population will affect your market? Who studies your market? How? • Profile an individual customer who represents your market as a whole. Summarize market studies by your trade association.

Marketing plans; philosophy; research; strategies; goals—How do you market your products/services? How does your marketing compare with the competition's? How can employees/members help people in marketing? • Feature a case study demonstrating a successful marketing plan.

Meetings planning; presentations; schedules; reports—What regular meetings do you have for members/employees/public? When/where does your board of directors/trustees meet? • Report about community meetings that affect you.

Membership dues; fees; activities; recruitment; renewals—How do members benefit from belonging to your organization (organizational support for goals they believe in, use of facilities)? Why have dues/fees increased? What activities serve the membership? How? • Publish a profile of your membership. Highlight benefits/activities/questions in a regular membership column.

Mission statement goals; purposes; objectives; strategies—Who developed your mission statement? How does it affect goals/operations? When/how is it reviewed? • Print your mission statement. Interview management/leadership about how the mission statement affects goals/budgets.

Patents copyrights; trademarks—What patents do you or your members/employees own? What protection do copyrights offer the organization/individuals? What products are exclusive to the organization because of trademarks? Why is protection important? • Profile the department that secures rights. Explain recent changes in patent/copyright law.

Personnel hiring; records; employment practices—Who authorizes new positions? Who advertises/interviews/hires? How are employees involved in screening/selection? What notice do current employees have about job openings/promotions? What records does personnel keep about employees? For how long? Who has access to files?

Presentations speeches; displays; meetings; conferences—What are goals/techniques of effective presentations in your industry/area of concern? What help can readers get with presentations? • Print a photo spread about how to prepare a presentation. Explain what makes presentations effective/ineffective. Describe a cost effective presentation that got excellent results.

Printing services in-house; design; typesetting; publishing; binding—What can in-house printing services do (color printing/types of binding/desktop publishing)? Who selects/monitors outside printers? What kind of jobs stay inside/go outside? How much money/lead time is required to print various kinds of publications (stationery, newsletter, annual report)? • Describe a day in the print shop. Interview a printer about requirements for camera-ready copy.

Productivity goals; programs; incentives; measuring—How do you define productivity? How do your most productive departments achieve/maintain their high levels? What

incentives do you offer to increase productivity? • Run a contest to find ways to increase productivity.

Products testing; prices; quality—Where do ideas for new products come from? How does product development work? How do you test products before they go to market? How do you test markets? • Follow a product from idea through testing/marketing. Feature a product that you offered twenty years ago.

Profits gross; earnings; proceeds; yields; margins—How do you compute profits? What do industry leaders consider a good profit margin? Did last year's profits meet management's goals? • Interview an organization leader about how profits/losses reveal the "health" of your organization. Explain the relationship between profits and productivity.

Promotions advancement; upgrading—Do you have specific requirements for promotions (e.g., length of service, outstanding sales record, college degree)? Do those promoted tend to stay in the same department/office, or are they usually transferred? • Interview the head of your personnel department about how your promotion policy fits with your goals/objectives. Feature an individual recently promoted.

Publications brochures; magazines; tabloids; newsletters; annual reports; manuals; directories; books; catalogs—What publications do you produce? What goals/audiences does each have? How can readers get publications that interest them? • Write a publication review column.

Public ownership annual report; employee stock plans; dividends; stockholder meetings; proxy; forecasts; outlook; value—How do the activities of members/employees/stockholders affect each other? What can employees read to learn about stock prices/market viewpoints about your organization? How can employees use stock plans for retirement planning? What is the main thrust of this year's annual report? • Summarize discussions that take place at stockholder meetings.

Public relations press releases; media relations; publications; speeches; meetings; hearings; image—Who is your "public"? Who speaks officially to the media about your organization? What information does the public want from you? What image/information do you want conveyed to the public? • Reprint important speeches made by your employees/members. Notify readers of radio/television/print coverage of your organization. Tell readers how they can help build good public relations.

Purchasing supplies; services; central supply; inventory control—Who decides what supplies/services to buy and when? What opportunities exist for cooperative purchases to save money/ensure supply? When is the best time to requisition various items? • Interview a purchasing agent about sales and special opportunities. Spell out how to plan for efficient purchasing.

Quality control standards; programs; incentives—How do you define quality? Who sets the standards? Who enforces them? How often do you check quality? Which of your products/services need the toughest quality control? Which departments have the best records? How do they keep their standards up? • Encourage readers to suggest quality improvements.

Records files; archives; minutes; proceedings; databases—What records do you preserve? Where/for how long? How do you keep records (file drawers, microfilm, piles in office corners)? What must be saved to meet state/federal requirements? For how long? How do readers use archiving services? • Tell readers what they must save/can discard. Explain legislation that affects record-keeping procedures.

Recreation sponsored activities; facilities; health benefits—What do you do to encourage recreation? Where are health/fitness facilities? Do you offer membership at a health club?

What teams/activities do you sponsor? How can readers get involved? • Publish a schedule of events/times/places. Write about the health benefits of different types of exercise. Give tips for stress management that include recreational activities that readers can do on breaks.

Recruitment hiring; membership—How do you recruit new employees/members? Who is planning your next membership drive? What does the plan involve? How can readers offer suggestions?

Recycling policy; importance; programs—Do you recycle paper/glass/metals/anything else? How does recycling affect the environment and the organization? Do you take part in community recycling efforts? What specific ways can employees/members help?

Repairs schedules; plans; costs—Who contracts for repairs on in-house equipment? How much money do you spend on repairs annually? What is the average time between damage/breakdown and repair? • Publish names/phone numbers of employees authorized to make repairs/contact repair agencies. Interview a service person about preventive maintenance.

Research and development testing; analysis; trial; experiment—What is R&D and how do you use it? How do R&D projects affect the rest of your organization? Do all new products/services begin in R&D? If not, do they all pass through R&D eventually? How can readers offer ideas for R&D? How can other departments work with R&D to produce new products? • Follow an idea through the R&D process to show readers what really happens.

Retirement activities; pension; age of; early—What are your retirement policies? How can employees work part time to retire gradually? What control do employees have over pension fund contributions? • Print a question/answer column with questions asked/answered by retired employees.

Safety programs; incentives; problems; procedures; needs—What job-related injuries/problems have occurred recently? What fire/medical safety programs do you have? Who runs them/how should readers get involved? Who is trained in first aid or in dealing with specific injuries that might happen to people on site? • Alert readers to hazardous procedures/tools/products. Print maps that mark fire extinguishers/exit routes. Announce training sessions in first aid/CPR.

Sales support; training; goals; techniques; materials; staff; costs—Do your sales have a seasonal pattern (strong in the winter, weak in the summer)? How do changes in sales volume affect the rest of your organization? How many sales calls go into the average sale? What benefits do you offer that would make customers want to buy from you instead of your competition? How are sales people trained? • Tell readers how they can help with sales. Describe a day in the life of a sales representative.

Security alarm systems; guards; precautions; problems; policies—What can readers do to increase the security of your buildings and facilities? What should readers do if they discover a theft/intruder? What should they do if they believe someone is stealing from the organization? • Interview the director of security for hints/suggestions. Summarize security problems/solutions.

Shipping services packages; common carriers; overnight; domestic; overseas—What should readers do if they need to ship packages in unusual circumstances? Which carriers do you use regularly? What services/discounts do they offer? • Write about true shipping costs (how much you spend on overnight delivery for packages that could as easily have gone by slower methods).

Software accessories; programs; utilities—What software do you rely on most? Do you have in-house/proprietary software? Who troubleshoots problems with software? • Print a directory of your most-skilled users of each software package.

Speaker programs public relations; meetings; school visits—What schools or other outside groups want to learn about you? Who are your speakers in most demand? • Explain how to make a successful outside speech. Describe what support you offer to the speaker. Print a photo spread showing the experience of a popular speaker at an outside event.

Special events anniversaries; openings; dinners; parties; picnics—What will your organization celebrate during the next year? How will branches/chapters participate? How will celebrations help build morale/enhance image? • Interview people planning/participating in events.

Sponsorships teams; events; performances; programs—What activities/groups do you sponsor? What benefits do you expect as a result? Who decides what to sponsor? • Feature an activity or group that couldn't continue without your help. Tell readers how they can suggest groups/activities to sponsor.

Structure reorganization; mergers, acquisitions; closures—What is the structure of your organization? How do branches interact with the main location? How has your structure changed over the years? What do those changes mean today? • Print your organizational chart. Do a series of forums following a reorganization (one on reactions to the announcement, one a month after the reorganization, and another one a year later).

Supplies materials; equipment; fixtures; furnishings—Who keeps track of what supplies your organization needs? Who orders supplies? What do supplies cost? • Report donations of supplies and how they help. Feature ways to reduce waste.

Taxes sales; property; business; withholding—What taxes do you pay? What taxes are withheld from employee earnings? How do taxes affect your bottom line? How can you reduce taxes? • Spell out where your tax dollars go. Explain hidden taxes (property taxes as part of rent, sales tax on supplies or services).

Technology helping do the job better; advances; effect on personal lives—What technological advances can help improve the lives of employees/members? How? What technology are you developing/testing to benefit customers/society?

Telecommunications conferencing; fax; e-mail; groupware; bulletin boards—How has telecommunications increased/decreased your operating costs? How can you take best advantage of your phone system? • Describe plans to add services/equipment. Profile your phone system ten years ago.

Trade shows exhibits—How do attendees get the most out of the exhibits? Who designs/staffs your exhibits? What are typical exhibit costs? How are people who staff exhibits trained to work effectively? How should readers decide whether exhibiting at a specific show is worth the time and money? • Write a feature, "one day at a trade show," through the eyes of someone staffing an exhibit for your organization.

Traffic car pools; public transport; biking; walking—What public transportation could your readers use? Do you have split shift/carpooling/parking policies that help reduce traffic problems? • Interview people with novel solutions to problems commuting/parking. Describe benefits like cleaner air/less stress from battling traffic/healthier pocketbook. Publish maps of bike routes that lead to your location.

Training symposiums; clinics; seminars; workshops—What training programs do you have? Who is eligible? In what specific ways do training programs benefit employees/members/volunteers? • Interview an employee who has benefited from a training program. Analyze what constitutes a good training program, and publish guidelines about evaluating training opportunities.

Travel policies; programs; planning; budgeting—How much do you spend each year on travel? What policies/regulations do you have? How do you handle credits for programs for frequent flyers/car rentals/hotel accommodations? • Publish guidelines regarding travel policies. Describe who travels a great deal and why. Interpret policies by spotlighting specific travel situations.

Vendors account executives; sales reps—How/by whom are vendors chosen? What makes certain vendors popular with you (credit terms, delivery)? How do vendors improve your customer service? • Spotlight a vendor with whom you have a long relationship. Ask readers to write letters to the editor about what they wished vendors did/offered.

Volunteers need for; productivity of; training; rewards—Why are volunteers important to your organization? What do they do? What supervision do they need? Who supervises them? How do you get volunteers? How do volunteers benefit? What do volunteers make possible that wouldn't be possible without them? • Describe what volunteers achieve. Explain how readers can best work with volunteers. Define how volunteer hours save/make money.

GLOSSARY

This glossary contains the technical and business terms used in this book plus many others. Terms come from the fields of publishing, photography, computers, graphic design and printing.

If you need more complete definitions of newsletter terms or want to know the meanings of other terms used in graphic design and printing, consult my book *Graphically Speaking: An Illustrated Guide to the Working Language of Design and Printing.*

AA Abbreviation for author alteration.

alignment Orientation of type with regard to edges of the column or paper, such as aligned right (flush right), aligned left (flush left), and aligned on center (centered). Also called range.

alley Space between images or columns of type on a page, as compared to gutter.

alteration Any change made by the customer after copy or artwork has been given to the service bureau or printer. The change could be in copy, specifications or both. Also called AA, author alteration and customer alteration.

artwork All original copy, including type, photos and illustrations, intended for printing. Also called art.

ascender Part of lowercase letters, such as h and b, that rises above its x height.

backup copy Duplicate of an original made in case of loss or damage of the original.

banding Defect in halftone screens or screen tints output by laser printers or imagesetters in which parallel breaks (stair steps) or streaks appear in the dot pattern.

banner Large headline, usually across the full width of a page.

base art Copy pasted up on the mounting board of a mechanical, as compared to overlay art. Base art usually has the copy to be printed using black ink.

baseline Imaginary line, under a line of type, used to align characters.

basis weight In the United States and Canada, the weight, in pounds, of a ream (five hundred sheets) of paper cut to the basic size. Also called ream weight and substance weight (sub weight). When writing basis weight, the word "pound" is abbreviated with the symbol "#." Fifty-pound coated is written 50# coated.

bindery Place where printed products are collated, trimmed, folded and/or bound. A bindery may be a department within a printing company or a separate business.

bleed Printing that extends to the edge of a sheet or page after trimming.

blueline Prepress photographic proof made from stripped negatives where all colors show as blue images on white paper. Because "blueline" is a generic term for proofs made from a variety of materials having similar appearances, it may also be called a blackprint, blue, blueprint, brownline, brownprint, diazo, dyeline, ozalid, position proof, silverprint, Dylux or VanDyke.

blurb Brief description of a person, such as a writer or speaker, appearing as part of an article by that person.

body copy 1) Copy set in text type, as compared to display type. 2) The bulk of a story or article, as compared to its headlines and decks.

bold type Type that appears darker than the text type of the same typeface.

bond paper Category of paper commonly used for writing, printing and photocopying. Also called business paper, communication paper, correspondence paper and writing paper.

book paper Category of paper suitable for newsletters and general printing needs. Book paper is divided into uncoated paper (also called offset paper), coated paper (also called art paper, enamel paper, gloss paper and slick paper) and text paper.

brightness Characteristic of paper or ink

referring to how much light it reflects.

build a color To overlap two or more screen tints to create a new color. Such an overlap is called a build, color build, stacked screen build or tint build.

bulk mail Alternate term for third-class mail.

bullet Bold dot used for typographic emphasis or to identify elements in a list.

business reply card Preaddressed card meeting postal regulations for size, caliper, bar coding and prepayment. Also called BRC and reply card.

byline The name of the author appearing at the beginning or end of an article.

callout Word that identifies part of an illustration.

camera-ready copy Mechanicals, photographs and art fully prepared for reproduction according to the technical requirements of the printing process being used. Also called finished art and reproduction copy.

cap height Height of capital letters in one type size of a font.

caption Identifying or descriptive text accompanying a photograph, illustration, map, chart or other visual element. Also called cutline, legend and underline.

change order Written instructions about changes to a job already in progress.

character Any letter, numeral, punctuation mark or other alphanumeric symbol.

Cheshire labels Names and addresses printed on wide computer paper in a format that can be cut into labels and affixed by machines developed by the Cheshire Company. Also called four-up labels.

clip art Copyright-free drawings available for purchase for unlimited reproduction. Clip art illustrations are printed on glossy paper or stored on computer disks. They are ready for placement on mechanicals or pages designed on computer screens. Also called standard artwork.

coated paper Paper with a coating of clay and other substances that improves reflectivity and ink holdout. Mills produce coated paper appropriate for newsletters in three major catagories of surface shine: gloss, dull and matte.

color separation service Business making color separations for four-color process printing. Also called engraver, prep service, separator and service bureau.

column rule Thin vertical line that separates columns.

commercial printer Printer producing a wide range of products such as announcements, newsletters and posters. Commercial printers typically use metal plates made from negatives. Also called job printer because each job is different.

composition 1) In photography, the manner in which an image is arranged and framed to give an overall effect. 2) In typography, the assembly of typographic elements, such as words and paragraphs, into pages ready for printing. 3) In graphic design, the arrangement of type, graphics, and other elements on the page.

comprehensive dummy Simulation of a newsletter complete with type, graphics and colors. Also called comp.

condensed type Characters relatively narrow in proportion to their height, thus seeming tall and tightly spaced.

continuous-tone copy All photographs and those illustrations having a range of shades not made up of dots, as compared to line copy or halftones. Abbreviated contone.

copy 1) For an editor or typesetter, all written material. 2) For a graphic designer or printer, everything to be printed: art, photographs and graphics, as well as words.

copyeditor Person who checks and corrects a manuscript for spelling, grammar, punctuation, inconsistencies, inaccuracies, and conformity to style requirements. Also called line editor.

copyfit 1) To calculate the space that a given amount of text requires in a specific typeface and point size. 2) To edit writing and adjust typography for the purpose of making text fit a layout.

copyright Ownership of creative work by the writer, photographer or artist who made it or, if work for hire, the organization that paid for it.

copyright notice Statement of copyright ownership that has the word "copyright" or symbol ©, the year of publication, and the name of the copyright owner. For example, "Copyright 1995 Mark Beach."

corner marks Lines on a mechanical, negative, plate or press sheet showing locations of the corners of a page or finished piece.

credit line Line of relatively small type next to a photo or illustration giving its source and/or the name of the photographer or artist. May include copyright notice. Also called courtesy line.

crop To eliminate portions of an image so the remainder is more useful, pleasing, or able to fit the layout.

crop marks Lines near the edges of an image indicating portions to be reproduced. Also called cut marks and tick marks.

cropping Ls Pieces of paper or cardboard cut into L shapes that, when overlapped, can be adjusted to frame a photograph. Also called cropping angles.

crossover Type or art that continues from one page across the gutter to the opposite page. Also called bridge, gutter bleed and gutter jump.

dash Typographic mark that indiciates a break between thoughts. An em dash (—) is longer than an en dash (–) and much longer than a hyphen (-).

descender Portion of a lowercase letter falling below its baseline.

dingbat Typographic symbol, such as a bullet (•), used for emphasis or decoration.

display type Type used for headlines, advertising and signs. Also called headline type.

drop shadow Screen tint or rule touching an illustration, box or type to give a three-dimensional shadow effect. Also called flat shadow.

dropped cap Large capital letter that extends down into the first two or more lines. Used as a design element.

dual-purpose bond paper Bond paper suitable for printing by either lithography (offset) or xerography (photocopy). Abbreviated DP bond paper.

dull finish Flat (not glossy) finish on coated paper, slightly smoother than matte. Also called suede finish, velour finish and velvet finish.

dummy Mock-up simulating the final product. Dummies range from very simple, showing only size or rough layout, to very complicated, showing position and color of type and art. Also called mock-up.

Dylux Brand name for photographic paper used to make blueline proofs. Often used as alternate term for blueline.

edition One version of a newsletter, such as the western regional edition.

element One part of an image or page. Elements of an image may include subject, background and foreground. Elements of a page may include headlines, body copy and halftones.

estimate Price that states what a job will probably cost. Also called bid, quotation and tender. Printers base estimates on specifications provided by customers.

extended type Characters wide in proportion to their height, thus seeming fat. Also called expanded type.

fair use Concept in copyright law allowing, without permission from copyright holder, short quotations from a copyrighted product for purposes of reviewing or teaching. Also called fair dealing.

feature Article that provides general knowledge, entertainment, or background on the news. Feature articles are usually longer than news articles.

fillers Short items, such as proverbs or announcements, kept on hand to fill small blank spaces in a layout.

film speed Measure of light sensitivity of photographic film. Fast film is highly sensitive, slow film less sensitive.

finish 1) Surface characteristics of paper. 2) General term for trimming, folding, binding, and all other postpress operations.

finished size Size of product after production is complete, as compared to flat size. Also called trim size.

fixed costs Costs that remain the same regardless of how many copies are printed, as compared to variable costs. The costs of copywriting, photography and design are examples of fixed costs.

flat 1) Printer's assembly of film taped to a carrier sheet ready for platemaking. Also called film mechanical and Goldenrod. 2) U.S. Postal Service term for a piece of mail whose length is from 5 to 15 inches and height from 3½ to 12 inches, as compared to letter mail, which has smaller dimensions. Flats include unfolded newsletters.

flat size Size of product after printing and trimming, but before folding, as compared to finished size.

floating rule Rule, usually between columns, whose ends do not touch other rules.

flop To change the orientation of an image so it is the mirror image of its orginal.

flush left Type aligning vertically along the left side of the column. Also called left justified and ranged left.

flush right Type aligning vertically along the right side of the column. Also called right justified and ranged right.

fold marks Lines on a mechanical, film, printing plate or press sheet indicating where to fold the final product.

font Complete assortment of upper- and lowercase characters, numerals, punctuation and other symbols of one typeface. A font is a concept, not a physical object. Fonts can be held in the storage or memory of a computer, on sheets of transfer lettering, on film, or in job cases holding metal type.

footer Information, such as page number or chapter title, that appears at the bottom of every page. Also called running foot.

format Size or layout, depending on context. "The format is 8½" x 11"." "Our newsletter has a one-column format."

for position only Refers to inexpensive copies of photos or art used on mechanicals to indicate placement and scaling, but not intended for reproduction. Abbreviated FPO.

freelancer Professional, such as writer or photographer, who is self-employed, thus free to accept work from many clients. Also called contract artist.

gang To halftone more than one image in only one exposure.

gloss finish Paper with a coating that reflects light well, as compared to dull- or matte-coated paper. Also called art paper, enamel paper and slick paper.

glossy print Photography term for black-and-white print made on glossy paper.

grade General term used to distinguish between or among printing papers, but whose specific meaning depends on context. Grade can refer to the category, class, rating, finish or brand of paper.

grain direction Predominant direction in which fibers in paper become aligned during manufacturing. Also called machine direction.

grainy Appearance of a photograph or halftone that has been enlarged so much that the pattern of crystals in the emulsion can be seen in the photo or its reproduction.

graphic arts The crafts, industries and professions related to designing and printing on paper and other substrates.

graphic design Arrangement of type and visual elements along with specifications for paper, ink colors and printing processes that, when combined, convey a visual message.

graphic designer Professional who designs, plans and may coordinate production of a printed piece.

graphics Visual elements that supplement type to make printed messages clearer or more interesting.

gray levels Number of distinct gray tones that can be reproduced by a computer.

grid 1) Pattern of lines representing the layout of a newsletter. A grid may be imaginary, or it may be printed on paper or displayed on a computer screen. 2) Pattern of nonprinting guidelines on a pasteup board or computer screen. Grids help align and organize copy.

grip and grin Staged photograph of two people smiling and shaking hands at a ceremonial event.

gutter Line or fold at which facing pages meet.

hairline Thinnest visible space or rule. Because visibility is determined by factors such as contrast between ink and paper and eyesight of the viewer, hairline has no precise meaning. Hairlines exist in the eye of the beholder.

hairline register Subjective term referring to very close register.

halftone A photograph or illustration that has been converted into dots for reproduction.

hard copy Copy on a substrate, such as film or paper, as compared to soft copy.

hard mechanical Mechanical consisting of paper and/or acetate, as compared to electronic mechanical.

hard proof Proof on paper or other substrate, as compared to a soft proof.

header Information, such as page number or chapter title, that appears at the top of every page of a newsletter.

hickey Spot or imperfection in printing, most visible in areas of heavy ink coverage, caused by dirt on the plate or blanket. Also called bull's eye and fish eye.

highlights Lightest portions of a photograph or halftone, as compared to midtones and shadows.

house organ Newsletter published for employees or members of an organization.

house sheet Paper kept in stock by a printer and suitable for a wide variety of printing jobs. Also called floor sheet.

house style Guidelines for grammar, typography, color and other graphic features, as adopted by a specific organization.

image Type, illustration or other original as it has been reproduced on computer screen, film, printing plate or paper.

imagesetter Laser output device using photosensitive paper or film.

imposition Arrangement of pages on mechanicals or flats so they will appear in proper sequence after press sheets are folded and bound.

imprint To print new copy on a previously printed sheet, such as imprinting an employee's name on business cards. Also called surprint.

indicia Postal permit information printed on objects to be mailed and accepted by U.S. Postal Service in place of stamps.

infographics Charts, graphs, tables and other visual representations of ideas and statistical information. Also called business graphics and management graphics.

in-house Refers to an activity, such as graphic design or printing, performed within an organization, not purchased from outsiders.

ink holdout Characteristic of paper that prevents it from absorbing ink, thus allowing ink to dry on the surface of the paper.

in-plant printer Department of an agency, business or association that does printing for a parent organization. Also called captive printer and in-house printer.

ISSN Abbreviation for International Standard Serial Number.

issue 1) All copies of a newsletter having content related to one theme, such as the tenth anniversary issue, or location, such as the western issue. 2) All copies of a newsletter published on the same date, such as the September issue.

issue date Year, month or date on which a newsletter was mailed or released.

italic type Type slanted to the right to resemble handwriting, as compared to roman type.

jump Point at which text moves from one page to another. When the second page does not immediately follow the first, the jump is indicated with "continued on p.__."

jumpover Type that continues from above a photo or illustration to below it, so the reader's eyes must jump over the visual to continue reading the copy.

justified type Type set flush right and left.

kern To reduce space between two or three characters so those characters appear better fitted together.

key To relate loose pieces of copy to their positions on a layout or mechanical using a system of numbers or letters.

keylines Lines on a mechanical or negative showing the exact size, shape and location of photographs or other graphic elements. Also called holding lines.

kicker Small, secondary headline placed above a primary headline to lead into the primary headline.

laser printer Device using a laser beam and xerography to reproduce type, graphics and halftone dots.

laser type Type made using a laser printer. Imagesetters also use lasers to make type, but the term "laser type" refers to type produced by toner on plain paper.

layout Sketch or plan of how a page or sheet will look when printed.

lead 1) Main story in a newsletter. 2) First paragraph in a news story. Pronounced "leed."

leaders Dots, dashes or other symbols that guide the eye from one item to another, as in a table of contents. Pronounced "leeder" because the term refers to the verb "to lead."

leading Space between lines of type expressed as the distance between baselines. Pronounced "ledding" because the term originated with strips of metal (lead) used to separate lines of hot type. Also called interline spacing and line spacing.

legible Referring to type having sufficient contrast with its background so readers can easily perceive the characters, as compared to readable.

letter U.S. Postal Service term for piece of mail whose height is between 3½ and 6⅛ inches and length between 5 and 11½ inches, as compared to a flat, which has larger dimensions.

letter fold Two folds creating three panels that allow a sheet of letterhead to fit a business envelope. Also called barrel fold and wrap-around fold.

letter spacing Amount of space between all characters. Also called character spacing.

line copy Any high-contrast image, including type, as compared to continuous-tone copy. Also called line art and line work.

lines per inch Linear measure of screen ruling expressing how many lines of dots there are per inch in a screen tint, halftone or separation. Abbreviated lpi.

logo Abbreviation for logotype, an artistic assembly of type and art into a distinctive symbol unique to an organization, business or product. Also called emblem.

mailing service Business specializing in addressing and mailing large quantities of printed pieces. Also called lettershop.

makeover 1) New design replacing an old design. 2) Printing job done over again—made over without changes—because of unacceptable flaws in the previous production run.

mark up To write on a manuscript or proof instructions about matters such as typesetting, color correcting or printing.

markup Amount of money that one supplier adds to the price of goods or services secured for a customer from another supplier.

mask To prevent light from reaching part of an image, therefore isolating the remaining part. Also called knock out.

masking material Opaque paper or plastic used to prevent light from reaching selected areas of film or a printing plate. Also called knockout film. Masking material is often referred to by brand names, such as Amberlith, Goldenrod and Rubylith.

masthead Block of information in a newsletter that identifies its publisher and editor and tells about advertising and subscribing.

matte finish Flat (not glossy) finish on photographic paper or coated printing paper.

measure Width of a column of type. With justified type, all lines have the same measure. With ragged type, measure equals the longest possible line. Also called line measure.

mechanical Camera-ready assembly of type, graphics and other copy complete with instructions to the printer.

merge/purge To combine two or more databases (merge), then eliminate duplicate records (purge). Usually refers to a function performed by a list house on address lists before mailing.

midtones In a photograph or illustration, tones created by dots between 30 percent and 70 percent of coverage, as compared to highlights and shadows.

modem Acronym for modulator/demodulator, a device that converts digital signals to analog tones and vice versa so computers can communicate over telephone lines.

moiré Undesirable pattern resulting when halftones and screen tints are made with improperly aligned screens or when a pattern in a photo, such as a plaid, interferes with a halftone dot pattern.

mottle Spotty, uneven ink absorption. Also called sinkage. A mottled image may be called mealy.

mounting board Any thick, smooth piece of paper used to paste up copy or mount photographs.

mug shot Photograph showing only a person's face.

multicolor printing Printing in more than one ink color (but not four-color process). Also called polychrome printing.

nameplate Portion of front page of newsletter that graphically presents its name, subtitle and date line.

newsletter Short, usually informal periodical presenting specialized information to a limited audience.

offset printing Printing technique that transfers ink from a plate to a blanket to paper instead of directly from a plate to paper.

opacity Characteristic of paper that prevents printing on one side from showing through to the other.

original art Initial photo or illustration prepared for reproduction.

out of register Characteristic of an image not printed in register. Also called misregister.

overlay Layer of material taped to a mechanical, photo or proof. An overlay has the same dimensions as the mounting board that it covers. There are two types of overlays:

Acetate overlays are used to separate colors by having some type or art on them instead of on the mounting board.

Tissue overlays are used to carry instructions about the underlying copy and to protect the base art.

overprint To print one image over a previously printed image, such as printing type over a screen tint. Also called surprint.

overrun Number of pieces printed or paper made in excess of the quantity ordered.

overs Printed pieces in an overrun.

page One side of a leaf in a newsletter. One sheet folded in half yields four pages. An eight-page signature has four pages printed on each side of the sheet.

page count Total number of pages that a newsletter has. Also called extent.

page proof Proof of type and graphics as they will look on the finished page complete with elements such as headings and rules.

PANTONE Colors Brand name of colors in the PANTONE Matching System.

paper distributor Merchant selling paper wholesale to printers and other buyers of large quantities.

paste up To paste copy to mounting boards and, if necessary, to overlays so it is assembled into a camera-ready mechanical. The mechanical produced is often called a pasteup.

pasteup board Any piece of paper or board used as the base for a mechanical. Also called lineup board.

phototype Type created by projecting light onto photosensitive paper.

pica Anglo-American unit of typographic measure equal to .166 inch (4.218mm). One pica has twelve points.

PMS Obsolete reference to PANTONE Matching System. The correct trade name of the colors in the PANTONE Matching System is PANTONE Colors, not PMS Colors.

point Regarding type, a unit of measure used to express size (height) of type, distance between lines (leading) and thickness of rules. One point equals $\frac{1}{12}$ pica and .013875 inch (.351mm).

position stat Photocopy or PMT of a photo or illustration made to size and affixed to a mechanical. Position stats show proper cropping, scaling and positioning.

PostScript Brand name for a page description language used in laser printers and imagesetters.

prepress Camera work, color separating, stripping, platemaking and other prepress functions performed by the printer, separator or a service bureau prior to printing. Also called preparation.

preprint To print portions of sheets that will be used for later imprinting.

presort To separate mail into categories, such as postal codes, before mailing it.

press check Event at which makeready sheets from the press are examined before authorizing full production to begin.

printer spreads Mechanicals made so that they are imposed for printing, as compared to reader spreads. For example, an 11" x 17" mechanical for an eight-page newsletter would have pages 2 and 7 opposite each other. See also imposition.

proof Test sheet made to reveal errors or flaws, predict results on press, and record how a printing job is intended to appear when finished.

proofread To examine a manuscript or proof for errors in writing or typesetting.

proofreader marks Standard symbols and abbreviations used to mark up manuscripts and proofs. Most dictionaries and style manuals include charts of proofreader marks. Also called correction marks.

proof sheet 1) Photographic term for sheet of images made by contact printing negatives. Also called contact sheet. 2) Printing term for any proof or press sheet used as a proof.

proportion scale Round device used to calculate percent that an original image must be reduced or enlarged to yield a specific reproduction size. Also called percentage wheel, proportion dial, proportion wheel and scaling wheel.

publisher 1) Person or organization that coordinates creation, design, production and distribution of newsletters. 2) Chief executive officer or owner of a publishing company.

pull quote Words from an article printed in large type and inserted in the page similarly to an illustration.

quality Subjective term relating to expectations by the customer, printer, and other professionals associated with a printing job and whether the job meets those expectations.

quick printing Printing using small sheetfed presses, called duplicators, using cut sizes of bond and offset paper. Paper, plastic or rubber plates are made directly from camera-ready copy, as compared to metal plates for commercial printing that require making film first.

quotation Price offered by a printer to produce a specific job, thus alternate for estimate. The quoted price is the printer's side of the contract based on specifications from the customer.

ragged-left/right type Type whose line beginnings/endings are not aligned vertically.

readable Characteristic of printed messages that are easy to read and understand, as compared to legible.

reader spread Mechanicals made in two-page spreads as readers would see the pages, as compared to printer spread. For example, an 11" x 17" mechanical for an eight-page newsletter could have pages 2 and 3 opposite each other.

register To place printing properly with regard to the edges of paper and other printing on the same sheet. Such printing is said to be in register.

register marks Cross-hair lines on mechanicals and film that help keep flats, plates and printing in register. Also called crossmarks and position marks.

rescreen To create a halftone of an image that is already printed as a halftone; for example, rescreening a photo appearing in a magazine for reprinting in a newsletter. When not done properly, rescreening yields a moiré.

resolution Sharpness of an image on film, paper, computer screen, disk, tape or other medium.

reverse Type, graphic or illustration reproduced by printing ink around its outline, thus allowing the underlying color or paper to show through and form the image. Also called knockout and liftout. The image "reverses out" of the ink color.

rights Conditions and terms of a licensing agreement between a copyright owner and a publisher.

roman type Type with serifs and that is upright, as compared to italic. Also called plain type. Roman is the basic typeface in any type family. Other typefaces in the family are based on the roman. For example, light is lighter than roman and bold is darker.

rough layout Sketch giving a general idea of size and placement of text and graphics in the final product. Also called esquisse and rough.

rule Line used as a graphic element to separate or organize copy. The width of rules is measured in points or millimeters.

runaround Type set to conform to part or all of the shape of a neighboring photograph or illustration. Also called wraparound.

saddle stitch To bind by stapling sheets together where they fold at the spine, as compared to side stitch. Also called pamphlet stitch, saddle wire and stitch bind.

sans-serif type Type without serifs. Also called gothic type.

satin finish Alternate term for dull finish on coated paper.

scale To identify the percent by which photographs or art should be enlarged or reduced to achieve the correct size for printing. An 8" x 10" photo to be reproduced as a 4" x 5" image should be scaled to 50 percent.

scalloped columns Page layout in which columns of unequal length are aligned at the top so their bottoms vary. Also called hanging columns.

scan To read an image using a pinpoint beam of light.

scanner Electronic device used to scan an image.

screen To convert a continuous-tone image into a halftone or a solid into a screen tint.

screen density Refers to the amount of ink that a screen tint allows to print. Also called screen percentage. Screen density is expressed as percent of ink coverage.

screen ruling Number of rows or lines of dots per inch or centimeter in a screen for making a screen tint or halftone. Also called line count, ruling, screen frequency, screen size and screen value. Common screen rulings for newsletters are

85 lines per inch/34 lines per centimeter

100 lines per inch/40 lines per centimeter

120 lines per inch/47 lines per centimeter

screen tint Color created by dots instead of solid ink coverage. Also called Benday, fill pattern, screen tone, shading, tint and tone.

second-class mail U.S. Postal Service classification for newspapers, magazines and other periodicals that meet specific requirements.

selective binding Placing signatures or inserts in magazines or catalogs according to demographic or geographic guidelines.

self-mailer Printed piece designed to mail without an envelope.

semibold type Type darker than normal but lighter than bold.

serial identification code Alphanumeric set that may follow an ISSN to identify the issue date and number of a periodical. Abbreviated SIC.

serif Short line crossing the ending strokes of most characters in roman typefaces.

service bureau Business using imagesetters to make high-resolution printouts of files prepared on microcomputers. Also called output house and prep service.

shading film Dry transfer materials used to make screen tints.

shadows Darkest areas of a photograph or illustration, as compared to midtones and highlights.

show through Printing on one side of a sheet that is visible from the other side due to insufficient opacity of the paper, as compared to strike through.

sidebar Block of information related to and placed near an article, but set off by design and/or typography as a separate unit.

small caps Capital letters approximately the x height of lowercase letters in the same font. Used for logos and nameplates and to soften the impact of normal caps.

smooth finish The most level finish offered on offset paper.

soft copy Copy viewed on a computer screen, as compared to hard copy.

solid 1) Any area of the sheet receiving 100 percent ink coverage, as compared to a screen tint. An area of an image on film or a plate that will print as 100 percent coverage is also called a solid. 2) Type set with no leading.

soy-based inks Inks using vegetable oils instead of petroleum products as pigment vehicles, thus being easier on the environment.

special fourth-class rate U.S. Postal Service mail category giving discounts to published material, such as books and phonograph records.

specifications Complete and precise written description of features of a printing job, such as type size and leading, paper grade and quantity, printing quality or binding method. Abbreviated specs. Specifications for newsletters typically include the following:

type specs define typeface, size, line measure, indentations, headlines, and other features of typography.

printing specs concentrate on press work, such as quantities, ink colors and dot gains, but often include prepress, paper and finishing.

finishing specs tell folding requirements and trim size.

spread 1) Two pages that face each other and are designed as one visual or production unit. 2) Layout of several photos, especially on facing pages.

standing headline Headline whose words and position stay the same issue after issue, such as "President's message." Also called slug.

strip To assemble images on film for platemaking. Stripping involves correcting flaws in film, assembling pieces of film into flats, and ensuring that film and flats register correctly. Also called film assembly and image assembly.

stripper Person who works in a stripping department.

style Copyediting rules for treatment of such matters as modes of address, titles and numerals.

style sheet Document containing rules for copyediting and typography to be used for a newsletter.

subhead Small heading within a story or chapter. Also called crosshead.

substance weight Alternate term for basis weight, usually referring to bond papers. Also called sub weight.

subtitle Phrase in a nameplate that amplifies or supplements information in the newsletter name.

summary deck Two or three sentences that condense the highlights of an article and appear between the headline and the lead paragraph.

tabloid Newsletter with trim size 11" x 17" aor A3.

tag line Alternate term for subtitle.

template Pattern used to draw illustrations, make page formats, or lay out press sheets. A template may be a physical object that guides a pencil, an underlay for a light table, or a computer file with preset formats or outlines for the final printed piece.

terms and conditions Specifics of an order for printing that a printer and a customer make part of their contract.

text Main portion of type on a page, as opposed to such elements as headlines and captions.

text paper Designation for printing papers with textured surfaces, such as laid or linen.

text type Type used for text and captions, as compared to display type. Also called body type and composition type.

thumbnail sketch Small rough sketch of a design.

tight register Subjective term referring to nearly exact register.

tombstone Two headlines next to each other so that, at first glance, they appear to be one headline.

toner 1) Powder forming the images in photocopying and laser printing. 2) Powder or liquid forming the images in some color proofing systems.

trade customs Business terms and policies codified by trade associations, such as Printing Industries of America. There are trade customs in the graphic arts for service bureaus and printers.

type Letters, numerals, punctuation marks and other symbols produced by a machine and that will be reproduced by printing.

typeface Set of characters with similar design features and weight. Garamond Light is a typeface. Also called face.

type family Group of typefaces with similar letter forms and a unique name. Garamond, including all weights and styles, such as light, semibold and bold italic, is a type family. Also called family of type.

type size Height of a typeface measured from the top of its ascenders to the bottom of its descenders, expressed in points.

type specimen book Book of printed samples of type families and typefaces offered by a type shop or a type font company.

type style Characteristic of a typeface, such as bold, italic or light.

typography 1) The art and science of composing type to make it legible, readable and pleasing. 2) The arrangement of type on a page.

ultrabold type Type that is heavier than bold. Also called black type.

uncoated paper Paper that has not been coated with clay. Also called offset paper.

underrun Quantity of printing delivered that is less than the quantity ordered.

unit cost The cost of one item in a print run. Unit cost is computed by dividing the total cost of the printing job—variable costs plus fixed costs—by the quantity of products delivered.

uppercase letters Alternate term for capital letters.

variable costs Costs of a printing job that change depending on how many pieces are produced, as compared to fixed costs. Costs for paper, printing and binding are examples of variable costs.

vellum finish Somewhat rough, toothy finish; smoother than antique, rougher than English.

Velox Brand name for high-contrast photographic paper.

washed out Characteristic of printing or a photograph whose images appear faded.

waste Unusable paper or paper damaged during normal makeready, printing or bindery operations, as compared to spoilage.

white space Area of a printed piece that does not contain images or type. Also called negative space.

wide angle lens Camera lens whose field of view is wider than the eye can normally see, as compared to telephoto lens. Also called short lens.

window On a mechanical, an area that has been marked for placement of a halftone. When photographed using graphic arts film, a window made using masking material (dark area) creates a window on the film (transparent area).

x height Vertical height of a lowercase x in a typeface. X height varies from one typeface to another. Also called body height.

ZIP code Acronym for Zone Improvement Plan code, five numerals that identify every Post Office and substation in the United States.

ZIP+4 Five-digit ZIP code plus four additional numerals giving more precise information about the address.

INDEX

More Great Books for Your Writing and Desktop Publishing Projects!